Voices in English Classrooms

Voices in English Classrooms

Honoring Diversity and Change

Classroom Practices in Teaching English
Vol. 28

Edited by

Lenora (Leni) Cook
California State University–Dominguez Hills

Helen C. Lodge
California State University–Northridge

National Council of Teachers of English
1111 W. Kenyon Road, Urbana, Illinois 61801-1096

Manuscript Editors: Robert Heister, Frances Camarena, Hamish Glenn
Humanities & Sciences Associates

Production Editor: Peter Feely

Interior Design: Doug Burnett

Cover Design: Victoria Martin Pohlmann

NCTE Stock Number: 16450–3050

Library of Congress Catalog Card Number 85–644740

Contents

Acknowledgments

During my tenure as co-chair of the CEE Commission on Minority Educators and Minority Education, a subcommittee chaired by Lois Matz Rosen began to explore the possibility of publishing a collection of program practices that reflected successful teaching in ethnically diverse and/or language-diverse classrooms across grade levels. A call for manuscripts was issued during 1991–1992, and twenty-one articles were initially selected for possible publication. As the Commission reorganized and members took on other responsibilities, I took on the work of editing the volume and persuaded Helen Lodge, recently retired, to serve as co-editor.

Many people share responsibility for this collection: Phillip Gonzales, co-chair, and members of the CEE Commission on Minority Educators and Minority Education (1989–1992), who solicited articles; Lois Matz Rosen, who collected the initial submissions, chaired the screening committee (made up of volunteers from the Commission and others), and prepared the first collection for submission; the authors themselves, who worked tirelessly on their manuscripts; and James Squire, whose spirit and dedication to the principles of educational equity and access provided inspiration and encouragement at all stages of the process.

Leni Cook
California State University–Dominguez Hills

Introduction

Change. We are in a time of exciting, yet seemingly chaotic, change in our nation and in our schools. Looking at schooling in general and schooling in English in particular, we see an ongoing transformation within our student bodies and a thoughtful reexamination of both content and practice within our classrooms. A flood of immigrants—from Asia, from the Near East, from Central and South America, from the Pacific Islands—has vastly increased the diversity within classrooms all across the country. Additionally, segments of our native population—Native Americans, Hispanic Americans, and African Americans—are asking that their experiences and their languages or dialects be respected within the classroom as well as in society at large. Adapting content and practice in English teaching to the needs of this diverse student population has resulted in changes in the teaching of language, composition, and literature.

Linguistic research has clarified the nature of dialects in society—their regularities, their richness, their suitability for conveying the experiences of the groups who use the dialects. Teachers have also become aware that knowledge about languages or dialects other than standard English can sensitize language users to the ways in which all languages work and to the relationships among languages. Teachers are constantly looking at ways to reshape and expand traditional language instruction and to use the language resources of their students.

Composition courses, at all levels, now use personal experience for more than traditional introductory autobiography. Indeed, personal experience is viewed as a resource useful in any form of composition, including argumentation. Writing about personal experience can lead to knowledge of self and of society. Coming from diverse cultures, languages, and environments, students who learn to value personal experience in writing maintain their sense of self while working toward skill in recounting ideas and arguing opinions.

The recognition of the presence of diverse groups in society has changed profoundly the literary canon taught in schools and colleges. A great variety of literature representing this diversity has been added to the traditional canon, making literature study richer, more vigorous, and more accessible to students.

The teachers whose practices are recounted here have embraced diversity, have planned for it, indeed, have regarded it as indispensable for achieving a sensitive acceptance of the differences in the ethnicity, language, and sexual orientation of their students. No longer is diversity in the classroom seen only as a wide range of reading and writing abilities. Perhaps more important, no longer is diversity seen as synonymous with remediation. Rather, this term connotes the challenge and reward of providing quality programs and instruction that tap into the experiences which students bring to their learning. All this diversity is part of the woof and weave of the fabric of American society in the 1990s.

Yet there is more than newness and diversity here. Implicit and sometimes explicit in the practices recorded in these chapters are important traditional goals and values associated with the best of American schooling. These practices point to the necessity of looking at the individual as unique in background and life experiences, not simply as a member of an ethnic or sexual minority. The practices here underscore two important traditional goals of the English classroom: (1) increased reading ability achieved through reading and discussing a broad range of literature and (2) increased competence and clarity in writing. And there are other important goals as well. Heightened self-esteem, confidence in writing in one's own voice, and empathy and sympathy for the life experiences and language of those coming from backgrounds vastly different from one's own are important requisites for full membership in American society in the twenty-first century.

The practices recorded here come out of curricula and classrooms that teach English as a unified subject, often with tightly interwoven strands of language, composition, and literature. They are classrooms which use collaborative learning groups with carefully structured feedback procedures for the whole class. For the purpose of this volume, we have separated out—indeed, in some instances, teased out—the strands we consider most innovative, most useful for teachers who may want to adapt what they read here to their own classrooms. Thus, the language strand emphasizes new ways of dealing with language differences by recognizing these differences and deepening and clarifying our understanding of dialects, language change, and the relationships between language and life experience. The composition strand indicates how the relationship between writer and audience can clarify the writing task, build a bond between writer and audience, and lead to an understanding of self and others. The literature strand deals with some traditional literature, part of the canon, but also with literary selections that reflect the experiences of diverse groups within American society. All of the literature is taught so as to evoke a more personal response because, we believe, the connection between literature and personal experience enables students to make literature their own.

While the activities and assignments of each selection come out of a specific classroom milieu, each has elements which can transfer to another classroom setting and another group of students, whether the assignment be letter writing from an ESL class to students in a regular composition class, or environmental writing, or the reading of regional novels by students of that region, who in turn assess the literature in terms of its faithfulness in depicting the region's cultural landscape and tone.

It is the hope of the editors that this book will show readers some successful programs and practices that can be adapted for use in schools, colleges, and classrooms throughout the English teaching community. Its contribution to the profession is seen as twofold: first, as a forum to affirm specific practices which have been successful and meaningful to the instructors and students that they've served; and second, as a pattern and support for teachers who seek innovative and different ways to help their students learn about ethnicities, cultures, languages, and themselves.

I Hearing Every Voice: Language Diversity as Classroom Resource

The three selections on language describe procedures that focus on the richness of language study. All three use language diversity as a valued classroom resource. The first selection, "Celebrating Diversity through the Language Autobiography," describes a writing assignment useful in helping students assess their own development and versatility in the use of language—the language autobiography. This assignment, useful and effective in both high school and university classrooms, helps second-language speakers and speakers of Black English to discover something about language systems and the way in which these systems have influenced the learning of standard English. The assignment also helps students realize that language plays a crucial role in their own lives and helps them evaluate themselves as writers.

The second selection, "Classroom Diversity as Strength: A Language-Centered Unit," focuses on a classroom with many different primary languages and a number of multilingual students. In this classroom, the creation of a polyglot dictionary, comprised of "survival words and phrases" from many languages, helps students not only to gain a better understanding of the English language but also to appreciate their own linguistic versatility.

The third selection, "'How You Not Be Knowin' Dat?': Using Language Study to Enfranchise Diversity," focuses largely on making students aware of dialects, of their regularities, of their power and appropriateness as the language of nurture for some ethnic and cultural groups. This examination of dialects, which looks at Black English and Appalachian dialect, encourages student interaction and supports all students as they work to find the appropriate voice for their situation and purpose.

1 Celebrating Diversity through the Language Autobiography

G. Douglas Meyers
University of Texas at El Paso

*The greatest prize one can receive is the knowledge that one can
speak, that it is possible to emit articulated sounds, enunciate words
that signify objects, events, and emotions. . . . No subsequent
phenomenon . . . is comparable in transcendence to the first
naming of the most elemental things.* (Cela, 11)

Señor Cela, the Spanish writer who won the 1989 Nobel Prize for
Literature, reminds us in his Nobel Lecture that language is central to the human condition. English teachers no doubt draw
much professional satisfaction from this truth, and one way we can
practice our pleasure is to model enthusiasm and curiosity about language, celebrating its diverse manifestations in our diverse student
populations.

No one would disagree that classrooms must be places where
every learner's uniqueness is valued. These days, to do our jobs conscientiously means sensitizing ourselves and our students to the ethnic
and cultural dimensions of that uniqueness. Minorities now account
for about 12 million students in public schools nationwide and consti-
tute the majority populations in nearly 90 percent of our country's
twenty-five largest central school districts (Greene, 4). Such demographics suggest that teachers must consciously develop ways to tap
students' linguistic diversity as a source of strength in whatever educational setting they may find themselves.

Educators are shaped by the contexts in which they work, and I
am fortunate to have had a career teaching students whose diversity
has been a great aid to me in strengthening their mastery of the traditional goals of the English curriculum. The university where I currently chair the Department of English, the University of Texas at El
Paso, is the largest Hispanic-majority university in the continental
United States. Having also taught at an inner-city high school in Balti-

more as well as at public universities in the metropolitan areas of New York City, Washington, D.C., and Miami, I have consistently mined the ore of my students' linguistic riches to help them acquire greater control over their language and, I hope, their lives. I have done this in each of these settings by having them prepare a "language autobiography," in which they tell their life stories as knowers and users of language.

The language autobiography is an assignment that would be of use to any English teacher, though teachers of minority students will find it a particularly powerful tool for raising their students' language consciousness and enhancing their self-esteem. By chronicling their successes and failures in learning to use language appropriately in a variety of social and academic settings, students come to value their language. Learning that no one talks or writes or reads or listens the same way all of the time, they discover for themselves what linguistic research shows: "It's an interesting paradox that the more we find out about how language development differs from individual to individual and situation to situation, the more we find out about how it is similar for all" (Lindfors, 39).

The remainder of this article will describe the assignment and its rationale, results, variations, and implications.

The Language Autobiography Assignment

When using this assignment with secondary and university classes, I give students the following instructions:

> This project provides you with a chance to research and report on the stages of your growth as a knower and user of language, from your birth to the present. The main task is for you to see, understand, and communicate to the other members of our class why and how you have become the kind of language user you are today, addressing all four of the language arts— speaking, writing, reading, and listening. You will need to examine how in-school as well as out-of-school experiences and people have affected you and your language. How, for example, have family, friends, teachers, entertainment, and travel experiences made a difference in the ways you use and understand language?
>
> Your language autobiography focuses more on your language than on your autobiography. It tells, in the fullest detail possible, your language's life story. While many of us share much in common, your language history probably also includes some rich and unique individual differences. If you speak more

than one language or dialect, for instance, pay close attention to those details in your language autobiography.

The format of your finished autobiography can be as creative as you would like. However you organize it, try to include as much documentation as possible—your own personal remembrances, quotations from interviews with significant people in your life, old papers and drawings, report cards, lists of influential books, etc.

The Rationale for the Assignment

Adolescents and young adults possess enormous linguistic resources. Creating and sharing their language autobiographies engages them in accessing those resources and, at the same time, in actively discovering and savoring a great amount about language variation. Students cannot prepare a language autobiography by consulting textbooks. Rather, it is a project which requires them to make meaning of the stuff of their own lives—by collecting, categorizing, and interpreting data discovered from original research.

The assignment is manageable enough for students. Because autobiography is a genre that all students seem able to master, they never lose control of it. Nonetheless, the challenges of creating one's autobiography in a piece of writing or an extended piece of oral discourse should not to be underestimated. Narratologists tell us that creating a narrative goes beyond just formulaically recording "first a, then b"; rather, narrative requires both a *core*—"a, then b"—to which is added an *evaluation*, which answers "so what?" Preparing this project thus demands a good deal of critical thinking from students because they must analyze, synthesize, and evaluate, balancing specifics against generalizations and marshaling evidence to support their theses. The classical rhetorical decisions about invention, style, and arrangement are ones that each language autobiographer must grapple with, for students must identify which details seem most crucial and determine what form their projects should take.

The rationale for the assignment thus stems from its message, its medium, and the contribution it makes to the classroom environment. First, the message: an appreciation of language—including the profound variety of influences accounting for language diversity—is an important objective for all students. Second, the medium: this assignment promotes process-oriented teaching and student-centered learning because teachers start the project by helping students to develop heuristics for discovering information. Throughout the project, teachers can engage students in cooperative learning activities for preparing, revising, and publishing their projects. As a student-centered piece of investigation, the language autobiography bestows all of the benefits of Macrorie's acclaimed "I-Search" approach to research. Third, the classroom environment: students and their sources are clearly the empowered experts here, and they genuinely teach their teacher and classmates something about themselves and about language.

The Results of the Assignment

The diversity of the finished language autobiographies is astonishing, and while space limitations prevent me from reproducing extensive examples, I would be happy to describe projects in detail to anyone who contacts me directly. Students have submitted extraordinary research papers that have been rigorously documented with extensive interview quotations as well as archival evidence that includes old report cards, old drawings and valentines, letters and old papers written half a lifetime ago (all preserved by their parents, much to students' amazement). They have authored novellas and children's stories (*The Story of _____ 's Language*), as well as plays, screenplays, and scripts for television shows ("This is Your Lingual Life"). Students have also employed their artistic abilities for these projects, creating mobiles, dioramas, comic books, as well as annotated scrapbooks and photo albums laden with memorabilia. They have composed original songs, and audio cassettes have lovingly recorded a language's life, complete with reenactments of major events (for which various voices are assumed to achieve verisimilitude) and commentaries by significant others (often family members from two generations).

An African American student wrote a play about her experiences being bused to an all-white school where she was forced to take speech therapy classes because she spoke differently. A student from New York created a series of interviews with significant others, remarking upon the influences of his Puerto Rican parents, his childhood in Japan, and his adolescence in Miami. A Chicano proudly proclaimed in his language autobiography, "Books were my best friends. One day I just began to read on my own, and I never stopped," celebrating how being a good reader got him placed in his school's gifted-and-talented program. Another language autobiography, composed by a first-year college student, was presented as a diary, parts of which were written in a code that captured the author's teenage experiences using coded language with her peers.

If only for the sheer creativity and the love of learning that this project inspires, the language autobiography is worth doing. While students may consider the language autobiography merely assigned work at first, it is nearly always the case that they eventually become proud "owners" of their finished autobiographies, an ownership facilitated by the connections among school, family, and community which this assignment encourages.

By investigating and reporting on their stages of growth as knowers and users of language, students learn a great deal about linguistic phenomena. In classes where linguistic study is a stated objective, they reach, inductively, some important conclusions about the nature of language. Many of these insights are especially profound for students in ethnically and culturally diverse classrooms.

Students understand concretely, for instance, a teacher's discussion of the difference between "competence" and "performance" because they recollect times when they were able to comprehend a good deal more than they could actually articulate. A teacher's coverage of the distinction between "deficiency" and "difference" takes on a special, personal significance for students. Some African American students, for example, arrive at newfound understandings of Black English, for the first time appreciating the systematic contrasts whose coherence legitimizes that dialect's integrity. Bilingual students gain a greater awareness of the gifts and challenges that their first language has bequeathed them, achieving new recognition of the patterns of overanalogizing between their native languages and English which have resulted in structures such as "These books are difficults" and "The problem with American students is that they don't take *the* school seriously." Students also learn that errors such as those illustrated above (pluralization of adjectives and the misuse of the definite article) spring from intelligent (over)generalization, not stupid carelessness. Like their bidialectal classmates, bilingual students find in the study of their own language experiences a validation of themselves as capable learners, appreciating that their "problems" really signify intellectual strengths, not infirmities.

Sometimes the trials of code switching also come to the surface in these autobiographies, as do issues relating to the public-versus-private use of language. Students have commented upon their new appreciation for the differences between writing and speaking; the important role their peers have played in their processes of language acquisition; the wealth of their out-of-school linguistic resources; and even the development of spelling and handwriting skills. They have also recalled the warmth, both physical and emotional, of being read to; the tactile pleasures of painting with finger paints and drawing pictures that told stories; the rhetorical interplay of playing the dozens or listening to a *cuento* told by one's *abuelita*; the accomplishment of being in school plays and assemblies or of having a poem published; the lively talk involved in playing games with family, friends (both real and imaginary), puppets, dolls, and pets.

Nearly all students discover how pervasive language has been in their development as people, how integral language is to being a whole person. The rare student who may not immediately apprehend this from his or her own language autobiography certainly comes to recognize it from the show-and-tell of the entire collection of autobiographies. As one literary critic has observed:

> Autobiography is the literature that most immediately and deeply engages our interest and holds it and in the end seems to mean the most to us because it brings an increased awareness, through an understanding of another life in another time and place, of the nature of our own selves and our share in the human condition. (Olney, vii)

Certainly, one of the most important results of this project is that it inspires students to join in a celebration of language's diversity. It also helps them to affirm a healthy constructivist understanding of language. They have, after all, used language to create themselves in this assignment.

Variations on the Assignment

The language autobiography assignment has been used with consistent success with students in grades 6 through 13. If a middle school student can write, "In the middle of my life, ages 5 to 8 . . . ," there is probably no reason why even younger children could not also prepare their own language autobiographies. Clearly, one doesn't have to be old or famous to have a language story worth telling, and this alone is a lesson worth learning for all students.

While I generally encourage a holistic approach in this assignment, promoting as I do a conception of language that highlights interplay among the four language arts, other teachers might find it profitable to have students prepare separate autobiographies for each of the different language arts. In reading or literature classes, for example, preparing a reading autobiography might serve a worthwhile purpose; in a speech class (or unit), a speaking-and-listening autobiography might also be useful. As a college composition teacher, I have asked first-year students to compose a writing autobiography, to give them practice in writing researched papers using primary sources. Their evaluations of this assignment have indicated that working up their writing autobiographies has helped them to learn more about their strengths and weaknesses as writers as well as about the different composing strategies that they use.

In methods courses for English and bilingual education majors, I have used the language autobiography as a way to help future teachers understand and value the diversity of influences on their students' language. It also helps to bring home the point, as one literacy specialist has noted, that "those of us who deal with children unlike ourselves need to see our classrooms and our students differently from the way we may have seen them in the past" (Fishman, 38). The language autobiography assignment also helps teachers to appreciate that their students are not empty vessels but that, like themselves, they probably already know a lot about language.

Implications

"Of all the richnesses that define the complex culture of this nation," on the one hand, "none is more sparkling, more fascinating, or more evocative of our diverse origins than our plural heritage of languages" (Daniels, 3). The genre of autobiography, on the other hand, by fostering specific understandings of individual persons, also contributes global insights about all people. Taken together, these two principles suggest the virtues of the language autobiography assignment. Through crafting their lives as language users and knowers within a context of respect for diversity, students transcend merely "knowing about" diversity to actually living it, joyfully and triumphantly. Sensing through this project that language changes and develops throughout an entire lifetime, they enter into a world of lifelong learning. Is there any more important outcome than this?

Whether or not they become future Nobelists, all students—simply through the nobility of being human—deserve to prize themselves as language-using beings. The language autobiography assignment awards them such esteem.

Works Cited

Cela, Camilo José. "In Praise of Storytelling." Trans. Agnes Moncy. *PMLA* 106 (1991): 10–17.

Daniels, Harvey A. "The Roots of Language Protectionism." *Not Only English: Affirming America's Multilingual Heritage.* Ed. Harvey A. Daniels. Urbana, IL: NCTE, 1990. 3–12.

Fishman, Andrea R. "Becoming Literate: Lessons from the Amish." *The Right to Literacy.* Ed. Andrea A. Lunsford, Helen Moglen, and James Slevin. New York: MLA, 1990. 29–38.

Greene, Leon E. "Where Minorities Rule." *Principal* 70.3 (1991): 4.

Lindfors, Judith Wells. "The Classroom: A Good Environment for Language Learning." *When They Don't All Speak English: Integrating the ESL Student into the Regular Classroom. Ed.* Pat Rigg and Virginia G. Allen. Urbana, IL: NCTE, 1989. 39–54.

Macrorie, Ken. *The I-Search Paper.* Portsmouth, NH: Boynton/Cook, 1988.

Olney, James. *Metaphors of Self: The Meaning of Autobiography.* Princeton, NJ: Princeton UP, 1972.

2 Classroom Diversity as Strength: A Language-Centered Unit

Kyoko Sato
California State University–Northridge

Bonnie O. Ericson
California State University–Northridge

with
Linda Flammer-Kassel
John H. Francis Polytechnic High School, Sun Valley, California

Many teachers in large urban school districts lament the difficulty of teaching students who come from diverse cultural backgrounds and who speak a variety of first languages. As a teacher in the Los Angeles Unified School District, our colleague Linda Flammer-Kassel counted seventeen primary languages spoken in her five English classes. Not one to throw up her hands and rely on the traditional curriculum, she called to ask whether we'd work with her to develop a unit for her tenth-grade classes which would somehow build on this diversity—that is, view cultural and linguistic diversity as a resource rather than a frustration. She wanted all of her students to appreciate the breadth of ethnicities and languages represented in her classes; she also wanted native-born English speakers to be sensitive to the plight of the foreign-born in their quest to adapt to their new English-speaking surroundings.

What resulted from our planning sessions was a three-week unit centered on language (see figure 1 for the unit overview). Linda taught the lessons, and we assisted and observed two or three times weekly. The main components of the unit included a language survey; group development of a "polyglot" dictionary (a dictionary with entries written in several languages); jigsaw reading of literature selections; reading, debate, and letter writing concerning the "English Only" issue; and regular learning-log entries. Explanations of these components follow, along with anecdotes and examples of student work.

Figure 1. Unit overview.

1	2	3	4	5
(1) Send letter home. (2) Complete language survey.	(1) Compare language surveys in discussion groups. (2) Groups complete chart of responses. (3) Whole class tallies different languages on overhead projector.	(1) Groups compare "twenty essential words and phrases." (2) Select "ten survival words and phrases" on overhead projector. (3) Introduce homework. Read aloud and role-play. HW: Read poem "Foreign Student," Barbara Robinson.	(1) Follow-up discussion and categorization of "ten survival phrases." (2) Discuss "Foreign Student." (3) Connect language survey and poem.	(1) Introduce Lewis Carroll's "Jabberwocky." (2) Students project meaning of nonsense words from context. (3) Begin practice dictionary entry using nonsense words or phrases from "Jabberwocky." Use class dictionaries as model for practice.
6	**7**	**8**	**9**	**10**
(1) Teacher gives lesson on phonetic alphabet and diacritical marks. (2) Practice phonetic alphabet using key words from "ten consensus phrases."	(1) Begin creating dictionary entries of foreign survival phrases, listing them according to English alphabet; e.g., A to Z. (2) Teacher assigns short story-expert groups and provides purpose for reading short stories. HW: Complete reading short stories.	(1) Discuss literature in expert story groups. (2) Regroup into mixed story groups. Students take notes and focus on language and multicultural issues. HW: Learning log: Three questions.	(1) Discuss issues from learning-log entries. (2) Regroup into language-expert groups. Create dictionary entries for "ten survival phrases" in native languages. HW: Letter to author of one of the stories.	(1) Continue compiling dictionary entries for "ten survival phrases" in language-expert groups.
11	**12**	**13**	**14**	**15**
(1) Students meet in new mixed language groups called "phrase groups." "Ten survival words and phrases" match ten groups. (2) Each mixed language group collates multilingual dictionary entries, taking information from language-expert groups.	(1) Complete polyglot dictionary entries and design cover. HW: Learning log: "Language Against the Law."	(1) Discuss learning-log HW. (2) Intro "English Only" issue. (3) Read "English Only" on voting ballot and define legal language. HW: Read pro/con articles on "English Only" issue. Write letter of persuasion.	(1) Discuss "English Only" letters. (2) Debate "English Only" issue. (3) Complete written evaluation of this "Classroom Diversity as Strength: A Language-Centered Unit."	(1) Discuss evaluations. (2) Distribute complete sets of polyglot dictionaries to all students and to school administrators.

1. What language/dialect do you speak at home?
2. What language/dialect do you speak with your friends? (If it is a mixture, describe.)
3. What language or dialect do you speak when you are at school?
4. When did you first learn English, and what were the circumstances?
5. Do you recall what English words or phrases you learned first? What were they?
6. What were your feelings when you were first speaking English?
7. What other languages can you speak, read, or write? How well? How did you learn the other languages?
8. What do you think are 20 essential phrases a person must learn and know in order to function in the U. S., specifically in Los Angeles? List them below.

Figure 2. Language survey.

The Language Survey

Since we really didn't know which students spoke what languages in these classes, the unit began with an informal language survey (see figure 2). A letter was sent home to inform parents of our reasons for conducting the survey, just to alleviate any suspicions they might have regarding our interest in their family's immigration status. Once the students completed the language survey individually, they met the following day in randomly selected small groups and tallied their responses to each question onto a group chart. Groups then shared their responses with the rest of the class, resulting in a whole-class, language-information chart.

We found that the home languages spoken included Spanish, Thai, Armenian, English, Tagalog, Visayan, Vietnamese, Cantonese, and, as reported by a number of students, "Spanglish," or a combination of Spanish and English. Students had newfound respect for each other when they discovered that many possessed limited but conversational fluency in an even wider variety of other languages: French, Arabic, Russian, Mandarin, Korean, Turkish, Japanese, Polish, Italian, and German. The feelings of students when learning English ranged from "proud" to "uncertain" to "embarrassed." Finally, the students enjoyed hearing each other's first English words—"Mommy," "Daddy," ketchup," "yum," "What's up?" and "Gimme five."

The Ten Survival Words: Function or Politeness?

The first seven questions in the language survey were intended to provide information about students' language use. A final, key question asked them to think of twenty words essential to survival in a foreign country. If we were to readminister the language survey now, we would ask students for twenty phrases or sentences rather than single words. We would make this change both because of our experiences with the unit and because of our expanded knowledge of second-language acquisition theory. Limiting students to single words for survival was artificial but nonetheless effective for our first run-through with this unit. The students came to realize firsthand that language develops in phrases that focus on meaning. The unit overview (figure 1) and the language survey (figure 2) have subsequently been revised to reflect our current position on the "words vs. phrases" issue, while our explanations in this essay detail how students actually responded to the original question focusing on survival words.

When the students met in their groups, this question about survival words, in particular, led them to a probing discussion in which they justified their choices and tallied the common words. Finally, Linda led a lively class discussion, honing the twenty words into a class-consensus list of "ten survival words": *bathroom, food, help, money, no, please, shelter, understand, work, yes.*

We were delighted and surprised at how the students argued about which words to include. They delved into the subtleties and connotations more than we had anticipated. For example, there was an extended debate about whether to use "bathroom," "restroom," or "toilet." Initially, the class decided to be direct and preclude any possibility of misunderstanding by using "toilet." But one student noted that "toilet" is rather crude and that the more commonly used term in America was "bathroom." Another said that the more public and perhaps neutral term he had heard was "restroom." When the debate was halted, the disagreement was put to a vote. The results: "bathroom" = 12; "restroom" = 7; "toilet" = 1.

The level of critical thinking was also impressive as the students tried to overlap and combine the precious few ten words. "Police" was submitted by two groups, but the word did not make the top ten because the other three groups felt that "help" was a more general and useful term. As one student noted, "If you're in the library and you need help, you don't need the police." Similarly, "stop" yielded to "no." The students opted originally to use gestures (a shake of the head) instead of "no," but another student successfully argued that gestures are cultural: "I happen to know that the gesture for 'come here' in our country means 'flipping off' to someone in England." Students concluded that politeness is especially important if you don't know the language: "It's better to use the proper words than risk shortcuts like gestures; otherwise, you might alienate the very people who could help you." We couldn't have said it better ourselves.

The Polyglot Dictionary

Students now worked toward a larger goal: the making of a dictionary for Poly students. To complete this portion of the unit, the students were divided into new groups, "language-expert groups," according to their respective native languages (four Armenian speakers, three Cantonese speakers, four Spanish speakers, etc.). In these language-expert groups, the students developed dictionary entries on separate pages for each of the ten survival words. Although students often view dictionary work as tedious and boring, the "polyglot" dictionary activity promoted creativity. For example, if a phonetic symbol did not exist for a Vietnamese sound, students needed to devise one.

The ten survival-word entries were completed by the language-expert groups over a two-day period. Then students were regrouped into "word groups"—e.g., a bathroom group, a food group, etc. The task of each word group was to compile a multilingual entry for the one word, taking their information from the entries developed earlier by the different language-expert groups (see figure 3 for an example of an entry). Student volunteers later assembled the completed dictionary and created a cover. Students named it a "polyglot" dictionary after struggling for a title that would convey the nature of the dictionary and its function in helping Poly students:

> ***poly•glot** (pol'-i-glot'), adj. [Gr. *polyglottos,* <poly-, many +*glotta,* the tongue], 1. written in several languages, 2. written in many languages by students from Polytechnic High School.

Copies of the polyglot dictionary were made for each student and for school administrators, and these were distributed on the final day of the unit.

Jigsaw Reading of Literature

No unit, not even a language-centered unit, would be complete without some literature. For this unit, our selections had to meet several criteria: literature for which the topic of language or communication was central, literature by writers from diverse backgrounds, literature that

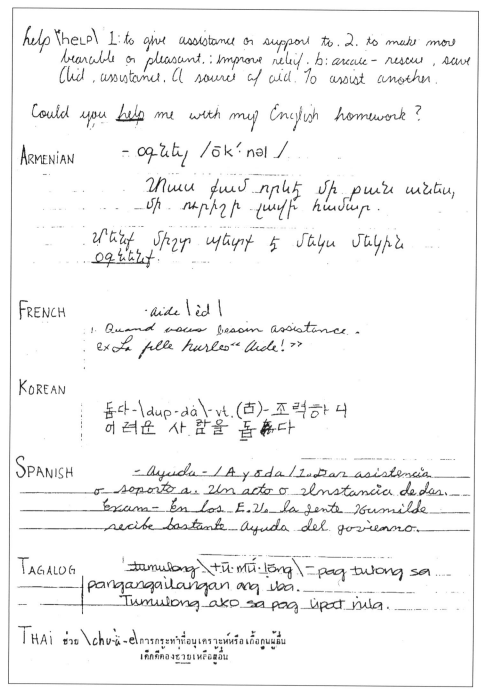

Figure 3. Survival-word entry sample.

students could read easily, and literature containing characters and situations with which students could identify readily. Using these criteria, we chose five selections: "I See You Never," by Ray Bradbury; an excerpt from *The Woman Warrior,* by Maxine Hong Kingston; "Coming to an Awareness of Language," by Malcolm X; "The Filipino and the Drunkard," by William Saroyan; and "The Kitten," by Richard Wright. Because students were the "experts" with the diverse language knowledge for this unit, we decided to continue with this approach: they should also be the literature experts. Thus, we decided to use the jigsaw strategy, which is described below.

Linda introduced these selections by encouraging the students to read for how characters struggled with their problems and for the role played by language. Students were divided into five "story-expert groups," and each group read and discussed one of the selections, using the questions in figure 4. The next day, they were regrouped, or "jigsawed," so that each new group was comprised of five representatives, one from each story-expert group. The experts summarized their selections and addressed any questions while the others took notes. Following these discussions, students responded in their learning logs to three questions: (1) What connections do you see among the five selections? (2) What role does language play in them? (3) Which selections were the most compelling for you and why? Sample learning-log entries appear in figure 5.

"English Only": Debate and Letters

When planning this unit, the three of us toyed with the idea of introducing the "English Only" issue. All of us had reservations because of the political overtones, so we decided to expose the students to this issue but to touch on it only briefly. Much to our surprise, the students not only understood the complexities of the issue but wanted to pursue it further. In fact, for the students, this was the most compelling part of the entire unit.

To dramatize the implications of "English Only" legislation, Linda had students complete a writing activity she called "Language Against the Law":

> How many of you learned to speak a language other than English first? Starting tomorrow it will be against the law to speak your language! Describe how your life will be different. For those of you who learned to speak English first, pretend that tomorrow you may no longer speak English because it will be

"I See You Never"

1. How is Los Angeles contrasted to a Mexican border town? Do the two have anything in common? How do these descriptions fit with your experiences?

2. What is the attitude of Mrs. O'Brian's children to Mr. Ramirez's being deported to Mexico?

3. Compare and contrast the attitudes, feelings, and thoughts contained in the sentences (a) "I see you never" and (b) "I'll never see Mr. Ramirez again."

4. What do you think of the characters in this story?

5. What do you think will happen to Mr. Ramirez? To Mrs. O'Brian? Why?

Excerpt from *The Woman Warrior*

1. Why do you think Maxine Hong and the other Chinese girls are silent in kindergarten?

2. Why does Maxine Hong have difficulty reading and understanding 'I' in English?

3. Compare and contrast Maxine's attitudes toward English and Chinese. If you speak two languages, what are your attitudes toward each?

4. How do the regular American school and the night Chinese school differ? Which does Maxine prefer, and why? Have you attended more than one school? Compare and contrast your experiences in the schools.

5. What sort of student do you think Maxine Hong was as she continued through school? Why?

"Coming to an Awareness of Language"

1. Why did Malcolm X write letters from prison? Why didn't he receive responses?

2. How did Malcolm X learn to read and write? How does this compare to your learning to read and write?

3. How is a dictionary like an encyclopedia, according to the author? Do you agree? Explain.

4. What does Malcolm X mean when he says, "I had never been so truly free in my life"?

5. Do you agree that reading is a liberating experience? Is illiteracy a kind of prison? Use your own experiences to discuss these questions.

Figure 4. Literature discussion questions.

"The Filipino and the Drunkard"

1. What does the drunkard resent about the Filipino?

2. What is a "real American" to the drunkard? How would you describe or define a "real American"? Compare and contrast the two definitions.

3. Describe how the drunkard and the Filipino talk. What do you know about each of these characters from what they say, and the way they say it?

4. Why didn't anyone in the crowd help the Filipino? Would people today refuse to become involved? Explain.

5. Was the Filipino right or wrong to stab and kill the drunkard? What alternatives could you suggest?

"The Kitten"

1. Do you believe Richard when he says he is killing the kitten because his father told him to? Why/why not?

2. Why do you think Richard's mother orders him to bury the kitten? Do you think she was right to make him do this?

3. What do you think Richard learns from this incident?

4. Explain the following: "I had made him believe that I had taken his words literally. He could not punish me now without risking his authority. I was happy . . . I had made him feel that, if he whipped me for killing the kitten, I would never give serious weight to his words again." Have you ever taken someone's words literally, when you knew the person didn't mean them literally? Describe the situation and the consequences.

5. What are Richard's feelings toward his father at the beginning of the story? Do you think his feelings toward his father have changed by the end of the story? Why/why not?

Figure 4. *Continued.*

> against the law. You can only speak Spanish. How will your life be different?

One student's description (figure 6) exemplifies the degree to which she and her classmates were moved both intellectually and emotionally by this hypothetical situation.

This activity was a highly effective introduction to the authentic Proposition 63, which passed in California in 1986 by a margin of 4 to 1. The actual ballot measure reads:

> OFFICIAL STATE LANGUAGE. Requires Legislature and State Officials to ensure English as official state common language. Provides for private enforcement. Fiscal impact: No direct effect on the costs or revenues of the state or local governments. (Election Commission, 8)

I believe the major connections among the selections have to do with cultures. People seem to have certain attitudes towards people from other cultures. Some of the people in the selections were from different countries or ethnic backgrounds and had to adapt to new situations. Maxine Hong found her new society totally different, and although we never found out about her later years, I think she gradually adapted. Others felt their cultures were superior such as in "The Filipino and the Drunkard." I thought there was a touch of jealousy as well as racism in that particular story. Then there was Mrs. O'Brian who saw beyond the nationality and cared for the actual person.

Another major role in the selections was language. Misunderstanding and misinterpretation took place several times. The guy in prison who wrote to politicians in slang was ignored because his style of writing was different and consequently misunderstood. The boy that killed his cat used deliberate misinterpretation to get back at this father. Other people like Maxine Hong found themselves in a new environment having to get used to a new language. In each of the selections the person made an effort to correct or adapt to the situation whether there was a cultural difference or a language barrier.

I found Maxine Hong's autobiography the most interesting mainly because it's the one I could relate to the best. As far as the selection went, Maxine kept silent in school because she found the English language strange and she felt uncomfortable with it. When I started kindergarten, I didn't know the English language except for the alphabet and a few words. Throughout most of the year I kept silent as well. I listened to the teacher and listened to the other students. By the first grade I had a good grasp of the English language, and I was anxious to learn more. Although I spoke Spanish rather well, I became so comfortable with English, I would always prefer to speak English in any situation.

Figure 5. Literature learning-log entries.

The students were eager to read what would normally be considered boring or complex legal language. They *wanted* to read the pros and cons of the ballot measure. They also read a collection of editorials and repeatedly asked Linda how she had voted, which she purposely, but with some frustration, refused to reveal so that she wouldn't bias the students' opinions.

Following a formal classroom debate, this component of the unit concluded with a letter writing activity:

Write a letter of persuasion to the opposing organization discussing and defending your position. Use specific information you learned from your readings and the class debate. Draw on your own experiences as appropriate to persuade the opposition of your position.

If I wasn't allowed to speak my first language which is Armenian, then I am left with English. I don't think speaking English only would affect my school life, but I think it would affect my conversations with my mother who doesn't speak English very well, only a few phrases and words here and there.

I am glad that I know how to speak more than one language because then I won't be really stuck. But I do wonder if I will forget the language after awhile. It would be interesting though to see how I will be without Armenian. Then I suppose my mother would learn English a little later.

As I am writing this page I wonder if my communications with my mom will change the relationship I have with her. It would be awful to think about losing contact with my relatives in Armenia who don't speak English. I wonder what I have to do and what they have to do [to communicate]. Do they have to draw pictures? Or sign language? But what keeps recurring is what will happen between me and my mom. Sure I can communicate with my sisters, but I really can't with my mom. I am thinking now that I will teach my mom English. I am really considering that.

Figure 6. "Language Against the Law" sample.

If you were to vote "NO" on "English Only," discuss your position by writing to U.S. English, 1424 16th St. NW, Washington, D.C. 20036.

If you were to vote "YES" on "English Only," explain your position by writing to the National Coalition for Language Freedom, 530 12th Street, Sacramento, CA 95814.

Final Evaluation

Students generally have little direct say in the evaluation of a unit. But in keeping with our "students-as-experts" approach, we invited them to complete an anonymous, written questionnaire and participate in a follow-up discussion based on their responses:

1. What is one word you learned and can say in another language?
2. What did you learn in this unit?
3. Which activity was the most fun or interesting for you? Why?
4. What did you have difficulty with during this unit? Why?
5. What suggestions do you have for the next time we teach this unit?

The written and oral responses confirmed our observations. Students not only learned a great deal about language, but they enjoyed playing with nuances of meanings and enthusiastically compared their own languages with others. Generally speaking, they wanted more: more time and information about the English Only issue, more information about the history and etymology of English, more time to discuss the literature selections, more samples of foreign-language dictionaries, and additional presentations by speakers of languages not represented in the class.

What We Learned

We learned—or relearned—how enjoyable and stimulating it is to plan with others, and we believe our short unit is a strong argument for building and maintaining university-public school ties. We benefited from our extended contact with "real" students, and we will be better teachers with greater credibility for the experience. We were able to provide Linda with the literature selections and much of the "English Only" information, and her students were proud to be part of an "experiment" associated with the university.

What we did not anticipate was the depth of students' thinking and involvement in discussions about the "survival words," the literature selections, or the "English Only" issue. We attribute these successes to Linda's expert teaching and to the numerous writing and cooperative group activities. When the students were asked to be responsible for their learning, when they assumed the role of experts, we found that they met and often surpassed our expectations.

At the outset, we were astonished at the range of students' languages. We knew that a large number of the students were bilingual, but we were impressed by those who were able to speak three and even four languages. We had hoped students would develop greater multilingual awareness and appreciation, but we had not anticipated the major shift in attitude when the monolingual English speakers came to regret their single-language limitation. As a result, both native and second-language speakers gained in their understanding of the English language.

Teaching this unit led us to two important conclusions: not only can diversity be a strength in the classroom, but it can also lead students to appreciate in a meaningful way that English is a dynamic, everchanging amalgam of words and phrases. Because there is every indication that the trend toward diversity will continue indefinitely, these are indeed important conclusions.

Works Cited

Bradbury, Ray. "I See You Never." *The Best American Short Stories.* Boston: Houghton, 1948. 32–35.

Election Commission. *Official Sample Ballot and Voter Information.* Sacramento: State of California, 1986. 8.

Hayakawa, S. I. *National Opinion Survey of Language Usage in the United States.* Washington, D.C.: U.S. English, 1986.

Henry, Sarah. "Fighting Words: Can America Be a One-Language Country?" *Los Angeles Times Magazine* 10 June 1990: 10–17, 37–38.

Hewitt, Nancy. "English Is Still the Best Language for Americans." *Daily Sundial* 14 Sep. 1990: 5. Northridge, CA: California State University.

Kingston, Maxine Hong. *The Woman Warrior.* New York: Knopf, 1976.

Malcolm X. "Coming to an Awareness of Language." *The Autobiography of Malcolm X.* New York: Grove, 1964. 171–74.

Newsletter. Jan. 1990. Sacramento, CA: National Coalition for Language Freedom.

Robinson, Barbara. "Foreign Student." Source unknown.

Saroyan, William. "The Filipino and the Drunkard." *The William Saroyan Reader.* New York: Braziller, 1958. 116–18.

Wright, Richard. "The Kitten." *Black Boy.* New York: Harper, 1945. 16–21.

3 "How You Not Be Knowin' Dat?": Using Language Study to Enfranchise Diversity

Barbara Osburg
Parkway North High School, St. Louis, Missouri

I love our school. Parkway North is located on the edge of an affluent area of St. Louis's rapidly growing west county and is thus the recipient of the monies of its citizens' upper-middle-class incomes and the wealthy local industries and businesses nearby. But our school is also located in an area of low-income and somewhat transient housing, such as condos and apartments, which draws a slightly different student population than that of the wealthier general district; thus, the socioeconomic levels of our students range from poverty to affluence. The ethnicity of our district is also wide-ranging. We have a large Jewish population, including several immigrants from Israel. We have a significant number of Asians—Koreans, Vietnamese, Thai, Indians. Some belong to the National Merit Scholar-bookworm league, while others belong to the local, family-owned Chinese (or other Asian ethnic) small-business community.

We have the largest African American population of the four high schools in our district, and we have an occasional Hispanic or Native American as well. Our school also participates in the St. Louis Voluntary Desegregation Program, which buses African American students into our district from the predominantly black sections of St. Louis City. The speech of our students ranges from tenseless Thai to Creole Black English, and from Farsi to Hebrew. These various ethnic and language populations make Parkway North an exciting, multicultural place in which to teach and to learn because they present us with tremendous differences that we need to capitalize on instead of bemoan. Our students' diversity can create delight or debate, can enrich our school or debilitate it. The results depend on our attitudes and the use of a linguistically multicultural approach to curriculum and to students.

African Americans, whose language of nurture has been Black English, Hispanics, whose first language is not English, and Asians, whose culture often demands what seems to be acquiescent, quiet, self-effacing silence, are often the victims of thoughtless linguistic prejudice. Unfortunately, these students are often accused by their teachers of "not talking so I can understand them." "I can't hear you" and "What did you say?" are asked frequently and repeatedly at the beginning of the year. Then something happens: these criticisms and patronizing queries begin to disappear. Teachers do not understand students any better than they did initially; they just get tired and give up. And just as soon, or sooner, the students give up, too. Typically, the African American inner-city students are my second quietest group of students—the foreign-born Asians are the first. Both groups are smart—too smart to continue the humiliation of "What? I can't understand you" and the rest of their classmates' eyes upon them in impatient disgust. They quit talking and are soon left alone to the ignominy of silence.

Such subtle language prejudices surface today, even at my wonderfully multicultural school, because our curriculum and our school, however open and accepting they are when compared with many other places, are designed primarily for a homogeneous group—the English-speaking, white, middle class. My honors students immediately labeled a new girl from Kentucky a "hillbilly." American literature students nicknamed a Vietnamese boy "I No Unnerstan." If I had Hispanic students, I am sure that similar labels would be produced for them by the majority-population students. Interestingly, when confronted with African American classmates from Black English backgrounds, these same ethnocentric, linguistic snobs are halted in their mockery by a sophisticated appraisal of their milieu—they know that to mock the speech of their black peers is an act of bigotry. But the Black English speakers know that their speech is different, that they do not always speak what they call "proper" English, and that they are being laughed at even though the laughter is of a silent, sophisticated type. Their silence in class parallels the silence of the other linguistic minorities.

So what should we do when, in fact, we middle-class, white Anglos have trouble understanding these multicultural students? How do we encourage them to talk? How do we facilitate their entry into and full membership in our classes? Our mandate is to develop content that fights language biases and, simultaneously, to create a classroom setting that encourages language interaction.

Informing Our Students

Those of us who wish to enfranchise our linguistically diverse students must take up the study of their dialects and linguistic diversities. In so doing, we may enter, to a small degree, their language worlds. And thus, if Benjamin Whorf is correct in saying that language shapes thought, we may also enter, again to a small degree, their *life* worlds. Years ago, I began an avocational study of Appalachian English. I did so, in part, because my father's speech contains many elements of that dialect and, thus, my own language of nurture contains many elements of that speech. I suffered in the early grades and still occasionally suffer now from purists' corrections. In undergraduate school, under the tutelage of a wonderful teacher, I formalized this avocation and also began to study Black English, a study which has proved to be very helpful because, in St. Louis and in southeast Missouri, I encounter many speakers of that dialect, especially among the populations of high schools and junior colleges. This avocational study of dialects led me to classes and seminars, to reading about and even to teaching workshops and graduate classes on these dialects. As my expertise grew, I began to incorporate some of my knowledge into my high school classes, at first on an impromptu basis and then as a regular part of the curriculum.

I am not able to include all of the activities outlined in this essay in all of my classes, but I do include a substantial number of them in my teaching assignments, picking and choosing the activities based on the age levels, content foci, and populations of my classes. Whether the primary focus of a particular class is literature, composition, grammar, or speech, the opportunities to discuss language diversity (levels, dialects, jargons, and other aspects of varying speech communities) abound. I can begin a Shakespeare unit with a discussion of Elizabethan dialect as one of the dialects of Modern English, and add Black English Vernacular and Appalachian to compare and contrast with the Elizabethan. I can use oral histories as opportunities for students to try to write what they heard in interviews and to preserve dialectical features as well as personal idiosyncrasies of speech. In my planning and evaluation of assignments, I provide opportunities to use a variety of levels of language as well as standard and nonstandard dialects. I introduce the term "Network English" in substitution of their learned terms like "good English" or "proper English" or "correct English." Network English implies the language that is used in radio and television news reporting and on the news pages of major newspapers—the language of our national media networks. With a clearer view of the distinctions among varieties of English, students leave my class feeling that the mastery of a variety of dialects and levels is preferable to the knowledge and use of only one. Some assignments will be graded for standard usage, others for dialect accuracy. Providing a multiplicity of opportunities to learn about and use varieties of Modern English is my overriding goal.

In the early weeks of a semester, I often use the language attitude inventory shown in figure 1, which is based on Harvey Daniels's essay, "Nine Ideas about Language." Students compare and discuss their answers to these basic language facts, and then I explain that, according to linguists, these ideas are all true. We then discuss the ideas one by one and follow that with an "informed group discussion" on various issues in language. Possible points of departure for this "informed group discussion" and suggestions for student role-playing are given in the handout pictured in figure 2. We are then able to discuss the idea of usage as a tool for creating personae effectively and appropriately in varying situations.

A colleague and I have taped a number of speakers, both native and foreign- born, who speak English with varying accents and grammatical patterns, and I play these while displaying the chart pictured in figure 3 (designed and revised by my colleague, Susan Teicher).

After each speaker has read an assigned article from the newspaper and then summarized it in his or her own words, I ask students to examine their language prejudice by hypothesizing about the speakers from their speech and marking responses on the chart. Later I reveal the identities of the speakers. The discussion which follows this exercise is very interesting: students often reveal their language bigotry quite honestly and openly (though their racism and cultural ethnocentricity would be masked and guarded in a similar discussion).

Oral histories are another excellent way to build language diversity into assignments. Oral histories are best told in the dialect of the taleteller, so this writing assignment is a natural lead-in to discussions about dialect features, such as pronunciation and variations in grammar. I encourage students to interview one another (not just "old folks" in the area), to record holiday customs, to speak to the new kid in school, and to learn about immigrant experiences. The class thus becomes a wealth of linguistically diverse primary sources requiring

---

Language Attitudes

Rank your agreement or disagreement with the following statements:

1 = Strongly disagree
2 = Disagree
3 = Confused or undecided
4 = Agree
5 = Strongly agree

_____ 1. Children learn their native language swiftly, efficiently, and largely without instruction.

_____ 2. All languages operate by rules.

_____ 3. All languages have three major components: a sound system, a vocabulary, and a system of grammar.

_____ 4. Everyone speaks a dialect.

_____ 5. Speakers of all languages employ a range of styles and a set of subdialects or jargons.

_____ 6. Language change is normal.

_____ 7. Languages are intimately related to the societies and individuals who use them.

_____ 8. Values and judgments about different languages or dialects are merely matters of taste.

_____ 9. Writing is derivative of speech.

Which of these statements seems least true to you and why?

Which of these statements do you most readily accept and why?

Figure 1. Student handout (based on Daniels, 18–36).

careful recording and documentation of language for accurate reporting. Students are used as experts for one another on various aspects of their languages of nurture. They use their ears as guides for subject-verb rules. For example, in Appalachian, number may be marked in nouns but not in verbs ("The boys was a-goin' into the fields when we met up with 'em"). In Black English, a single notation of number is sufficient for the entire sentence ("We, the student of North High, *is* ready to learn"). In Network, or standard, English, the language of the majority of students at our school, subjects and verbs agree in number and students *hear* that agreement as natural and harmonious ("The boys were going. . . . We, the students, are ready. . ."). Students compare their responses and learn that most language is a matter of unconscious learning and that what "sounds" right is what we have heard most often.

**Language Position Statements
for Informed Group Discussion**

1. Terms like *spick, mick, Nazi, kike, jock,* and *slut* are not what harm people, but the attitudes behind them do harm.

2. Terms like *Ms., African American, Hispanic, Asian, woman,* and *athlete* can help to fight biases and unfair treatment.

3. Differences among people are important and need to be stressed to keep the pluralism of America strong.

4. When teachers reject the native speech of students, they do those students great harm.

5. One of the goals of the American school system should be the standardization of the English language.

6. A teacher should correct a student's use of nonstandard English.

7. Black English must be accepted if pride is to develop among African Americans.

Figure 2. Position statements for informed group discussion (with possible role-playing of U.S. English and English Only groups, the NAACP, the Center for Applied Linguistics, laypersons, and educator groups).

An excellent exercise for an initial study of grammar is an inductive one, which allows students to discover the method in the seeming madness of dialects. I offer sentences which employ the standard use of the subjunctive, those which employ the Black English use of be, and those which employ the Appalachian use of the a- prefix. Mixed in with these are sentences which do not employ these forms, so that a contrasting set of examples can be used to work out the rules. These exercise sheets are shown in figures 4, 5, and 6. In groups, students ponder these examples and try to work out the rules that govern their uses. Whether or not students have an ear for what is standard, all of them are on equal footing in trying to hypothesize rules to explain the uses. All dialects are equally enfranchised in this operation because all are shown to be rule- governed and logical

Etymology papers also offer interesting opportunities for language study, and the wealth of resources available—from the *Oxford English Dictionary* to the *Dictionary of Black English* to the *Dictionary of American Regionalisms*—makes this a wonderful research project as well as an exciting primary-source exploration; students can consult both texts and people in the information-gathering stage. This project includes a brief study of the history of the English language and its

Figure 3. Chart for student responses based on tapes of speakers gathered by Susan Teicher (St. Louis 1990).

Speaker Analysis Chart

Speaker	Sex	Age	Region	Education	Employment	Class	Reliability
#1							
#2							
#3							
#4							
#5							
#6							
#7							
#8							
#9							
#10							

Induction of Rules for Standard English Subjunctive

Some sentences in Network English require the use of a special form of the verb *to be* which seems to contradict the usual use of this verb. In fact, the standard use of this verb form, called the subjunctive, may sound rather fancy, old-fashioned, or even wrong to your ears, but it is considered educated and appropriate in writing and in formal speaking, such as that done in courtrooms by attorneys, in Congress by legislators, and on special occasions. The following sentence pairs reflect the pattern of Network English, that English which we hear on radio and television news broadcasts and read in large city newspapers. Try to induce rules to explain the following sentences. Write the rules you come up with on a separate sheet of paper, noting the sentences which led you to your conclusions.

1. a. If I were you, I would speak to him immediately.
   b. I was not with you when you spoke to him.

2. a. I was not with him when the accident occurred.
   b. I wish I were not going to ride home with him.

3. a. His parents insist that he go to work.
   b. His parents watch him as he goes to work each morning.

4. a. Because he was new, he did not know where the cafeteria was.
   b. If he were not new, he would know where the cafeteria is.

5. a. The committee will see to it that the wage scale is lowered.
   b. The committee recommended that the wage scale be lowered.

6. a. I desire that she stay.
   b. I will be sure that she stays.

7. a. I will give in to him when he begs me on his knees.
   b. I would never give in to him, though he beg me on his knees.

8. a. She wished she were not the first one to be selected.
   b. She was not the first one to be selected.

9. a. Jill would tell her if she were here.
   b. Jill told her when she was here.

10. a. If that be true, I will eat my hat.
    b. If that is true, I will have to reconsider my position.

Figure 4. Sentence pairs to make possible the induction of standard use of the subjunctive. The rules for standard use of the subjunctive are in situations of conditionality, wishes, advice, command, or great doubt.

relationship to other languages. Students with foreign-language backgrounds (preferably native speakers, but second-language students are also good resources) become guest lecturers, sharing interesting aspects of their non-English tongues. Sometimes these students include a discussion of their language's slang and their ethnic customs and cultural mores. Sometimes they include a number of words

---

Induction of *A-* Rules

Some dialects of English put an a-type sound before words that end in *-ing*, so that we get phrases like "A-hunting we will go." In fact, you will sometimes find headlines that have these forms, such as one in *Time* magazine that read, "Carter goes a-wooin' and wins some." The following sentence pairs reflect that pattern. Try to induce rules to explain the following sentences. Write the rules you come up with on a separate sheet of paper, noting the sentences which led you to your conclusions.

1. a. John likes sailin'.
   b. John went a-sailin'.

2. a. The woman was a-comin' down the stairs.
   b. The movie was shockin'.

3. a. He makes money a-buildin' houses.
   b. He makes money by buildin' houses.

4. a. She got sick a-workin' so hard.
   b. She thought workin' was good for her.

5. a. Sam was a-followin' the trail.
   b. Sam was discoverin' the cave.

6. a. The dogs were eatin' the food.
   b. The dogs were a-drinkin' the water.

7. a. The man was confessin' his crime.
   b. The man was a-hollerin' at the dogs.

8. a. I've never messed with dogs a-fightin'.
   b. I've never messed with fightin' dogs.

Figure 5. Appalachian sentences which demonstrate correct use of the *a*-prefix. This worksheet is taken from materials supplied by Walt Wolfram, Federal City College and the Center for Applied Linguistics. The rules for the *a-* prefix in Appalachian dialect are (1) used only with verbs, not verbals; (2) used only before verbs beginning with a consonant; (3) used only before verbs which contain a heavily accented first syllable or only one syllable (before the *-in'* suffix). Occasionally, the *a-* prefix takes the place of prepositions like *by* or *of*, thus changing a verbal (which served as the object of a preposition) into a verb.

English has borrowed from their language. This sharing becomes additional research available for the etymology paper since a large number of everyday words, like *shampoo* and *ketchup,* are borrowings from foreign tongues, while the development of slang vocabulary includes many borrowings from Black English and other forms of Modern English, including American, British, Australian, Indian, and South African dialects. Many of the borrowed words are naively mispronounced by standard English speakers, such as *chaise longue* ("chase

---

Induction of *Be* Rules

In at least one dialect of English, there is a form of *be* that is used where other dialects use forms such as *am, is, are,* or *will be.* We thus get sentences like *He be fooling everybody.* In that same dialect, forms such as *am, is,* and *are* are absent in certain contexts. The following sentence pairs reflect those patterns. Try to induce rules to explain the following sentences. Write the rules you come up with on a separate sheet of paper, noting the sentences which led you to your conclusions.

1. a. His ears itching (right now).
   b. His ears be itching (after he swims).

2. a. He be my partner when we play tennis.
   b. The woman in the picture my mother.

3. a. He busy (today).
   b. He be busy on Tuesdays.

4. a. He be home tomorrow.
   b. He home today.

5. a. The man in the brown suit my father.
   b. My father be my teacher when we go swimming.

6. a. He be thirteen in three weeks.
   b. He thirteen years old (today).

7. a. John be late for school (habitually).
   b. John late for school (today).

8. a. He sleeping (now).
   b. He be sleeping (usually) in the afternoon.

Figure 6. Black English sentences which demonstrate correct use of the be form. This worksheet is taken from materials supplied by Walt Wolfram, Federal City College and the Center for Applied Linguistics. The rules for the *be* form in Black English are (1) for actions which take place habitually over time, and (2) used for simple future tense.

lounge"); such "pronunciations of ignorance" provide opportunities for discussions of what constitutes "acceptable" and "unacceptable" pronunciation, what is standard and what is nonstandard, and the manner in which pronunciation and grammar become standard. Students are amazed to learn that *ain't* has an intellectually reasonable etymology, that *fox* was Black English long before it was white teenage lingo, and that, in Missouri, the town is properly called Ver-sailles (ver-sales), not Versailles (vehr-sigh).

When I begin an introduction to Shakespeare, I do not start with information on the Elizabethan theater, but on the Elizabethan dialect: "I hate that Old English stuff," they say, when I announce the beginning of our unit on *Macbeth*. So I show them Old English, Middle English, and Modern English, clearly demonstrating that Shakespeare is not "Old English stuff," but Modern English stuff. I show them the similarities between his dialect and ours, stressing the commonalities our dialects share rather than their differences. I also ask my students to isolate the Appalachian *a-* prefix as they find it in the play, to point out the lingering threads of sixteenth-century grammar in modern Appalachian speech. Granny Clampett isn't a hillbilly after all; she's just Elizabethan (at least in that one linguistic variable).

Another opportunity to enfranchise linguistic minorities comes during the writing process, when we have nearly completed the first major paper and the time has come for polishing and conforming to conventions. We begin by taking a Black English test in grammar. Sometimes I use Geneva Smitherman's (247–50), and sometimes I use Walt Wolfram's (shown in figure 7). I also use Wolfram's Black English vocabulary test (shown in figure 8). If students are to deliver their papers as speeches, I include a pronunciation test as well (see Smitherman, 247). Some of my inner-city students from Black English backgrounds score very high on this test; everyone else fails miserably. That's when my standard English speakers say, "How did you know that?!" And my Black English speakers reply, "How you *not* be knowin' dat?"

I then say I will make it easier by allowing them to take a test in Appalachian grammar designed by Walt Wolfram (figure 9) and an Appalachian vocabulary test designed by me (figure 10). Many Missouri students have Appalachian "ears" from listening to their grandparents' speech and therefore fare better on this test. But once again, the language-majority students fail and the language minority excel (though education is beginning to wipe out the natural "ear" of many of my students, and many of them are more or less immersed in Network English). This process can be continued with Hispanic patterns of dialect variation or with some Asian dialect patterns (many of which lack tense and number inflections and both definite and indefinite articles—as in "Boy walk six mile" for "A boy walked six miles").

The next assignment is to change several sentences from Network English into dialect. These exercises are shown in figures 11 and 12. Once the testing is over, I require students to edit a paragraph from their own papers for nondialect usage—that is, students must make sure that their paragraphs conform to the chosen power dialect of the day, either Black English or Appalachian. This assignment can also be used in conjunction with literature that is written in dialect. The trans-

---

Reactions to *Be* Forms

In at least one dialect of English, there is a form of *be* that is used where other dialects use forms such as *am, is, are,* or *will be*. We thus get sentences like *He be foolin' everybody*. The following sentence pairs each contain an *am, is, are,* or *will be* word in standard English. Choose which of the sentences you think would require the *be* form, but choose only one sentence in each pair. If you are not sure, take your best guess. On a separate sheet of paper, note the sentence (either a or b) which you think requires the form *be*.

1. a. His ears are itching (right now).
   b. His ears are itching (after he swims).

2. a. He is my partner when we play tennis.
   b. The woman in the picture is my mother.

3. a. He is busy (today).
   b. He is busy on Tuesdays.

4. a. He will be home tomorrow.
   b. He is home today.

5. a. The man in the brown suit is my father.
   b. My father is my teacher when we go swimming.

6. a. He will be thirteen in three weeks.
   b. He is thirteen years old (today).

7. a. John is (habitually) late for school.
   b. John is late for school (today).

8. a. He is sleeping (now).
   b. He (usually) is sleeping in the afternoon.

Figure 7. As noted already, the rules for the use of the *be* form in Black English are that it is used for habitual actions which occur over time and for future. This worksheet is taken from materials supplied by Walt Wolfram, Federal City College and the Center for Applied Linguistics. The answers are 1b, 2a, 3b, 4a, 5b, 6a, 7a, 8b.

lation of passages from *Huckleberry Finn,* for example, provides a very difficult academic task which helps students understand the subtleties of Jim's speech and the liveliness of Huck's when compared with the rather bland standard texts generated by their translations.

My majority students struggle with these exercises and come to understand how difficult the acquisition of a new dialect is. Nonstandard-English-speaking minorities already feel this, but they may not yet understand it. Nonetheless, they enjoy being right and having it come easily. By this time, majority students have gained a strong respect for the rules of minority dialects and some measure of academic understanding of them as well. This study is not just affective in its orienta-

Vocabulary Test

In the following sentences, choose the meaning(s) of the sentences as you would normally understand them. In a few cases, a sentence may have more than one meaning, but you should normally look for only one meaning. Different sentences may mean different things to different people, and we're simply interested in what they may mean to you. If a sentence doesn't really mean anything to you, write "Don't know" under the sentence.

1. I hear that Mrs. Jones has *a crumb snatcher.*
   a. a dog that begs at the table.
   b. a cat.
   c. a pet that begs at the table.
   d. a baby.

2. Don't *waste the milk!*
   a. spill the milk!
   b. drink the milk!
   c. drink all the milk!
   d. taste the milk!

3. Curtis was *hitting on Edna.*
   a. flirting with Edna.
   b. beating Edna.
   c. lying to Edna.
   d. teasing Edna.

4. John was *doing a slow drag.*
   a. dancing a slow dance.
   b. driving in his car slowly.
   c. smoking his cigarette slowly.
   d. walking very slowly.

5. James *is a punk.*
   a. is a troublemaker.
   b. is a young child.
   c. acts like a young child.
   d. is a homosexual.

6. The Jones's just bought a new *hog.*
   a. animal for the farm.
   b. car.
   c. Cadillac.
   d. house.

7. James *is bright.*
   a. is intelligent.
   b. has light skin color.

Figure 8. This worksheet is taken from materials supplied by Walt Wolfram, University of District of Columbia and the Center for Applied Linguistics and has been revised by Barbara Osburg. The answers are 1d, 2a, 3a, 4a, 5d, 6c, 7a, 8d, 9b, 10b, 11d, 12b, 13c, 14c, 15b.

   c. is cheerful.
   d. is fat.

8. Don't *roll your eyes at me!*
   a. let your mind wander when talking to me!
   b. flirt with me!
   c. let your eyes go crossed when talking to me!
   d. be disrespectful to me!

9. James *is color struck.*
   a. likes sparkling colors.
   b. likes light-skinned persons.
   c. is color blind.
   d. can't stand the bright sun.

10. Linda *has an attitude about Gene.*
   a. likes Gene.
   b. is angry with Gene.
   c. is nice to Gene.
   d. knows what she thinks about Gene.

11. Mrs. Johnson *blessed out Dolores.*
   a. blessed Dolores.
   b. prayed for Dolores.
   c. liked to pick on Dolores.
   d. scolded Dolores.

12. Melvin *had tight jaws.*
   a. had a thin face.
   b. was very quiet.
   c. was angry.
   d. had the mumps.

13. Don't *poke your mouth out at me!*
   a. laugh!
   b. cry!
   c. be mad!
   d. be surprised!

14. *It's boocoo candy in the box.*
   a. There's good candy in the box.
   b. There's chocolate candy in the box.
   c. There's a lot of candy in the box.
   d. There's no candy in the box.

15. It's time for *the haints.*
   a. saying no.
   b. the ghosts to be out.
   c. visiting.
   d. going to church.

Figure 8. *Continued.*

Reactions to *A-* Forms

Some dialects of English put an *a-* type sound before some words that end in *-ing,* so that we get phrases like "A-hunting we will go." In fact, you will sometimes find headlines that have these forms, such as one in *Time* magazine that read, "Carter goes a-wooin' and wins some." The following sentence pairs each contain an *in'* (or *ing*) word. Choose which of the sentences you think require the *a-* prefix, but choose only one sentence in each pair. If you are not sure, take your best guess. On a separate sheet of paper, note the sentence (either a or b) which you think requires the form *a-* before the *ing* word.

1. a. John likes sailin'.
   b. John went sailin'.

2. a. The woman was comin' down the stairs.
   b. The movie was shockin'.

3. a. He makes money buildin' houses.
   b. He makes money by buildin' houses.

4. a. She got sick workin' so hard.
   b. She thought workin' was good for her.

5. a. Sam was followin' the trail.
   b. Sam was discoverin' the cave.

6. a. The dog was eatin' the food.
   b. The dogs was drinkin' the water.

7. a. The man was confessin' his crime.
   b. The man was hollerin' at the dogs.

8. a. I've never messed with dogs fightin'.
   b. I've never messed with fightin' dogs.

Figure 9. As noted already, the rules for the use of the *a-* prefix in Appalachian English are that it is used for verbs, not verbals, with initial consonants, not vowels, with first-syllable stressed words, and in place of prepositions such as "of" and "by." This worksheet is taken from materials supplied by Walt Wolfram, Federal City College and the Center for Applied Linguistics and has been revised by Barbara Osburg. The answers are 1b, 2a, 3a, 4a, 5a, 6b, 7b, 8a.

tion or its goals; we are not just trying to empathize with speakers of nonstandard English dialects or with those whose language of nurture is not English. This study is cognitive and highly intellectual, just as the study of standard English usage has been in school for years. Genuine academic attention to dialect enfranchises both the speech and its speakers. My students' newfound knowledge of non-Network variations of English provides a basis for their growing understanding of and empathy for non-Network English speakers. And this under-

---

Vocabulary

In the following sentences, choose the meaning(s) of the sentences as you would normally understand them. In a few cases, a sentence may have more than one meaning, but you should normally look for only one meaning. Different sentences may mean different things to different people, and we're simply interested in what they may mean to you. If a sentence doesn't really mean anything to you, write "Don't know" under the sentence.

1. Ginny brought corn pone for supper.
   a. corn on the cob for the evening meal.
   b. cornbread for the evening meal.
   c. corn on the cob for the noon meal.
   d. cornbread for the noon meal.

2. He *like to died.*
   a. He enjoyed funerals.
   b. He resembled a dead person.
   c. He almost died.
   d. He was dead.

3. He ate *a mess of beans.*
   a. bean soup.
   b. pork and beans.
   c. a helping of beans.
   d. all of the beans which had been prepared.

4. She toasted a piece of *light bread.*
   a. bread made with bleached flour.
   b. bread made with yeast.
   c. store-bought bread.
   d. cornbread.

5. He brought us a peck of *pickles.*
   a. dill-pickled cucumbers.
   b. green peppers.
   c. fresh cucumbers.
   d. pickled green tomatoes.

Figure 10. This Appalachian vocabulary test was designed by Barbara Osburg. The answers are 1b, 2c, 3d, 4b, 5d.

standing and empathy become coupled in my classroom format, which is designed to get students to talk.

Interaction and Engagement

If we are to create truly equitable multicultural classrooms, we must design student-centered classrooms which not only encourage but also require student interaction and speaking. This interaction is the key to a classroom community. From the first day of class, I use an oral

---

A- Prefix in Appalachian English

Appalachian dialect includes an *a-* type sound before some words that end in *-ing*, so that we get phrases like "A-hunting we will go." You have discovered and studied the rules governing this prefix use and should now be able to correct the following Network sentences so that they conform to Appalachian usage. Please be sure that you also correct the verb forms to conform with Appalachian pronunciation.

1. Mary's gone dewberry picking.
2. Mary's always liked picking dewberries.
3. Mary's picking dewberries.
4. Mary's money comes from picking dewberries.
5. Mary earns a little money picking dewberries.
6. I was feeding the dog when he turned and bit me.
7. She got tired of studying for so long.
8. The hog was eating his slop.
9. The woman was singing to her baby.
10. The boy wanted whittling to make a living for him.
11. The calf was drinking her ma's milk.
12. Lily was reciting her verses.
13. The teacher was punishing the disobedient.
14. He makes a living by whittling.
15. Walter was shooting at squirrels.

Figure 11. Using the rules already outlined in the earlier exercises, students should be able to correctly turn these Network sentences into Appalachian dialect.

language-centered model which engages students, puts them in leadership roles, and allows them to practice both their language of nurture and the "English of Wider Communication" (see Smitherman-Donaldson, "Toward a National Policy") in a variety of situations. Students must lead discussions, be accountable for what is said, and further one another in the discussion at hand (that is, ask questions of the speakers before stating their own views). Students begin to ask one another, "What did you say?" with sincerity, not disparagement. This respectful furthering results from both the format and the language study in which we are simultaneously engaged. Quieter students begin to talk, having just learned that their talk is valid, logical, equal. They begin to

---

Be in Black English

Black English includes a *be* use in certain instances to function as the future and for habitual actions or actions which happen over time, so that we get sentences like *He be foolin' everybody.* You have discovered and studied the rules governing this verb form and should now be able to correct the following Network sentences so that they conform to Black English usage. Please be sure that you also correct the verb forms to conform with Black English pronunciation. Use a separate sheet of paper to rewrite the sentences into Black English.

1. The principal is in the lunchroom (during lunch every day).

2. My sister is always talking on the phone.

3. James is watching TV (right now).

4. That girl will be seventeen on Friday.

5. Allen is always early for school.

6. Allen is always early, so he will be early tomorrow.

7. Cheryn is a cheerleader.

8. Cheryn will be crowned homecoming queen at the dance.

9. My mama is a teacher.

10. I will be late if I am talking to you when the bus comes.

Figure 12. Using the rules already outlined in the earlier exercises, students should be able to correctly turn these Network sentences into Black English.

speak loudly and articulately enough to be understood by their class-mates (see Osburg, "The Student-Centered Classroom," for details).

From the first day of class, the period begins with a brief pre-lesson (anticipatory set) writing experience. For example, on the first day I begin English I (ninth grade) with a brief study of symbolic communication and group dynamics. I then assign an entry that asks students to make judgments concerning my income, age, hobbies, taste in music, favorite movie, and marital/family status by looking at my clothes and hairstyle, the decorations in the room, and the title I have chosen for my name (Dr./Ms. Osburg). I then ask for a volunteer to lead the journal-sharing time. (Someone always can be counted on to volunteer, although a little prodding might be needed in the form of "Volunteer or I will volunteer you.") The leader then explains the list of rules concerning our class discussions, which are shown in figure 13 (the students have handouts of these in front of them). Following these rules, the leader begins by asking for volunteers to read or paraphrase their journal entries and to comment on the entries of others. Students

---

Guidelines for Class Discussion

1. Calling on persons must be done fairly and equitably, not capriciously or vindictively. In other words, discussion leaders cannot protect their friends from involvement or unfairly give them too much attention; they cannot call on people in order to embarrass them or to get even with them.

2. Everyone must listen when someone is reading aloud or speaking, and the speakers must speak loudly enough to be heard by everyone.

3. As a check on listening and clarity of communication during journal sharing and other discussions, before calling on the next respondent, discussion leaders must summarize each person's response or ask someone else to do so. During class discussion, students wishing to respond to another's comments must first briefly summarize those comments before giving their own; for example, "I see. You think that Beatrice meant to entrap Giovanni. I believe her when she says she 'thought only to love' him."

4. Discussion should usually include references to the text at hand. Note the example in Guideline #3, which includes a line from the story under discussion ("Rappaccini's Daughter").

5. The discussion leaders must act primarily as moderators and summarizers, not as the focus of discussion.

Figure 13. These guidelines were developed for all kinds of classes, not just literature study, and are more clearly illustrated in Osburg (22–26).

who do not speak loudly enough to be heard are hailed ("I can't hear you!") by their classmates, who may be called upon to paraphrase their comments. Students who do not have their own responses often use questioning as a way of participating: "I don't see why you said that she has kids. Where did you get that idea from her looks?" I encourage students who are especially timid to do paraphrasing and questioning because it does not force them to reveal their own thoughts and opinions and thus make themselves vulnerable to criticism.

Because the writing has no right answer and because the responses are often funny and poke fun at me, the session goes well. The students have been encouraged to participate, and they have enjoyed the experience. Everything is positive. I use a guideline that I call "participation in good faith." This means that different students will participate in varying ways according to the situation and their own temperaments. But I expect them all to participate fully in their own fashion "in good faith." Listening, leaning forward to hear better, smiling, and encouraging are important parts of communication, too, and go a long way toward making our classroom community work. I take aside especially shy students and encourage them to consider questions instead of answers during the discussions. I often tell them the next day's assignment so that they can prepare ahead of time. Often, these more reticent students choose to lead discussion rather than share journals. As the year progresses, I add more and more responsibilities to the discussion leader, such as planning the actual journal assignment, arranging small-group discussions, and even picking topics for discussion. And the rules for class discussion encourage students to speak and listen and to demand that others speak clearly enough to be heard.

This classroom model for interactive and egalitarian language use also promotes appreciation and understanding as well as genuine interaction and language practice. I often find that those African American students who initially were quiet, low-profile, invisible people develop as class leaders. Some of them choose to keep their Black English speech but now use it for effective, coherent classroom contributions. This enfranchises their language of nurture and helps acclimate the majority to Black English dialect and its intricacies and expressiveness. Some of the Black English speakers choose Network English for classroom discussion. These students are provided opportunities to practice a developing dialect. When inner-city Black English speakers speak only to other Black English speakers, they have no occasion to use Network English. In a student-centered, interactive classroom, these students and their "foreign" peers find an audience that actively listens to their ideas, and they simultaneously gain an audience for their "English of Wider Communication." Majority students learn to listen to meaning instead of form and thus gain an "ear" for both dialect and immigrant pronunciation. Asian students, who often outright refuse to speak their own minds at first, find comfort in the form of asking questions which further the comments and discussion of others and which require less personal revelation and seem less abrasive to Asian concepts of respect and politeness.

But all of the students find new language experiences in listening and in speaking—and in writing. They begin to make choices about their levels of language and about dialects, choices based in part on their own self-concepts and their own felt needs and in part on their new knowledge about language, not on some teacher-imposed rule of "standard usage." Students talk more at the end of the class than at the beginning. And whether that talk is standard or dialect, Network or immigrant, they are talking to learn as well as learning to talk in an atmosphere which encourages talk without reference to the outmoded model of "correctness."

This approach and these assignments open up much more than just discussion: they open up minds and hearts to the delight of diversity and the intellectual validity of dialect. They provide actual information about our language and its many delightful forms. Both standard English and dialects receive grammatical analysis of equal status. Slang and esoteric vocabulary are both explored, and their usefulness is shown. Within a very few weeks, my students know what James Sledd has maintained for many years: that "Good English" is not a matter of form but is what good people use English to do; that "Bad English" is deceptive and manipulative instead of clear and communicative. Our discussions of "good" and "bad" language center on doublespeak and advertising, while our discussions of usage focus on appropriateness and power, history and heritage, personal preference and conformity. The result of my students' newfound knowledge about their language and its various forms is a newfound affection for language and for differences. They no longer disparage their dialects nor fall prey to doublespeak. They know the history and evolution of their linguistic differences, and they feel the power of language to heal as well as to harm. Minority students speak more loudly and confidently, taking leadership roles more willingly than they did before I used these strategies. They become active members of class rather than a peripheral, passive audience. They and their majority peers not only accept their differences, they embrace them.

Two years ago, after a brief presentation of the Black English substitution of *it* for *there* in sentences like, "It's a pencil on the des'" ("There is a pencil on the desk"), three of the most talented students in the class stayed to ask lots of questions about Black English, so I offered to bring in Smitherman's and Dillard's books. When I returned with the texts the following day, the three were delighted and set out on a month-long program to master the basic rules of Black English grammar. They came in each day with questions about the correctness of various negatives and tense formations and pursued their study with a fervor rivaling that in any of their other academic interests. These white, middle-class students had found a nonstandard dialect highly worthy of study and extremely fascinating, and this respectful attitude spread to their classmates. We wound up correcting each other's errors in Black English *and* in Network English as well; we all conformed to varying standards throughout the semester.

When I ask each semester for responses to the rather outdated Black English vocabulary test, white students are completely puzzled by the knowledge of their black peers: "How do you know what a crumb snatcher is?" Inner-city black students are amazed at the ignorance of their white peers: "How you *not* be knowin' dat?" Ironic laughter begins; eye contact is made. Interaction is initiated because of this contradiction of traditional school roles: after all, students, black and white, know that, in the final analysis, school is white and middle class in its curriculum, its values, and its climate. To reward knowledge of a subculture is humorous, iconoclastic, and motivating. Each year, my Black English speakers delight in informing me that my vocabulary test is out of date. They offer me substitute items to update my "olddddddddddd-fashionedddddddd—Negroes" (Hansberry, II, iii, 273) test: especially new vocabulary like "paper" (money), "homey" (close friend), "dope" (something approved by the majority of people), "strapped" (armed with a weapon), and "hard" (to express approval).

All of this contributes to the fluency and flexibility of my students' language and to their involvement in the community of my class. But this by no means guarantees the perfection of their conformity to Network English or to their native dialects. Like all of us, high school students—even those from homes where Network is the language of nurture—struggle to find accurate and appropriate voices for their situations and purposes. Students are almost always in transition between languages and dialects, formal and slang usage, and are quite frequently the masters of none of these forms. And though their knowledge is often adequate for testing, their own usage in writing is a complex blending of their various tongues. Sometimes I evaluate their use of Network English; other times, I read their pieces without marking or evaluating this aspect of writing. Sometimes I require dialect for authenticity.

The implications of Smitherman-Donaldson's term, "English of Wider Communication," is obvious here in that students begin to realize that a Network dialect allows them a wider audience for their communications and a more agreeable reception from that audience than would a minority dialect. As well, and in line with Smitherman-Donaldson's mandate to require foreign languages in public schools, those of us who speak only English may soon find that—at least in the Western Hemisphere—English alone is not sufficient or effective to gain the widest audience for our communications and the most agreeable reception when speaking, for example, with Hispanics and Asians. The key, I believe, for students and for all of us, is to be aware of diversity and its possible consequences—for success and failure, acceptance and rejection, good and evil—and to try to become the kind of people James Sledd is talking about when he says "Good English."

Long ago, only white adolescent males were educated in Latin grammar schools, away from the negative personal influences of home and native tongue. The homogeneity of those schools and of those who left these educational factories of 50-plus students in a class, translating Latin into English and back again, created a common culture of a homogeneous, educated elite. Perhaps the most idealistic and noble part of the great American democratic experiment was to educate every one of our future citizens—girls and boys, rich and poor, native and immigrant. Local school districts, though, still reflect the ethnicity and socioeconomic mores of the white, middle-class male.

But, if we are lucky—as I am—we find classrooms full of diversity. And, if we are lucky, we make use of this diversity to improve the education of all our students. We take their disdain and shame and transform them into delight and democracy. We lead them to the knowledge that diversity is neither inferior nor superior. We help them to see that language diversity enriches both majority and minority students, enfranchises them all, and helps them to begin to realize the ideal American democracy we have only begun to build.

Works Cited

Daniels, Harvey. "Nine Ideas about Language." *Language: Introductory Readings.* Ed. Virginia Clark, Paul Eschholz, and Alfred Rosa. New York: St. Martin's, 1985. 18–36.

Dillard, J. L. *Black English: Its History and Usage in the United States.* New York: Vintage, 1972.

Hansberry, Lorraine. *A Raisin in the Sun. Understanding People: Four Representative Types.* Ed. Julius Liebb. New York: Globe, 1971. 204–309.

Osburg, Barbara. "The Student-Centered Classroom: Speaking and Listening in American Literature." *Talking to Learn.* Ed. Patricia Phelan. Urbana, IL: NCTE, 1989. 22–26.

Sledd, James. "Sticks and Stones Break Only Bones." Lecture. Southeast Missouri University. April 1979.

Smitherman, Geneva. *Talkin' and Testifyin': The Language of Black America.* Detroit: Wayne State UP, 1977.

Smitherman-Donaldson, Geneva. "Toward a National Policy on Language." *College English* 47.1 (1987): 29–36.

Teicher, Susan. "Speaker Analysis Chart." Handout created for unit plan in fulfillment of course assignment and subsequently revised. St. Louis. 1990.

Wolfram, Walt. "Black Vocabulary Test." Handout from workshop for National Humanities Faculty grant. University of District of Columbia and the Center for Applied Linguistics, 1985.

———. "Reactions to *A*- Forms." Handout from workshop for National Humanities Faculty grant. Federal City College and the Center for Applied Linguistics, 1985.

Additional Sources for Teachers

Christian, Donna, and Walt Wolfram. *Exploring Dialects.* Arlington, VA: Center for Applied Linguistics, 1979.

Gere, Anne Ruggles, and Eugene Smith. *Attitudes, Language, and Change.* Urbana, IL: NCTE, 1979.

Non-Native and Nonstandard Dialect Students. Urbana, IL: NCTE, 1982.

Shuy, Roger. *Discovering American Dialects.* Urbana, IL: NCTE, 1967.

Smitherman-Donaldson, Geneva, and Teun A. Van Dijk, eds. *Discourse and Discrimination.* Detroit: Wayne State UP, 1988.

Wolfram, Walt, and Donna Christian. *Dialogue on Dialects.* Arlington, VA: Center for Applied Linguistics, 1979.

II Preserving Voices: Writing as a Reflective, Clarifying, and Expressive Force

This section focuses on writing—all forms of writing—and how it is used to clarify, reflect, and analyze both self and society. The first three chapters address writing programs for basic writers at the community college level. "Becoming Centered in the Students: What a Teacher Can Do for Underprepared Learners" points out how a sensitive teacher who listens carefully to students and who reads carefully and empathetically what they write can attain a student-centered classroom. Here "people of various language backgrounds come together to get work done." "'Worldview' Publication as an Incentive for Excellence in Writing" describes a program where developmental writing and English composition courses are taught in distance learning to students statewide from an Inupiat Eskimo village thirty miles above the Arctic Circle. Completed assignments find publication in regional newspapers and magazines throughout Alaska. Teaching via satellite to reach remote students, the instructors augment audio-conference classes with telephone, fax, and surface-mail contact. Thus, distance learning, a force for the future, is already being shaped in a state where distance and weather are impediments to traditional modes of teaching. "Autobiography as a Liberating Force in the Basic Writing Classroom" recounts how students in basic writing courses write autobiographical letters and notes that serve as a springboard to understanding audience and voice as the students share, revise, and refine their ideas about themselves and their world.

The fourth and fifth chapters deal with writing programs for second-language learners. "Bridging Cross-Cultural Differences through

Writing" describes a letter writing exchange between ESL students and freshman composition classes. The pen-pal exchange helped ESL students learn about American English and American culture, while the regular composition students learned more about the components of effective written communication. Both groups learned about people from other cultures. "'Delicious of the New': ESL as Poetry, EFL as Literary Analysis" describes the use of "refined found poetry" in language fluency and language appreciation. This poetry is used as a means of helping students to discover both narrative voice and the richness and diversity of English. As part of their discovery process, students attempt to translate a poem or short story into their second language (or their first language, in some cases). This translation is, as the author says, a task that calls for keeping the "mood and feeling" of the original.

The next chapter in this section, "'Break On Through': An Interdisciplinary Approach to Composition," describes a unit useful for both second-language learners and native speakers at a number of grade levels. The unit brings cohesion to a remarkably diverse group of secondary school students that includes many ethnicities, cultures, and languages. Here students reveal their impressions and their memories of neighborhoods as they disclose the new patterns of their lives in an imaginary, underground city, where they have survived disaster.

The last two chapters examine writing classes that focus on contemporary issues. "Environmental Writing and Minority Education" describes an advanced composition workshop that has proved successful for African, Native, Hispanic, and Portuguese American students. These students integrate personal environmental concerns with personal history in a wide range of essays that includes an environmental autobiography, a landscape history, a nature essay, and a landscape-perception study. The final chapter, "Successful Teaching Practices for Sexual Minority Students in Writing Courses: Four Teachers at Work," concerns sexual minority issues in the composition class. This chapter details four courses where university students explore sexual minority and gender issues and culture through literature and their own writing. Three courses described in this chapter are elective for university students who wish to explore the issues involved, while the fourth course is a more broadly based university course containing a unit that explores these issues. All of the courses nonetheless focus on writing from experience, analyzing literature, and using this knowledge to interpret one's own place in society.

4 Becoming Centered in the Students: What a Teacher Can Do for Underprepared Learners

Smokey Wilson
Laney College, Oakland, California

There has been talk for a long time about classrooms becoming more student-centered. It sounds like a simple idea and easy to practice. But, in fact, I have found that figuring out how to conduct myself and my curriculum in ways which are authentically centered in students' needs has occupied most of my teaching life, now approaching (can it be?) thirty years.

I had always believed the phrase "student-centered" was coined by James Moffett. My colleague with a Master's in counseling assumed that the phrase evolved from Carl Rogers's ideas about client-centered therapy. And that's how it generally is, I believe, when teachers begin to uncover the theoretical roots of their practice. We find that we have worked using notions from many sources, from the air we breathed in our formative teaching years. We rarely take time to examine this conventional wisdom.

My effort to think through the idea of student-centered teaching and learning came from my reading of Paulo Freire's notions of marginalization. The reasoning behind marginalization goes something like this: People of color, those who are poor, those who cannot read or write in ways that the academic world acknowledges, must inhabit regions on the edges of the real world while others who are more fortunate (like ourselves) occupy the center. These marginalized people, it is said, are disadvantaged; our advantages of income, status, and education are what they must be given. Their level of illiteracy is remediable; the remedies are found in our assessment and treatment and in their achievement of measurable objectives. Set out in stark simple lines, the ethnocentrism of this view becomes unmistakable. Yet, of course, Freire warned us years ago about the dangers of such ethnocentric reasoning, warned us about the folly of setting up any group of people as marginal.

As I looked at the way American schools treated youngsters who were people of color, poor, or in one way or another on the outside of the academic enterprise, I could see that these groups had been treated as exactly that—marginal, not "in the mainstream." Schools set up special programs of study—a semester-long course on sentence structure, whole tracks for "non-college-bound" learners, all in an effort to meet their needs. Programs test students, "diagnose" the problems of those who are below grade level, treat them in pull-out tutorials or by using programmed texts, and test them again, looking for miraculous improvements. These transfusions of knowledge often fail to fix anything, and we fall into the trap of blaming the victim—or blaming the schools. We less often search for the ways that school failure is produced by unresolved conflicts between the needs of the learner and the goals of the school.

None of this is new to teachers at any grade level who struggle daily with preparing students for the end-of-the-semester standardized tests or the college entrance exams. But what these unpleasant facts point up is that we need to think about the implications of having marginalized those who do not share the opportunities of mainstream, middle-class America, those who have been called "underprepared" (for the next English class, for the world of work, or for the current English class), those who are at high risk of failure (in school—to say nothing of the high risks they face to survive). And as a profession, we teachers need to figure out how to stop doing this.

As I worked with adults whose test scores reported that they read on a third- (or fifth-, or eighth-) grade level, who wrote a few painful sentences in response to a writing assignment and had not mastered the multiplication tables, I tried to stop and think. The writings by Freire helped me think productively. In fact, each group is a center, he said: children are born into a culture which gives them their worldview. If I accepted this assumption, then I had to discover ways to see no margins but only many centers. Therein lay the rub—for I, like all teachers, must somehow bring about the desirable ends of education, "meet standards," teach a curriculum, and at the same time respect each person's center. These heavy and sometimes contradictory demands produced a friction for me. As anyone who has ever tried to make a class complete an unpopular assignment can attest, the friction can rub teachers raw, and I left class many times nursing sore spots created by my missteps in judging where the students were in relation to where I wanted them to go.

But as I continued my attempts to match more closely the learning tasks I proposed with the students' readiness, I learned ways to lessen the gaps between what I proposed and what they were disposed to take on. As I accepted the challenge, a decentering took place. I became less ethnocentric, and what was once a contradiction became my method—that is, I found ways to meet the desirable ends of education by respecting each student's center.

As I said, it has taken my whole teaching life to begin to understand the practice shaped by this theoretical notion of student-centeredness. I started my teaching career in the mid-sixties, assigned to a course called "Remedial Reading" at an urban community college in northern California. Then (as now), the unemployment rate, the infant mortality rate, and the high school dropout rate were (and remain) impressively high for some of the members of the community this college serves. Recently, crack cocaine and gang violence have added new pestilence.

I have stayed so long, teaching now the children of my first students, because I fell in love with Franklin in 1969, Tommy in 1974, Stella in 1979, and LaShana just yesterday. Each of these students, and I could have named others, helped me, in some way, to understand how to adjust what I taught to what they needed. Franklin taught me how one could prize education even after being treated badly at its hands—and that understanding forms one of the vantage points from which I still regard my students. Tommy taught me how to say, without embarrassment, "I don't understand." Once, in a writing conference, he told me that his "so-called friend" did something to him; he "crep on his pocket." I was terribly confused, and to cover that confusion, I told him he had not picked a good subject to write about. It took me several conferences to admit to him that I had failed to understand his story, an admission which finally allowed him to explain that his friend had robbed him, a clarification that led to his first, full-blown, written narrative. Stella taught me to recognize the power of the mind to generalize—for while I could only measure her learning of a single concept—the variant sounds spelled with the letter C—the fact was that she went on from that point and "taught herself to read." And LaShana . . . but wait. While each of these students taught me something valuable about conducting student-centered classrooms, these were, for me, preliminary, almost accidental, learnings. It was much later that I began to know what I was doing, and it is this more explicit sort of knowledge, as it plays itself out in a couple of case studies, that I want to focus on in this paper.

Before proceeding to the cases, I need to add a bit more personal history to clarify how certain tacit teaching practices became more explicit. That course listed in the schedule as "Remedial Reading" was my first job. Since my Master's degree had prepared me to teach how to read Shakespeare, rather than to teach others how to read, period, I soon found myself back in graduate school—for it was clear (to me and to my students, I am sure) that I did not know what I was doing or what I should be doing for students who could read with ease neither Shakespeare nor the morning newspaper. While still teaching at Laney, I studied at the University of California and became, by academic training, a classroom microethnographer of communication—that is, I learned how to look long and carefully at specific interactions between teacher and student so that I could understand how larger social structures are shaped (and sometimes modified) through talk and text.

My graduate work refined my interest, impelling me to study Franklin and Tommy and Stella and others like them in the act of learning. I wanted to document the various routes to literacy which I felt sure people could take, by reporting how students like these succeeded rather than failed at school. Heaven knew, we had heard enough about their failure. It may seem the long way around, but before I could systematically study what I wanted to know more about, I first had to develop classroom environments in which this learning was happening. My long-term research agenda had to be based not on the occasional "good-luck" connection with an individual, but on classrooms that were programmatically focused on empowering this target population to attain success in school.

Toward this end, two colleagues and I began an interdisciplinary block program in basic skills. We started the program because, as reading, writing, and math teachers, respectively, we learned through our casual, over-coffee conversations that we were each working with the same students but that we were not coordinating our instruction in any organized way. We wrote a very small grant, enough really just to buy "talk time" for the three of us, and for three hours each week for one semester, we talked about what we wanted in a basic skills program. The driving force behind our planning was, first and foremost, the notion that skills should be subordinated to content. Our battle cry was "Ideas are intrinsically interesting. If the college experience is rich in ideas, the skills needed to read and write and compute about these ideas will follow." But these could not just be "topical-issues" courses. Rather, we had to develop curriculum about topics the students could connect with, and we had to convey this curriculum in ways that did not entirely depend upon the written word for instruction. The students we had in mind did not, would not, perhaps could not, read texts like *Antigone* as "homework" and come to class "prepared for discussion." But together, using the support of teachers, tutors, and more accomplished peers, we found it was possible to do in tandem what no one could have done alone: to read thought-provoking text and to reflect upon its meanings in discussions and writings.

We named this program Project Bridge, enrolling 75 students each semester in reading, writing, and mathematics courses; as time went on, we added a computer-applications class and a course in an academic discipline in the social sciences or the humanities. Four hours a day, four days a week, staff and students worked together to build a supportive academic community in which skills forgotten could be refreshed, those never acquired could be introduced and mastered, and a sense of excitement about learning could be passed on. This program has been operating now for over a decade; some of its students have gone on to graduate with two-year or four-year degrees, and a few have come back to tutor in the program. But for my teaching and research life, the payoff has been in getting a good look at the ways in which underprepared adults begin to use literate behaviors for college and for the world of work.

There are many interesting elements in Project Bridge: its focus on multicultural literature, its use of oral language, its work on self-esteem. All of these aspects of the program are crucial to students' learning and success. Various articles which discuss Project Bridge as an attempt to change the remedial education model are available, both in published and manuscript form (see, for example, Griffith et al.). But I have already mentioned that I look for large meanings in small spaces, so you may not be surprised by my focus on case studies of two students to explore just one notion—what does it mean for a teacher to be student-centered in a program where students represent so many centers, so many different ways of regarding things academic?

Teachers committed to an emphasis on each student's needs are crucial, no doubt, for many students' success. But for the student who wrote the following response to Project Bridge's first-day assignment, which asked for a letter of introduction, teachers with this theoretical base are indispensable:

> I am coming to project Bridge in hopes of battering my life in the since of, reading wirteing and spelling.
> I driped out out of school When I was in the 7th graid, I stop learning in the 4th graid.
> at home I there was one Big partee going on, I could not do my home work so one day I started parting to.
> I was an acolick at thirteen and that is that.
> today I am trying to live a good life I love peple and life I have came a long ways and I am not stoping because of my Schooling. . . .

This student is the kind of learner who plucks at my coattails to have some part of his story told. He began as a most unwilling writer, became deeply involved with his writing and with hopes for his future, and then one day, and with no explanation, disappeared after weeks of perfect attendance. I felt his loss keenly then, and I feel it still, after several years. What happened, and how was my instruction implicated? I know now what I did right. I did not flinch at the misspellings or write "FRAG!" in the margins, and because he felt a welcoming, this student got his foot in the door of the academic enterprise. I am less clear, however, about what went wrong (though I am working on this question in my current investigation on the resistance of underprepared learners). For the moment, I only can say that my teaching history has its share of those who took up the educational invitation—for a while—and then—far short of the training or competencies needed to exchange a minimum-wage life for a better one—said, "No, thank you," or "No, not now," or just, "No." But I can't think the time spent with the student was time wasted.

When Mike Rose wrote about students like these in *Lives on the Boundary*, he reminded us that, for them, coming back to school is more than a promise of just being able to earn a few extra dollars: it is "intimately connected with respect, with a sense that they are not beaten, the mastery of print revealing the deepest impulse to survive" (217).

For such students who return to school late in life—those whose chances of completing a college education are so slim, the students whom Mike Rose writes about and whom I teach—what is it that the teacher can do? From a programmatic point of view, I would argue that the teacher can either foster a learning environment which is safe and from which students can take what they need, or else create an atmosphere which perpetuates the students' previous school failures. But that is very general advice and less than helpful.

I suppose if I were to sum up the single most important notion about what to do in the real-time, minute-by-minute orchestration of instruction, that notion would be to assume nothing and pay attention to things which do not necessarily sit easy with me as teacher. The lesson is simple, but I keep forgetting. Even though Project Bridge classes focus on ideas, there are nevertheless skills I want to explain. I walk into my reading class energetically, going to the board to write in large letters, "SEQUENCE." I tell students the goal of the lesson: "Okay," I say, "today we are going to focus on sequence, on how events in this story are put together, on what happens first, second, third." Off to a good start—providing visual cues and clear definitions. Then, from the back of the room, a hand waves frantically and a voice says, "I know about sequins, little shiny, uh, shiny, uh, like all over my dress for the prom." These participants in the classroom make me listen, and they remind me that their sequences and my sequences do not always begin from the same place.

We are not a ready-made "academic learning community," my students and I; we hold in common so few ways of reading or writing that what community we have, we forge line by line. Underprepared learners become functioning members in communities of readers and writers only insofar as I successfully center myself and my instruction in what these students need. I want to provide two snapshots that catch me in the act of learning lessons about student-centeredness, profiles that suggest how the teacher can play a vital role in the development of literate behaviors without following either a "banking" model approach to instruction (see Freire) or a laissez-faire opting out of instructional responsibilities.

Snapshot 1: Darleen, Reading

The first snapshot is of Darleen Gutierrez, reading. When I first met her, she did not strike me as a particularly promising student. I overlooked her strengths of persistence and unfailing good humor, heard only her desperate bids for attention. One of our class activities, which was really one of my ongoing, teacher-research projects, helped me to appreciate her obstacles and see her possibilities. This activity, a tape-recorded reading journal (described more fully in Wilson, "Construction of Text"), requires that students read into a tape recorder for two minutes from any story they want, and then tell why they picked that particular passage to read. I then respond, on their tape, and give them a few pointers for their next reading.

On her first tape recording, Ms. Gutierrez read a story written by another student in a previous Project Bridge class about learning to drive. The tape went on for more than the two minutes, as she read the whole story instead of selecting what she regarded as the most important part. With fifteen tapes still to listen and respond to, I was peeved. The tape went on and on, and I grew more impatient with each sing-song sentence. I remember hoping, irritably, that she would at least catch the writer's point about becoming more independent. But her response was not to the author's message, but rather spelled out her own unique reading of the text. She said (and I quote from the tape):

> I don't drive. Lotta times I have the nerve to get up and do it but then I back away. Like everything else, you have to take that first step. Like everything else, I'm nervous to drive. I don't find myself doing that.

It had never occurred to me. For me, anxiety is something you grin and bear. For her, anxiety is a deterrent. But when I heard her, I understood how nervousness could stop someone not only from driving but from everything else. I recognized with a start that everyone is not like me, and I saw Darleen as separate and distinct and thus, mysteriously, somehow more approachable. And in the same minute, I knew what the "everything else" was that she felt anxious about. It was reading—in particular, it was my class. I grasped a larger scenario, and what had been impatience gave way to empathy. On tape I responded:

> Learning how to drive is no joke. You might want to try some things that help you get over your nervousness. I am really impressed you are trying so hard to read when I know it makes you nervous.

Two weeks later, she read again into the tape, this time from a class handout called "History of English" which I had written to communicate my love for this language. In her response to what she read, she continued to develop a line of her personal reading evolution. She said:

> I'm finding out more and more each day that I read that I understand English more, and the more I read the more I like it. There's a lot more for me to learn. But it's a start and I think I'm headed in the right direction. And that's why I picked this story. The story "History of English" is very fascinating to read.

Talk about fascinating. Suddenly I couldn't wait to listen to her tape. I became fascinated by the history of literacy Darleen was making as she was reading the history of English, at her process as she was becoming more "literate." I became less dismayed that she didn't fully share my enthusiasm for Hengist and Horsa. I was ready to listen to her making meaning, knowing that she was struggling with her life-long fear of reading failure. I was pleased that she felt she had made a start at overcoming it, a little bit engaged with written matters. And of course, she had engaged me, built a link with a teacher. And we all understand how significant this link is (as old as master to apprentice, as expert to novice) between one who is a bearer of literacy and one who seeks to acquire it.

Listening carefully, I can almost hear literacy being transmitted in our tape-recorded exchanges. It moves unobtrusively, osmotically, as I listen to her reading and her interpretations and make suggestions couched in phrases that show her my own ways of reading. This transmission of literacy might not have happened had I not become interested in her reading process, rather than seeing it as a poor reflection of my own. As I left for the moment my own center to see things from her perspective, she came a little closer to reading in ways that my experience told me would be more rewarding. On the second reading, her tape was less sing-songy; she had selected an important passage rather than reading the whole thing. She was, in short, closer to meeting a teacher's expectations than she had been before. And here lies the paradox of student-centered teaching: As soon as the teacher takes on the perspective of the student (for however brief a moment), the student is more able to adopt the strategies the teacher is suggesting.

Darleen spent one year working with me. As she progressed, she began to memorize her favorite poems. She began to write, rather than tape-record, her responses to what she read. This development of writing is no less fascinating than her development of reading. There is not space here to examine this process in detail, but as this response to one of Langston Hughes's poems suggests, she continued to work out new understandings of old themes. However, there is an important difference: she began to learn to intersperse her own words with written text to make meaning, and the meanings she learned to make became more generalized.

Darleen's Written Response

[A]s a Puerto Rican I learn to deal with a lot of the outside prob-
lem as well but I, too, laugh and eat well and grow strong
because I, too, am an American. . . .
As American, I am not ashamed of who I am
or What I Can and Cannot do, and I don't
Care who is ashamed of me
"I too sing America.
I am the darker Brother
They send me to eat in the Kitchen. . . .
This line means to me that if Someone
was to send [me] in the kitchen when
Company Come" I would feel not wanted. . . .

Five or six years have now passed. After several years in the
community college, Darleen has received her two-year college degree.
After she left the courses in which I had a chance to monitor her
progress, she was tested by the campus learning disabilities specialist
and qualified for the Learning Disabilities program. This course of
instruction provided her with valuable, additional basic-skills work
(particularly in math), invaluable tutorial support as she moved into
college-level classes, and even more invaluable advocacy. Both the
counselor and an instructor in Disabled Students' Programs and Services contacted her teachers, arranged for extended time on tests, provided Darleen with awareness about her learning difficulties, and
helped her through financial-aid crises, graduation requirement crises—more difficult moments than I can remember or even know
about. In addition, she received weekly tutoring from a community
library project called "Berkeley Reads." She also acquired some clerical
skills from her work-study job under the direction of the college's faculty secretary. Without this array of support people, each meeting a
specific need with a specific set of skills and practice, Darleen might
not be the competent and confident person she is today.

But I can only reflect on the early steps which I witnessed firsthand. For Darleen and students like her, the battle with school pro-
ceeds simultaneously on both personal and academic fronts. Acknowledging the importance of the personal is the lifeline that allows
progress on the academic. By moving toward the learners who may be
very far from the world of school, teachers can invite them into the academic community we hope they will successfully enter. Had I maintained my less-than-sympathetic judgments, had I listened impatiently
only for the answers I expected, Darleen's story of school could have
dead-ended as it had done before. Darleen's unfolding story has inter-

ested me for six years; her hunger to achieve has called up the best in those who worked with her. A more complete explication of Darleen's early school experience has been published (Wilson, "What Happened"), but I am sure her story is far from finished.

Snapshot 2: Charles Eastmont (pseudonym), Writing

This second snapshot is of a student, whom I will call Charles Eastmont, writing. The lesson he taught me is not, I suppose, so different from the one I learned from Darleen, so although I was long in learning it with Mr. Eastmont, I can be brief in describing it. The classroom activity which led me to first begin thinking about Charles was Project Bridge's decision to use portfolio assessment; as a staff, we read every student's complete writing folder. Charles had completed one semester of Project Bridge (and hence I had a whole body of his work to examine), but his writing remained highly problematic. Though he had been in other teachers' sections during that semester, I knew he would join my writing class when school began again in the fall.

As with Darleen, Charles put me off at first. His demeanor and his reputation as someone who had spent many years in a Federal penitentiary intimidated me.

About August, I began recollecting the spring semester in tranquillity. I read reams of Charles's writing, listened to tape-recorded readings and to interviews with almost everyone who had worked with him during his year in the program. I remember especially Charles's end-of-year interview with a counselor. I recall being struck by how far out in left field his answers seemed. The counselor asked him what he had learned during the semester. Charles said (in various ways), "I was . . . better able to maintain my temper and myself as a human being." Nothing in Project Bridge's curriculum dealt with temper control, so I disregarded his version of what he had learned. Even when, in a portfolio interview with me, he had spoken repeatedly about how important his control over his bad temper had been, I neglected to transcribe—and hence ignored—these comments. I did not regard temper control as valid learning.

August turned into September, and Charles appeared in my writing class. How to begin with this man, a veteran of a lifestyle so different from my own? I had studied his work; I had thought about him a lot. And yet the semester was beginning, and I had no clear sense of direction. I found this direction just in time, though had I not been involved in a teacher-research group through the Bay Area Writing Project, I might have missed the moment. In one session, the leader of the teacher-research group asked us to write in our logs about a "day that had gone well." I wrote (and I have italicized the relevant portion):

> It's 3:30 Wednesday, and class has been going for an hour. It's one of those days I can do no wrong. I have just read Mark Twain's "I Can Remember" piece, and though the air outside is balmy, in this room we can feel the snow blowing in the attic windows, curbing the wild desire to get up in case there was any (as Twain says). I suggest at the end of the reading that everyone close their eyes and remember a place—I am going for imagery today, not stories. The room is quiet with writing, and as I go around the room asking people to read, I realize that I have gotten it. LaShana in church, a little girl praying the preacher will finish early so she can go watch TV, moving from side to side because her bottom's asleep, her mom telling her to be still. *Charles, his ten-inch-long braid newly trimmed, his jail-angry isolation broken, moves his hand rhythmically across the page, remembering detention homes, and the woman who "made a clean fool out of me so I did something about it so I cut and cut until I seen red all over cause if there were any black left I would cut more."*

When I read my log entry the next day, Charles's violent history and his emphasis on learning to control his temper finally fused together, and in one hot second everything made sense. The reason he associated control of violence with learning in the classroom was, at least in part, because his temper had so often been tangled with negative views of himself as a learner. Then I remembered how he reported in flat tones the years in prison when he was called "Dumbbell Cholly" because he tended to fly into a rage without thinking and assault others; in fact, he had told me that he was often goaded into violence by other prisoners who used that appellation. When he reported a new-found ability to respect others and care for himself, he had indeed been describing a new readiness to learn to read and write.

The themes which Charles was focusing on—of violence, strains on family ties, and loving—touched chords that resonate in most of us. I was at last able to bring something to the teaching exchange; I found ways to help him write about these themes that absorbed him. During the semester, his writing softened. The man who wrote initially that he "had no pity for others" wrote later about people being "good to each other." I cannot say that his spelling was perfect or that his sometimes idiosyncratic sentence structure met academic standards. But in his last major project of the fall semester, a twenty-two-page booklet prepared for his children about his life, he wrote in the introduction, "I will tell you boys and girls life does not have to be only pain." And for him, the lessening of pain was connected to his learning to control his temper, to feel "smart" enough to write, and eventually to write a family history.

By way of conclusion, I want to consider what student-centeredness does for the education of underprepared learners. It is, first, a way of balancing the power in the classroom. An "anything goes" laissez-faire classroom is a disaster, but so is a classroom that regiments learning into skills that must be mastered before the students are allowed to read and write about topics that engage them. Student-centered teaching requires us to recognize the narrow path between too much direction and too little control and to try to walk it. If I play my role as teacher while I am centered in my own ideas about what constitutes learning, or if I hammer at the content in the book whether students are engaged or not, or even if I continue to ask students to "find their own voice" when they have checked out of my freewriting classroom assignments, then I, as the teacher, hold all the power while the students are disempowered. Too little steering, too much "Well, what do you want to do today?" and the students perceive a teacher who is incompetent, who "doesn't care." When I center myself in the students, I can include in my thinking and planning the students' perceptions of what they need as well as my instructional agenda. This wider vision does not obliterate teacher-student power relations. It does, however, redefine them and allows students to participate more actively in their education. And second—and this is what I called earlier in this paper the paradox of student-centered teaching—when the teacher validates the students' ways of doing or seeing or thinking or reading or writing, the students are more able to accept the academic invitation that the teacher is offering.

To put what I have learned back into a theoretical frame, I can say that what my students teach me daily is to decenter certain academic expectations. As a profession, we English teachers are learning that same lesson on many fronts. We are learning not to privilege (or to privilege less) the writings of the canon over all other writings by women and people of color. We are learning not to privilege published writings over the often-fine works of student writers (or, at least, to do so sometimes). And we must learn to not always discount the writings of the new writer or reader, to think we know what is best because of our experience with those whose styles are more academic, more "correct." To gain a new openness in my classroom with underprepared

learners, I cannot always regard my reading as the one correct interpretation of a piece or myself as the sole decision maker of what is
worth learning.

I cannot state that working in a student-centered classroom necessarily produces students whose development leads them in the
direction of the demands of the institution. It would be inaccurate to
leave the impression that through this principle of student-centered
instruction, those who start very far from the academic enterprise
always, or even often, move in an orderly fashion through the various
courses leading to graduation. For every student who meets academic
goals, there are other someones who take from class learning which
does not seem to "go anywhere" beyond some personal satisfaction.

To be honest, I have given up a narrow construction of basic
skills courses as service courses that prepare the underprepared for the
next class in the academic sequence—not because students do not
often go on to that class, but because I can no longer conduct dull and
dutiful lessons on the grounds that such lessons are dictated by "the
remedial curriculum." When only half the class remains at the end of a
course, teachers must wonder if it was worth the boredom, hostility,
and irritation that allowed so many to remain disengaged, just to
move the remaining handful to the "next" class. I don't wonder about
that question any more. I know it isn't worth it. What I have placed in
a new center is the history in our classroom which is being lived now.
My students and I forge that academic learning community by reading
about what (given a fairly broad selection of kinds of writing) the students seem to gravitate toward now. We write about what makes sense
now. For some students, there may be no next English class or even no
next semester.

Such a shift in perspective can free us to head in new directions
with both our teaching and research. As John Gumperz and Mary Louise Pratt have argued, public institutions are not a single, unified community. Instead, we operate in a contact zone where people of various
language backgrounds come together to get work done. In urban
classrooms, the task often seems daunting. Because there is no fail-safe
method, we are thrown back upon listening to ourselves interacting
with our students about text. In a very different academic world, Jane
Tompkins's use of student-centered teaching proved revolutionary,
both for her graduate students at Duke University and for herself as a
teacher. When teachers in urban classrooms are alert, our learnings
and findings can be equally revolutionary. Teachers who work with
underprepared learners are uniquely situated to improve on present

practice and to add to a growing body of empirical research which teachers are helping to construct. This research will lead to better and more accurate theories about how people from various social contexts within American life learn to read and write.

Works Cited

Freire, Paulo. "The Adult Literacy Process as Cultural Action for Freedom." *Harvard Educational Review* 40 (May 1970): 205–55.

———. *Pedagogy of the Oppressed.* Trans. Myra Bergman Ramos. New York: Continuum, 1970.

Griffith, Marlene, Bruce Jacobs, Smokey Wilson, and Margot Dashiell. "Changing the Model." *Quarterly of the National Writing Project and the Center of the Study of Writing* 11.1 (January 1989): 4–9.

Gumperz, John J. *Discourse Strategies.* Vol. 1. Cambridgeshire, England: Cambridge UP, 1983.

Pratt, Mary Louise. "Arts of the Contact Zone." *Profession '91.* New York: MLA, 1991. 33–40.

Rose, Mike. *Lives on the Boundary: A Moving Account of the Struggles and Achievements of America's Educational Underclass.* New York: Penguin, 1989. [See especially pp. 213–21.]

Tompkins, Jane P. "Pedagogy of the Distressed." *College English* 52.6 (October 1990): 653–60.

Wilson, Smokey. "The Construction of Text by Adult New Readers." *Writing Our Lives: Reflections on Dialog Journal Writing with Adults Learning English.* Ed. Joy Kreeft Peyton and Jana Staton. Language in Education: Theory and Practice, no. 77. Englewood Cliffs, NJ: Prentice, 1991. 36–45.

———. "What Happened to Darleen? Reconstructing the Life and Schooling of an Underprepared Learner." *Two-Year College English: Essays for a New Century.* Ed. Mark Reynolds. Urbana, IL: NCTE, 1994. 37–53.

5 "Worldview" Publication as an Incentive for Excellence in Writing

Susan B. Andrews
Chukchi College, University of Alaska–Fairbanks

John Creed
Chukchi College, University of Alaska–Fairbanks

The "worldview" of minority groups is seldom portrayed through the national media, but educators can help remedy this lack of cross-cultural perspective and representation of minority experience by creating a mechanism to publish writing by minority students. For instance, in Alaska, which has the highest per capita aboriginal population in the country, where roughly 16 percent of the state's 550,000 residents are "Alaska Native" (the official name in Alaska for the Eskimo, Indian, and Aleut peoples), the press usually covers only one or two kinds of native events: tragedy related to drugs and alcohol, or cultural celebrations and activities such as the World Eskimo Indian Olympics and handicrafts. Typically, the day-to-day concerns and experiences of native peoples in Alaska are ignored. However, a university publication project in Alaska called the Chukchi News and Information Service helps fill this void by publishing student pieces, news stories, and argumentative essays (known to journalists as "opinion pieces") in the Alaska press.

This kind of project offers many benefits to the students and to the public, from the newspapers' and magazines' readerships to the communities they serve. In addition, when students write from their own worldview, they must learn more about their own culture, thereby strengthening rather than diminishing it, as so often happens in the pursuit of Western higher education. At the same time, a publication project such as this provides students with a powerful incentive to improve as writers.

Background of the Chukchi News and Information Service Project

This innovative publication project was developed in 1988 at Chukchi College, a branch campus of the University of Alaska, which is located in Kotzebue, an Inupiat Eskimo village 30 miles above the Arctic Circle in northwest Alaska and about 175 miles northeast of the easternmost tip of the former Soviet Union. (The Chukchi name comes from the fact that Kotzebue sits on a spit that juts into the frozen Chukchi Sea, a part of the Bering Sea.)

Chukchi's student population lives in remote settlements scattered across the vast, sparsely populated wilderness of Alaska where few roads connect to the outside world. Chukchi courses reach students via audioconference in the students' home villages from the Aleutians in southwest Alaska, to the Canadian border in the east, to Barrow in the north. By taking courses in their home villages, Alaska Native students can continue their traditional subsistence activities, such as hunting, gathering, fishing, and trapping, a way of life not available to on-campus students. Despite the obvious constraints of teaching and learning "over the telephone," rural Alaska communities also benefit because distance-delivery education does not create a leadership vacuum that typically occurs in these small communities when students leave home for a campus setting. While distance learning by television is available in Alaska's urban centers, this technology has yet to become universal in the more than 200 rural Alaska communities because of the cost of providing this technology and the difficulty of maintaining it across thousands of miles not yet accessible by road. Given these circumstances, most classes in rural Alaska currently are offered by audioconference rather than teleconference.

The majority of distance-education students in rural Alaska are Alaska Natives. Generally, Yup'ik Eskimos inhabit southwest Alaska; Inupiat Eskimos live in the north and northwest; Athabascan Indians are in the Interior; Tlingit, Tsimshian, and Haida Indians live on Alaska's Panhandle; and Aleuts live along the windswept Aleutian Islands. Each group has its own language and cultural traditions. For instance, even though Yup'ik and Inupiat Eskimos live "next" to one another geographically, they speak distinct languages.

All writing students of Chukchi College may participate in the Chukchi News and Information Service if they are enrolled in a variety of classes ranging from developmental English to sophomore composition to magazine and news writing courses. Although the Chukchi

News and Information Service publishes primarily the work of Alaska Native students, other minority and nonnative students also are published. Indeed, this is the kind of universal project that can be duplicated in classrooms nationally.

While the campus serves mostly students aged 25 or older, selected high school students and recent high school graduates also take classes at Chukchi. A profile of a typical Chukchi student would be Alaska Native female, 35 years old with four children and a full-time job. She lives in a native village with a population ranging from 50 to 3,000 people. She pursues a traditional subsistence lifestyle—hunting, gathering, fishing, trapping—while taking six credits per semester toward an associate's or bachelor's degree in rural development, education, or social work.

More than 200 pieces have been distributed through the Chukchi News and Information Service, and these have run in publications as diverse as Alaska's largest newspaper, the *Anchorage Daily News,* to smaller regional papers such as the *Tundra Drums,* to specialized periodicals such as *Mushing* magazine.

How the Project Works

This approach differs from other publication projects, such as *Foxfire,* for example, in that the Chukchi News and Information Service publishes student work through existing media, while other programs typically create their own vehicles for publication, such as a magazine or newspaper or desktop-published document. Another option, perhaps the simplest, is to work with campus newspapers. Regardless of which type of publication is used, participants in projects such as this gain valuable writing skills as a result of following the type of process outlined below.

Beginning with Classroom "Publication"

The idea of publication is planted in students' minds, starting with the very first piece they typically write in most classes, a short autobiography. Given a trusting classroom atmosphere, students will share their life stories with other students and the professor in a writing workshop, despite their initial fears about reading aloud. Students are required to rewrite this first paper, so that they quickly become used to rewriting, which is what professional writers must do in order to be published. If the students then express an interest in publishing the piece or simply in refining it further, they may then pursue additional optional rewrites; however, optional rewrites beyond the first one do not improve their grade. (This prevents students from rewriting only to improve their grade incrementally.) Essentially, at this stage, students must be willing to polish their writing without the incentive of a grade.

In any case, after students have rewritten their piece at least once, typically the final versions of their autobiography are mailed to all students (remember: this is distance delivery). The message here? Students understand right away that their audience includes everyone in the classroom, not just the professor. By sharing their work in class, students not only inspire each other, they also get adjusted to the idea of sharing their work with a wider audience.

Learning to Write through Revision

This method of teaching writing to both Alaska Natives and nonnatives centers on rewriting, not just once or twice, but multiple times in order to prepare a piece for publication. Instructors' emphasis on the kind of clear, straightforward writing that is suitable for newspapers serves native students particularly well as they struggle to sort out the challenges of bilingualism as well as "village" Englishes, local Englishes unique to Alaska Native people.

Students and professors must work closely together on this round of editing and rewriting. Because the majority of students are participating by distance delivery, which makes distributing students' drafts to their peers overly cumbersome, peer work is typically limited to an in-class workshop in which students read their pieces aloud. After this kind of peer input, the faculty member then works with those students who wish to be published on polishing their work. Although students occasionally indicate that they are interested in being published, more often the faculty member contacts students individually, suggesting one or more pieces that show potential for publication. Students understand that publication is not guaranteed because this decision is not made by the faculty member but by the newspaper and magazine editors to whom the pieces are submitted.

Typically, it is most effective for students and faculty to fax drafts back and forth as they are polished. Of course, students who attend Chukchi Campus in Kotzebue, where the project originates, may work with the professor face-to-face. In their syllabus, students are provided with a guide to proofreaders' marks for the basics of editing. As for the more complex issues of style, structure, and content, typically the faculty member provides extensive comments suggesting how to improve the piece in these areas. It is important to note, however, that if professors were to take it upon themselves to "transform" a student piece without engaging in the process with the student, a whole host of problems would naturally arise, not the least of which is that a great opportunity for learning would be missed. Also, professors must be as careful, as all good editors must, to respect the nuances of their writers' work.

Preserving Individual Voices

In working student pieces through a series of rewrites, professor-editors also must try to preserve the student's voice while providing guidelines for proper usage and grammar. For instance, the conversational tone of Siberian Yup'ik Eskimo Linda Akeya was left intact when she describes what is done with a polar bear once it has been butchered: "Some people can't stand eating the meat, and I am one of these people. But I wouldn't mind keeping the fur" (13). Certainly, these sentences could have been edited to make them more succinct, but not without destroying the unique voice that belongs to Ms. Akeya.

Another telling example of how important it is to preserve individual student voices can be found in a Chukchi News and Information Service piece by Inupiaq Eskimo Dollie Hawley, who tells her readers how a missionary teacher came to her village on the northwest coast of Alaska and "civilized the Natives":

> I can also remember the teacher teaching us our manners, such as saying "Please," "May I?" or "Excuse me" and "Thank you." She also taught us not to slurp whenever we ate our meals. Slurping was a very big problem in those days. Thanks to God we all learned not to slurp. (14)

Certainly, the sentence "Slurping was a very big problem in those days" could have been edited, if nothing else to delete the "very," but here is an instance in which the apparent simplicity of the voice reveals so much more. Ms. Hawley strikes at the core of the complexities of contact between aboriginal peoples and Western culture. On the one hand, she appreciates the "civilizing" benefits that the missionaries brought, while on the other hand, her humor satirizes the self-righteousness she sees in Western culture.

Meeting Standards of Accuracy

As students record traditional activities, the faculty and students work together to ensure that the piece of writing will meet the rigorous standards of accuracy that audience-based writing entails. For example, in preparing written communication for a larger readership, Inupiaq Eskimo Genevieve Norris takes great care to be precise in describing traditional activities of her own culture because she is going to share her worldview with thousands of readers, among them, her own people, who are familiar with such activities.

"I have seen my mother prepare a whole caribou hide to make leather rope," writes Ms. Norris from Shungnak, one of northwest Alaska's most traditional Inupiat Eskimo villages. "My mother then washes and strips the hide with a sharp knife, making strips as thin as spaghetti. When this thin leathery rope is dry, my father can use it to make snowshoes and basket sleds" (8).

Classroom research has, in fact, demonstrated that when students are presented with the "real-life" situation of having their work published, they fully understand, perhaps for the first time, the importance of accuracy and, consequently, revision. Karen Durrant and Charles Duke found such results in a class of twenty-five creative writers, who first were asked to analyze popular magazines to determine their target audience:

> Initially students were not informed that they would be submitting the pieces for possible publication. We did this to see how students would approach the assignment. Several students were ready to turn their pieces in after one revision; however, when students learned that they actually would be required to submit the pieces, they requested more time for revision and went back to their analysis to check on how well their articles seemed to meet the expectations of the magazine's audience. Such a reaction merely reinforced our belief that students need to write for genuine audiences and have their work submitted to those audiences for consideration. (169)

Targeting and Placing the Pieces

Once students have polished their pieces sufficiently for publication, the professor(s) works with editors at the various dailies and weeklies to place the work. This, of course, takes a sustained effort to first develop and then maintain relationships with editors and also a basic understanding of how to target a piece for a particular publication or even a particular section of a newspaper. (In fact, the effort to target a piece should have begun with instructing the student on how to accomplish this, as addressed in the findings of Durrant and Duke above.)

Cultural/Social Benefits of a Publication Project

Ultimately, for all Chukchi students who participate in this publication project, their incentive reaches far beyond the challenge to "get an A"; the six or seven rewrites necessary to develop a publication-quality piece must be driven by a profound desire to "educate" both natives and nonnatives about the traditional Inupiat Eskimo way of life. But the academic accomplishments are not the only benefit. Important social benefits also result from publication projects such as this, many of which are summarized below.

(1) Benefit: Educating the Public

All publication projects benefit students by empowering them to speak for themselves—especially on complicated issues that affect their own lives. At the same time, they teach the readers of these publications more about minority "worldviews"—in this case, the unique culture of Alaska's native peoples, the Eskimos, Indians, and Aleuts, who have lived off this vast remote land for the past 10,000 years.

For example, consider the following excerpt from Hannah Paniyavluk Loon, an Inupiaq Eskimo who writes about the sensitive issue of speaking "village" English:

> There's no such thing as "correct" village English. I structure
> my sentences any way I desire. Rules don't limit village English
> as long as the listener understands. (13)

Those who read Loon's entire piece in Alaska's newspapers undoubtedly came away with a better understanding of village English. Such an essay can do much to dispel many of the negative feelings about village English that are harbored by nonvillage and nonnative Alaskans and even by some native peoples themselves.

(2) Benefit: Expanding Coverage of Minority Issues

Chukchi News and Information Service participants most often write on issues typically ignored by the mainstream press, in particular about culturally relevant subjects, such as growing up in a family of reindeer herders; averting the tragedy of fetal alcohol syndrome; facing substance abuse among Alaska Natives; hunting, fishing, and gathering in a traditional subsistence economy; coping with the changes brought about by the clash of the Western and native cultures in this century; and performing such traditional tasks as drying and smoking salmon or tanning animal skins. At the same time, rural Alaskans' worldview also includes interests and concerns shared by other minorities as well as the mainstream audience across America, topics such as the health hazards of smoking; computers; fish farming; tourism; corporal punishment; mutual funds; cancer; and AIDS.

Issues of importance to a particular minority group often can be best highlighted by a member of the group that is most affected, such as in the following excerpt in which Athabascan Indian Georgianna Lincoln laments the lack of Native American emphasis in school textbooks.

> When American children reach the seventh grade, they may read the history text, *People, Places and Change,* which devotes but one page to American Indians. . . . American history textbooks must give a fair, historical perspective of American Indians, not a vision of half-naked savages scalping people and burning wagons. They must portray the Indian as the first explorer, the first colonist, the first conqueror of the North American continent. THE FIRST AMERICAN! (13)

As a native, Ms. Lincoln's worldview encompassed choosing to perform this kind of research initially and then being able to thoroughly explain the textbooks' imbalance in regard to the reality of her experience as a Native American.

(3) Benefit: Providing Permanence for Minority Voices

This type of publication project not only enhances cultural awareness and understanding for all peoples, it also provides a kind of permanence for voices not otherwise heard in the mainstream press. In other words, this type of project helps to write and preserve "the people's" history. For the Chukchi News and Information Service, specifically, the project's unique writings on a vanishing way of life join Alaska's historical record, which will be available to future historians, anthropologists, and other researchers, and, most importantly, to the people themselves.

Similarly, *Foxfire* founder Eliot Wigginton found himself concerned with the very same issue of preserving a culture when he initiated the now-famous publications of high-school-age writers in Rabun Gap, Georgia. Early on in the *Foxfire* experiment, though, he discovered that students need a deeper purpose than simply recording local history and lore:

> I'm talking about the peculiar, almost mystic kind of reso-
> nance that comes and vibrates in one's soul like a guitar string
> with an understanding of family, who I am and where I'm from,
> and the fact that I'm part of a long continuum of hope and
> prayer and celebration of life that I must carry forward. (75)

An example of this kind of breadth of generational understanding is apparent in native student Blanche Jones Criss's writing about
how missionaries wrongly beat her people for speaking their own language and for dancing traditional dances:

> "We as members of this (Western) religion were not allowed
> many of the fun things that others did, such as going to local
> dances, including local Eskimo dances," writes Inupiaq student
> Blanche Jones Criss (Higman) about what has happened among
> her people since "people carrying Bibles" came to her village in
> the early 1900s. "After a century of regrouping and reorganiz-
> ing, I have a sense that the next generation will have stronger
> faith and values to pass on to their children. With the Friends
> Church members' blessings, perhaps succeeding generations
> will participate in Eskimo dance festivities." (4)

(4) Benefit: Building Self-Esteem

For minority students participating in a publication project, the affir-
mation of not only culture but also self can be especially powerful. For
instance, Inupiaq Eskimo Geri Reich is a nontraditional student (as are
most writers for the project) who works as an electrician at the Red
Dog Mine in northwest Alaska. She was asked in class if workers at the
mine had noticed her byline in the local paper. "Oh, yes," she replied.
"Practically everybody." She said even "the white guys" who work at
the mine and live out of state are now taking an interest in the region,
including the problems faced by the local native people. She said
many of the nonnatives now seem to look at her as a real person and
do so with respect for the first time. She wasn't, in her words, "just a
dumb native anymore."

(5) Benefit: Retaining Cultural Activities

Finally, with the reinforcement inherent in researching and writing
about traditional activities and then publishing these works, students
are more inclined not to abandon ancient practices such as native
dancing, but rather to pass them on to their progeny. For instance, a

student who writes about traditional Eskimo dancing must sharpen her skills, not just with the written word, but also on the dance floor: "It happened that my dance was the last one for the night," writes Yup'ik Eskimo Luci Washington about performing at a traditional pot-latch in her village. "Gradually, the beat got faster. As I danced harder and faster, the fear and nervousness disappeared; instead, happiness and excitement flowed within me. Happy tears formed in my eyes. A tear dropped for my late grandmother, who wasn't there to watch me dance" (7).

Conclusion

Even if a publication project does not use existing media, similar academic and social results are mirrored in *Foxfire* spin-offs and other kinds of publication projects. For instance, Ann Vick, an educator who ran a *Foxfire* project in southwestern Alaska high schools in the mid-to-late 1970s, defines the essence of this kind of project as

> experienced students from Bethel and Emmonak conducting a workshop session in Mountain Village and, with no adults present, the whole group staying a half-hour after the bell had rung because they were involved in the discussion of whether or not to begin a magazine. And it is students writing article drafts or painstakingly preparing camera-ready copy over and over again, willing to do whatever is necessary, however time-consuming, to get it "right." (xix)

Regardless of who or what medium publishes the material, minority and other students who have been published take writing seriously and begin to equate good writing skills with "real life." Indeed, when coursework is tied to the "real world" of publication outside of academe, it enables students to see the practical value of taking an array of writing courses, ranging from developmental English to upper-level composition and journalism offerings. Ultimately, a publication project provides developmental students with not only a tremendous incentive to acquire the skills they need to succeed in college, but also a means to build self-esteem and to begin equating writing with power. Also, this kind of project encourages students' pride in their cultural experiences at the same time that they heighten their readers' awareness of a different worldview.

Works Cited

Akeya, Linda. "Elders Offer Advice on How to Butcher a Polar Bear." *Tundra Times* (15 October 1990): 13.

Criss, Blanche Jones [Higman]. "When the People Carrying Bibles Came, I Learned." *Arctic Sounder* (21 November 1990): 4.

Durrant, Karen R., and Charles R. Duke. "Developing Sensitivity to Audience: Connecting Theory and Practice." *Teaching English in the Two-Year College* 16.3 (October 1989): 165–73.

Hawley, Dollie. "Growing up in Kivalina on the Remote Arctic Coast." *Sun Star* (14 April 1992): 14.

Lincoln, Georgianna. "Textbooks Lack True Native American History." *All-Alaska Weekly* (14 September 1990): 13.

Loon, Hannah. "There's No 'Correct' Village English." *Tundra Times* (17 December 1990): 13

Norris, Genevieve. "Mother Nature Supplies Needs." *Tundra Times* (30 April 1990): 8.

Vick, Ann, ed. *The Cama-i Book: Kayaks, Dog Sleds, Bear Hunting, Bush Pilots, Smoked Fish, Mukluks, and Other Traditions of Southwestern Alaska.* Garden City, NY: Anchor/Doubleday, 1983.

Washington, Luci. "Dancing at a Traditional Potlatch." *Sun Star* (2 November 1990): 7.

Wigginton, Eliot. *Sometimes a Shining Moment.* New York: Doubleday, 1986.

6 Autobiography as a Liberating Force in the Basic Writing Classroom

Brenda M. Greene
Medgar Evers College, CUNY

The autobiographical narrative has always been the literary form that provides individuals with opportunities to present their awareness of the social and political realities in their lives, their sorrows, frustrations, and anger, and their hopes, wishes, and dreams. Autobiographical writing provides a natural means whereby the power of the word can reveal itself in rich, commanding, and provocative ways.

Using the autobiographical narrative in a writing classroom can provide students—particularly those who have had little writing experience or who are part of a culture where the oral tradition is valued over the written tradition—with a means to reflect on their pain and fears, their joys and desires; autobiographical writing can reveal the multidimensional self within our society. Because it represents writing that is closest to oneself, the autobiographical narrative can also reveal the tension generated by the conflict between the inner self and the self one represents to society. For students who are perceived as being on the margins of the dominant culture, who, in short, are viewed as minorities within a majority culture, autobiographical writing can offer a means for resolving conflicts and tensions within their own lives. This form of discourse can provide these students with a way to present the other side, the other perspective, the other point of view.

The need and rationale for presenting the other side are illustrated in an essay on literature and authority by Myra Jehlen. Jehlen, in addressing the overall need to explore other ways of reading and, specifically, the need to ensure that students read from multiple perspectives, notes that we need to read the *other*, "not only for the sake of the other, but in order to understand the one more fully, to see it and its room in the context of the house and the street it inhabits" (15). Literature, and in this case, autobiographical literature, provides students with an opportunity to present their sides and their perspectives on their lives, and in doing so, to teach us about themselves. As a result, both sides—those in the minority and majority cultures—gain.

Elizabeth Nunez-Harrell, a Caribbean fictional writer and educator, illustrated this point clearly at the 1990 NCTE Summer Institute on teaching multicultural literature to undergraduates. She pointed out that, as a Caribbean student who read and studied American culture, she learned about herself as she learned about American culture and values. In other words, by looking at others, she had looked at herself. She reinforced for the group the need to study the cultures of those around them as one path to knowledge of oneself.

In the writing classroom where I teach, autobiographical writing provides a means for students to validate their voices by sharing those experiences which have affected their lives in strong and powerful ways. Students read autobiographical excerpts, discuss the writing in small groups, and generate their own forms of autobiography through freewriting, letters, essays, or short stories.

One of the texts that I have found most useful for generating autobiographical writing by students is Robert Lyon's *Autobiography: A Reader for Writers.* This text, an anthology of autobiographical writings, provides models of different forms of autobiographical discourse. Students read excerpts from journals, diaries, and essays of contemporary writers. The excerpts on writing for oneself, for example, motivate students to compare their childhood memories with those from Lorraine Hansberry's *To Be Young, Gifted, and Black.* Students reflect on the uniqueness of their childhood experiences and examine how those experiences help to shape their views about family, love, work, play, etc. In Lyon's section on addressing a reader, students read accounts of how one writer varies the style and form of his letters to different members of his family. These letters clearly illustrate how audience and point of view can affect the content and form of a text, and they serve as models for how students can write about one subject for a number of audiences.

Thus, as students read and discuss autobiography, they examine the effects of voice, point of view, and audience. They use the readings to find points of comparison in their own lives. These points of comparison may not always be obvious to students, but through discussion and freewriting, students can use them to bring to life some aspects of their own backgrounds or cultures. Through this reading and discussion, they begin to see the value of validating their own voices, of realizing that their experiences are worth writing about and sharing. Hence, despite the fact that they may be basic writers and have not had many experiences in reading and writing autobiography, they nonetheless engage themselves enthusiastically.

The majority of the students at my college come from some part of the African diaspora. Approximately two-thirds of them are either first- or second-generation immigrants from the Caribbean. Although they have elected to attend a college where they are in the majority or have come from a country where their ethnic group is in the majority, they are now faced with being classified as a minority in this country. For many, this is the first time that they have encountered this experience; for others, they have been in this situation all their lives because, as African Americans, they have always been made aware of how others in our society perceive them. Hence, the students in my classes have made a conscious decision to attend a college where they are not in the minority.

I was interested in providing my students with a forum that would enable them to express their views and experiences on how being classified as a minority has affected their lives in our country. In posing this question to my students, I wanted to offer them an opportunity to reflect on their experiences as a minority in this culture, to articulate their views related to this experience, and to analyze how their views could be expressed from several perspectives. Autobiographical writing provided a natural means for accomplishing this.

Because I knew that, as a result of their diverse backgrounds, a number of students might have difficulty coming to grips with this question, I decided to share my own perceptions of growing up as African American in an educational system that was dominated by others. I shared my experiences and then asked students to freewrite on other or similar experiences. After students freewrote on those experiences and/or viewpoints, they shared their freewriting in a large group. Students wrote about being victims of racism in stores, in school, and in housing. Some wrote about coming from a different culture and feeling alienated because of their speech and accent. Others wrote about their awareness of the struggles of their people for equality and civil rights. Still others wrote about conflicts resulting from being, for example, the only Latino among a group of blacks or from looking like a member of one ethnic group while in reality being part of another.

After students shared their freewriting they were asked to create three different letters where they described these experiences to a friend, a family member, and an editor of a newspaper. The letter format provided students with a means to make personal, political, and social statements about race and ethnicity. They then critiqued the drafts of these letters in groups of three. They were required to comment on

the content of each letter;

the differences among the letters; and

the parts of the letter which were problematic and could be improved.

After critiquing the drafts, each group selected one series of letters to read to the entire class. Students then revised their letters and submitted them for my comments and feedback. They completed the final drafts of each letter in the microcomputer writing center. The following series of letters was written by a young, articulate black male student who, after participating in a voter registration rally, was arrested for a crime he did not commit:

Letter to a Friend

Dear Michelle,

How are you? How is Maryland? Fine I hope. Well things aren't too good up here. In New York, black people are treated like dirt.

On Sunday, October 7, I was arrested for something I didn't do. Two or three black kids robbed a white man in the same car I was in. When the train reached the next stop, the robbers fled. The victim came back with the police but couldn't identify anyone. Then a man who was supposedly a witness pointed out all the black youths, including me, as the robbers.

Now you know I'm not the type to be robbing anyone. Now just imagine how many innocent people this has happened to. I wouldn't advise you to come visit New York because since you're black, you never know what may happen to you here.

Yours truly,
Mike

Letter to a Family Member

Hi Mom,

What's up? How is everyone doing? You're so lucky to be out of state. I just wanted to thank you for standing by me when I needed someone. Something has to be done about the racial problem in New York. It's a shame that I had to go through the system for something I didn't do. Why should I even be threatened to have a crime put on my record when I'm innocent?

Well, I have to go now. Say hi to Dad for me. As that saying goes, "See you in court."

> Your son,
> Mike

Letter to an Editor

Dear Editor:

New York has a serious racial problem. Being a black young male may be hazardous to your health. Every black youth may be affected by racism in some way.

On Sunday, October 7, I attended a register to vote rally. It took place in front of the Harlem State Office Building on 125th street. The attendance reached at least 1500 people. At the end of the rally, most of the people headed for the train station. It was so crowded, I had to let the first train pass. I got on the second train. During the non-stop ride from 125th to 59th street, a man was robbed by two or more black kids. When the train arrived at 59th street, the doors opened. The man who was robbed and the robbers all got off the train. The doors closed until the police arrived. The man who was robbed didn't identify anyone. A man who was supposedly a witness, pointed out almost all the black kids on the train, including me. That means we were all arrested because we were black.

Since this has happened to me, I wonder how many innocent people have been arrested because they were black. How long will we as humans allow things like this to happen? Something must be done quickly about this problem.

> Sincerely,
> Mike Washington

The reading of these letters had a quietening and cathartic effect on the students in the class. After quietly reflecting on the reality and trauma associated with this experience, many students opened up. They knew other persons who had had similar experiences, and they began to share stories. A feeling of helplessness, frustration, and anger permeated students' comments and stories.

The next set of letters reveals the effects of being a minority from a more subtle perspective. These letters were written by a young black female student who, upon entering a jewelry store, was immediately suspected of being a potential thief:

Letter to a Friend

Dear Tanya,

How are you and your family doing? Fine I hope. I just had a little trouble last week when I went shopping in Kings Plaza. I had just gotten off work and decided to do a little pre-Christmas shopping. Since Kings Plaza is near my job, I went there. I was browsing around the store and the saleslady who was white followed me around the store. She did not ask me if I needed help. I thought maybe she was following me around in case I needed her to assist me, but I noticed that she had this funny look in her eyes. This look told me that she was following me around because I was the only black person in the store. Well, you could just imagine how embarassing it was for me. I felt humiliated and angry. So, I walked over to her and asked her if I could assist her with anything as though I was the saleslady. She turned so red and I could see that she felt embarassed. I did it on purpose. Maybe, then she will think twice about the way she treated me and others like me. I have to finish up my letter now. Take care and tell everyone I said "Hi." Write soon.

> Yours truly,
> Sherry

Letter to a Family Member

Dear Susie,

What's up? How is everything going? Fine I know. I am doing fine. I'm still working hard and going to school. Do you remember when you told me about that incident at Macy's? Well, the same thing happened to me. I went shopping the other day at Kings Plaza. I went inside this jewelry store to browse around. This white saleslady followed me around as though I was going to steal something. I thought about it and then realized that I was the only black person in the store. She made me feel like I had no business being there. The way she treated me made me so mad. Girl, I wanted to tell her off, but I thought about it and changed my mind. I knew that telling her off would only make me stoop down to her level. Instead, I went over to her and I asked her if I could help her with anything. I acted as though I was the saleslady. Susie, if you were there you would have been laughing. Her face turned so red. She gave me the evil eye, turned and walked away from me. I'll bet you she will think twice about the way she treated me. I hope that I made her day. Well, I have to go now. Tell everybody that I said "Hi." I'll be talking to you soon.

> Love Ya,
> Sherry

Letter to an Editor

To the Editor:

My name is Sherry Young and I live in Brooklyn, N.Y. I am writing to you in reference to the minority groups in New York City. I am concerned with the way they are treated. I am a part of this group and I feel that sometimes we are not treated with respect. I had an incident recently when I went shopping. I was in a jewelry store and this saleslady followed me around the store as if I were there to steal. I am not a thief and I did have money in my pocket at the time. I also had my charge cards and two shopping bags from Macy's with me. There was no need for her to be suspicious of me. I was the only black person in the store, but I did nothing wrong. She made me feel as though I had no right in being there. She did not ask me if I needed assistance. She just followed me around the store. I felt that this was an embarassing situation. I hope that you can make your readers aware that we have the same rights as others. It is time to put all of the racial conflicts behind us. Thank you.

> Sincerely,
> Sherry Young

Sherry's letters, as did Mike's, had a powerful effect on the class. After the letters were read, there was first silence and then anger. Again, students began to share similiar stories, and the class was not ready to leave at the end of the session.

Mike's and Sherry's writings reveal the liberating and powerful role that autobiographical writing can have in a writing classroom. This type of writing can give readers an injection of reality as well as motivate them to act as agents for change. If we accept Freire's concept that the act of teaching is a political act— that, as teachers, we have a responsibility to provide students with the strategies and learning environment that will enable them to use their voices to respond critically to social and political issues in their society—then using the autobiographical narrative in the writing classroom is an effective strategy for accomplishing this goal.

The timing for using this form of writing as a liberating force could not be more perfect. We are currently witnessing in film and in literature voices which have been repressed and silent for decades. We are being presented with the reality of subjects, such as racism, drugs, and interracial marriage, from points of view usually dismissed or omitted. We are being forced to confront our biases, prejudices, and stereotypes, to examine our values, to look beneath the surface for hidden agendas.

Reading and analyzing each other's autobiographical writing can provide an excellent forum for such confrontations, enabling students to articulate their views on controversial issues which have affected their lives and the lives of their families and friends in personal and powerful ways. Thus, we need only provide an arena—the writing classroom—in which students are encouraged to tell their own stories in voices that flow in a natural and liberating way.

Works Cited

Jehlen, Myra. "Literature and Authority." *Conversations: Contemporary Critical Theory and the Teaching of Literature.* Ed. Charles Moran and Elizabeth F. Penfield. Urbana, IL: NCTE, 1990. 7–18.

Lyon, Robert, ed. *Autobiography: A Reader for Writers.* 2nd ed. New York: Oxford UP, 1984.

7 Bridging Cross-Cultural Differences through Writing

Sarah Coprich Johnson
University of Alabama at Birmingham

Julia Stutts Austin
University of Alabama at Birmingham

How can language arts teachers best reach out to students in view of the great diversity and cultural differences represented in composition classes today?

Many university professors are charged, at present, with a dual responsibility in the teaching of composition. They not only must face the often difficult task of teaching basic writing to not-so-enthusiastic students, but they also must deal with the matter of teaching a socially and culturally varied community of students. Many students in university composition classes are also faced with difficulties. They are often hindered from participating in academic dialogue because of the language used within the academy. A letter exchange project was one way that we sought to assist basic and/or beginning writing students in becoming more proficient in using written language as a means of communication. By setting up a letter exchange between English-as-a-second-language (ESL) students and freshman composition students, predominantly native English speakers, we also believed that many of the cultural barriers would be lessened.

Rationale

When planning the letter exchange between ESL students and freshman composition students, our purpose was to assist them in improving their writing skills while increasing their knowledge of cultures different from their own. Another primary objective was to increase student awareness of the readers (the audience) of their texts. Because the students would not know each other and, therefore, would have shared little, if any, cultural or social background knowledge, they would become more aware of the need to write more detailed and explanatory prose in order to communicate successfully with their audience. Since the letter writing project would last for most of the quarter (approximately seven weeks), we anticipated that the extended exchange would provide students with opportunities to develop topics and to clarify perspectives. Feedback from a student's pen pal, asking for additional explanations or more descriptive details, for example, would be more effective, in most cases, than an instructor's comments written on an essay or journal entry, telling the student to develop or clarify a point. Also, because the students would be writing to uninformed readers about their personal experiences and their native countries, we believed that the student writers would be required to plan what they wanted to say and to pay close attention to details.

In addition to the writing objectives mentioned above, we also believed that an important goal of this project was to provide students with an opportunity to expand their perceptions and ways of thinking about other cultures, while perhaps helping them to gain a sense of self-discovery and more objective evaluation of their own culture as well. The American students in the freshman composition classes had, for the most part, extremely limited contact with persons from other cultures (or even from outside their own social strata). Even if they had noticed international students on campus, they evidenced little communication with them other than in cursory greetings or occasional, brief discussions about class assignments. The international students in the ESL classes spoke frequently about being isolated from their American counterparts and assumed that Americans disliked them simply because the American students rarely included them in their social activities. After all, from the ESL students' perspective, it was the natives' responsibility to initiate a friendship with a visitor. Based upon these obvious gaps and deficits in understanding by both groups, we felt that the letter exchange would be a nonthreatening way of fostering a rich dialogue between them.

A by-product of this exchange that we hoped for was an increased sense of self-awareness on the part of the students. By interpreting their own cultures, these students would need to examine their own experiences and beliefs more carefully, and perhaps more critically, than they ever had before. Also, the responses—often in answers to probing questions about *why* something is done in a particular manner or done at all—from their pen pals would help them to be more objective or at least to see that other people have different beliefs and valid reasons for doing what they do. We were neither advocating a mass rejection of formerly held beliefs nor attempting to provoke alienation from home cultures; rather, we hoped that all the students would be able to see their native cultures through new eyes and, from that experience, to develop a keener sense of inquisitiveness while becoming more tolerant of differences in others. For the students to see that this could be accomplished through writing would give them firsthand experience at seeing and using this powerful tool—language.

Although we have, at times, suffered the technical difficulties of getting letters back and forth between the classes in as swift and efficient a manner as we would like, we have experienced the joy of seeing students from different cultures and backgrounds engage in rich and fruitful dialogues that we believe serve to make language empowering rather than disempowering for those who often remain silent or passive in other classroom situations.

Methodology

The letter writing project usually ran for six or seven weeks of each quarter. We found that the project was most successful when begun during week two of the quarter, after class rolls had stabilized, and ended in week eight or nine before the end-of-the-quarter crush occurs. At the beginning of the project, an assignment sheet explaining the project and each student's responsibilities was handed out (see figure 1). The sheet was read aloud in class, and students were allowed to ask questions and voice concerns. Students frequently verbalized their fears about finding enough to write about for seven weeks. The instructors tried to generate some enthusiasm for the project by discussing the potential benefits. A group brainstorming session with the students to suggest benefits was one effective technique for doing this. By the end of the class discussion on benefits, even students who were not enthusiastic about the project were willing to suspend judgment until after they had written a few letters.

On one occasion, students who were particularly apprehensive about the project brainstormed possible problems. The problems ranged from concerns about handwriting to uncertainty about how to handle sensitive subjects, such as religion and politics. Then we discussed how these problems could be solved or at least minimized; students first suggested solutions, followed by the instructor ranking them for effectiveness or appropriateness. This brainstorming for

Letter Writing Assignment

This quarter you will have the unique opportunity to write to other students at UAB. These students, who in most cases will be Americans, are enrolled in EH 101. You will have two pen pals whom you will be corresponding with. Over the quarter, you will write six letters to them. In these letters, you can tell them about yourself, your country, your family, or anything else you would like to. You may also ask them questions about themselves, their families, and their interests. This exercise will allow you to correspond with someone besides your instructor. You will be able to ask questions about America, UAB, Alabama, or anything else you have been wondering about. In addition, it will be a unique experience for your pen pal to find out about your country, culture, and customs.

It is very important that you turn in your letters when they are due. Failure to turn in letters when they are due will result in a severe penalty for you, and it will also adversely affect the person you are corresponding with.

One time during the quarter, you will also serve as the letter carrier for our class. You will be responsible for giving out the letters from the EH 101 class, checking off who has received letters, taking up letters from the EH 100 class, and checking off who has written letters to their pen pals. There will be a Master List of all the students and their pen pals on which you will record the information. During the first week of class, we will assign the letter carrier duties.

You may write on notebook paper or any other type of paper you wish. You may write your letters on a typewriter or on a word processor. If you write the letters in longhand, it is important that you write clearly so that the letter is easy to read.

When you turn in the letter, fold it in half, lengthwise. On the outside of the letter, write:

TO: Your pen pal's name
FROM: Your name
DATE:

Do not worry about grammar or spelling. The major objective of these letters is *to communicate*. So, your focus should be on the content of your letters, not the form.

Figure 1. The project assignment sheet.

problems proved so helpful in reducing obstacles that we recommend it highly.

The letter writing project began with the ESL students writing letters of introduction to the American students. The American students answered with their own letters of introduction and with answers to the questions raised by their pen pals. The instructors suggested that students begin by telling about themselves and their families. Information about where they attended high school, what they were majoring in, and why they chose to attend school in Birmingham were common in these initial letters. In order to keep the exchange of ideas flowing, the instructors also suggested that each letter should contain at least one information question (yes/no questions don't usually initiate extended discourse).

The next order of business was to match up pen pals. The freshman composition instructor handed out the letters to her students and recorded the names of the American students and their ESL student pen pals. During most quarters, the instructors did not attempt to match students in any particular manner. Students were allowed to trade pen pals the first day, but most of the time they didn't. On the few occasions when students did trade, they did so because they wanted to write to a member of the opposite sex. The matching-up process was varied only once; the third quarter that we used the letter exchange, we allowed students to meet and choose their pen pals. This proved to inhibit students. As it turned out, they were more comfortable writing to someone whom they had never met. The instructors also felt that allowing students to meet at the beginning of the quarter lessened the overall effectiveness of the project.

Once the pen pals were matched up and any trading completed, a master list was compiled and distributed to each participating instructor. The ESL classes were normally half the size of the freshman composition classes, so each ESL student usually wrote to two American students. Of course, the classes were not always evenly divided. Whenever this occurred, we solicited volunteers to write to two pen pals. Students usually volunteered eagerly; only rarely was it necessary to encourage students to volunteer to write extra letters.

Four instructors participated over the course of the letter exchange project. Each instructor was allowed to make some modifications in the way the letter exchange was handled to better meet the needs of the individual classes. The constant for all classes was the physical exchange of letters. Mailboxes with the instructors' names and course numbers were provided by the English department in the faculty mailroom. Immediately following class, the letters were placed in the appropriate mailbox and were available for pickup before the next class period. Teachers or assigned "mail carriers" were responsible for picking up and distributing the letters.

Grading

Students received a grade for the letter exchange project at the end of the quarter. Each instructor decided on how the project would be counted in her class. In the ESL classes, the letter writing assignment usually counted 10 percent of the final grade; in the freshman composition classes, this assignment counted 20 percent. For all the classes, the letter exchange grade was based on the student's participation in the project—writing the required number of letters and fulfilling the minimum length requirement of one single-spaced page per letter. The content of the letters was not evaluated per se, but instructors did spot-check the letters to be sure that the students were following the assignment.

"Letter Day"

"Letter Day" was determined by our academic calendar. Regular classes meet Monday/Wednesday and Tuesday/Thursday at our university, giving a four-day break between the end and the beginning of the week. We decided to give the ESL students the longer, four-day weekend to write their letters since they were writing to two pen pals and generally needed more time per letter. Therefore, in the ESL classes, "Letter Day" was usually Monday or Tuesday, and in the freshman composition classes, "Letter Day" was generally Wednesday or Thursday. When the instructor or the letter carrier entered the classroom on "Letter Day," students immediately began asking questions: "Did I get a letter?" "When are we going to read the letters?" "Can we read the letters now?" Rarely do students get so involved in writing assignments that they clamor for them.

Letters were handed out at the beginning of class or immediately before the midpoint break. Time was always provided for students to read their letters. Frequently, they wanted to share parts of the letters with their classmates and their instructors. Sometimes they wanted to compare responses or to share questions. One of the most popular questions for the international students to ask was about slang or colloquial expressions. They loved to write the slang words on the board and discuss them with their classmates. The ESL students wanted to try out these new words immediately; then they practiced them for weeks, again something which they rarely did with their "academic" vocabulary.

Problems

Two related logistical problems that arose each time we used the letter writing project were student absences and withdrawals. In theory, students, whether present or absent, were responsible for seeing that their pen pals received letters each week. Some students did send letters when they had to miss class. But, of course, there were occasions when letters were absent along with their authors. The standing assignment was that students were to write their pen pals each week even if they did not receive a letter. The absent pen pals were responsible for answering all the letters they received as soon as possible upon their return.

The problem became a bit stickier with student withdrawals. Student populations in our classes rarely remained constant throughout an entire quarter. Each quarter, several students withdrew from the classes, sometimes as late as midterm. Whenever this happened, volunteers would once again be solicited to write additional letters. The worst problem with student withdrawal occurred when students did not withdraw officially for several weeks, leaving their pen pals in limbo. It might be two or three weeks before the instructor knew the exact status of the absent student. After attempting several solutions, we finally settled on a procedure. Students who did not receive letters from their pen pals were to continue writing to them for two weeks. During the second week, they were also to write to the instructor of the absent student, alerting the instructor to the problem. The instructor answered the student's letter, thus ensuring that the student would receive at least one letter on the next "Letter Day." Then the instructor would find a volunteer to write to the absent student's pen pal until the student returned or until the end of the quarter, if the student withdrew. Another way to address this problem would be to compile a list of volunteers at the beginning of the project who would write letters when students were absent. These "replacements" would prevent any pen pal from missing more than one letter.

In addition to the logistical problems, several student-centered problems have occurred during the course of the letter writing project. The matter of names has been a dilemma each quarter, albeit a minor one. Neither the American nor the international students can easily distinguish the gender of their pen pals from their names. The male students, in particular, find this a disconcerting situation. The instructors quickly learned to suggest that students tell their age and gender in their letters of introduction. Some international students solved the name problem by choosing (or having their classmates give them) American names. The American students were impressed by this gesture. This spirit of cooperation demonstrated by the international students heightened the interest of the American students in participating in the letter exchange.

Another common complaint voiced by students was that some of their questions did not get answered. While the students viewed this as a problem, the instructors used such instances as learning opportunities. Sometimes the international students did not answer questions because they thought they were too personal. Malaysian students were often shocked by the directness of their pen pals' questions about their dating practices. American students were surprised by some of the questions about money and the cost of personal items, such as clothes or cars, from their Latin American pen pals. Class discussions about what is and is not considered polite in various cultures were extremely revealing to both groups. The international students were surprised at how informal American students were when writing to strangers; they had anticipated longer "introductory" periods. At other times, students did not answer questions because they did not understand them. The reasons for this varied. Sometimes students had not phrased questions well; other times they had assumed that their pen pals knew more about a topic than they actually did. Instructors encouraged students to ask for clarification from their pen pals when there were questions or other items which were confusing in the letters. As a result, students began developing a keener sense of audience. This was evident during peer-review sessions. After the letter exchange, students were more likely to identify places in essays that needed additional information or more explanation. Students also commented that they proofread more carefully, especially those students whose pen pals had written questions prompted by what turned out to be a misspelled or carelessly omitted word.

Major problems between pen pals arose only on two occasions. In one situation, a thirty-year-old divorced mother was writing to a nineteen-year-old Saudi Arabian male. The Saudi student was not very tactful in the questions he asked about her personal situation; he quite adamantly voiced his opinions about women's roles, imposing his Saudi views on American women. The American student was simultaneously surprised, hurt, and angry. She discussed the situation with her instructor and with her pen pal's instructor. After writing her response, she again requested feedback from the instructors. She attempted to explain the American perspective on women's rights; her answer was polite but firm. Unfortunately, the Saudi student was not receptive to the American student's letter. He refused to acknowledge his pen pal's letters. Intervention by his instructor did not alleviate the problem; new pen pals were assigned, with the Saudi student being given a male pen pal. Although we would have preferred that the students work through the difficulties, the situation was a learning one. Discussions about cultural differences, conflicting belief systems, and the power of written language were productive outgrowths of this situation.

The only other major problem between pen pals was the result of religious differences. While the instructors had anticipated that students might encounter some difficulties because of the wide variety of religions represented in our classes, we did not anticipate that a problem would arise between two Christians. An eighteen-year-old American student, who was an enthusiastic Christian, was writing to a twenty-year-old Chinese Christian. While they shared many of the same beliefs, the Chinese student was interested in many other things besides religion. She was continually disappointed because her pen pal would not answer any of her questions unless they were about religion; every letter from her American pen pal was filled with long explanations about how happy her life as a Christian was. This one-subject discourse became quite tedious for the Chinese student. While the instructors did not forbid writing about religion, they did warn students about using their letters as tools for proselytizing. We encouraged curiosity but discouraged preaching.

Student Reactions

Throughout the three quarters that this letter writing project has been used, certain aspects of this exercise have remained the same, even though we have been continually fine-tuning it. The students in both the freshman composition classes and the ESL classes are usually surprised by the assignment. A few are resistant to the idea of writing letters, as is expected. But one of the most surprising elements of this activity is how quickly this ambivalence and opposition changes into enthusiastic participation. As soon as the first set of letters arrives, the students begin to get into the spirit of the project. Each week on "Letter Day," they want the letters handed out immediately. Writing becomes more than a requirement to be fulfilled; it becomes a means of communication, a way of reaching out, discovering, and exploring. Being able to use writing in this manner is a new and exciting experience for most of these students. They begin to see the potential that effective writing holds.

One of the greatest treasures of the exploration that has surfaced in the exchanges between the two classes is the questioning. The American students, for example, are frequently asked about everything from "safe" topics about school and home life in the U.S. to "hot" issues concerning politics, gender, and social class. Students have raised questions concerning the celebration of holidays in various societies as well as how education is defined and valued in different cultures. Through the stream of questions flowing between the groups, American students have gained insight concerning how America is viewed by various nations, whether friendly or hostile, while developing a sensitivity to the fact that international students are people who live, love, and experience problems just as Americans do. ESL students, on the other hand, have developed lasting friendships and cleared up many misconceptions about Americans and American life. They are amazed that American families can be loving and supportive while simultaneously fostering independence and critical thinking.

At the end of two of the letter exchange projects, student reactions have been solicited (see figure 2). Only one student has responded that the letter exchange was not enjoyable. Fewer than 10 percent of the students who returned the survey expressed a preference for keeping a journal instead of writing to a pen pal. The most common responses about what they liked most about the letter exchange fell into the following categories: (1) knowing someone from a different race, culture, or religion; (2) communicating informally with other people; (3) learning about things they didn't know about before; (4) making friends. One response to this question from an ESL student revealed how quickly the friendships developed and how meaningful they had become for some of the students: "We met new people and sometimes we shared special things and problems with them." More than half of the students declined to answer the question about what they disliked about the letter writing assignment because they said they liked everything. These were undoubtedly students who never missed any letters. The other dislikes listed were related to not receiving letters on "Letter Day."

Students offered several specific benefits of the project. Many ESL students said that they felt more comfortable writing in English because they had written to a native speaker who wasn't a teacher and had been understood. Other students said that they proofread things more carefully now. The American students liked learning about other countries; they also liked learning about how America is perceived by others. Several students commented that it was refreshing to be able to write about things which interested them. A few students wrote that it helped them to write about their past experiences. A number of Amer-

---

Letter Exchange Project Questionnaire

This quarter we have been involved in a letter writing project. The instructors are interested in knowing what you think about this assignment. Please answer as accurately and as honestly as you can.

1. Did you enjoy the letter writing project?

   YES   NO

2. Would you have preferred to write a journal which your instructor read instead of writing letters to other students?

   YES   NO

3. What did you like most about the letter writing project?

   _____
   _____

4. What did you like least about the letter writing project?

   _____
   _____

5. How do you think this assignment has helped to improve your writing abilities?

   _____
   _____

6. What suggestions do you have to improve the letter writing project?

   _____
   _____

Figure 2. Project evaluation questionnaire.

ican students were astounded by how well some of the international students could write in a second (or third) language. The ESL students, on the other hand, found it helpful to see how native speakers actually wrote (especially compared with textbook examples of standard English).

Students suggested that the letter exchange project continue. A few students commented that they would have liked to have had the letters kept in a folder and the folder "mailed." These students thought it would be helpful to reread the letters they had written as well as reread their pen pals' letters. Many of the students who wrote letters during class said they wanted more time; some suggested writing the letters as homework instead of answering them in class. Other comments were concerned with the logistics of exchanging letters, several of which were implemented.

Overall, American and international students agreed that the letter exchange was a positive experience. It nurtured friendships and broadened understandings for many of the students involved.

Benefits

The American students participated enthusiastically in the letter exchange, even those who were a bit apprehensive at first. The greatest benefits for the American students were learning about non-American cultures and practicing writing for very diverse audiences. Most of the American students wanted to learn about the dating and marriage customs of the international students. Some were curious about the reactions of international students to American life and to their American student counterparts, while others wanted a clearer understanding of the political conditions and climate of particular countries. The American students were usually impressed with the international students' expertise in mathematics. It was a common occurrence for tutoring exchanges to grow out of the letter exchange. American students helped with English, history, sociology, and psychology, while international students helped with math, physics, and chemistry courses. The American students were often travel consultants. They provided their international pen pals with information about Atlanta, New Orleans, and Memphis as well as local attractions around Birmingham. The American students always questioned their pen pals about their trips; the reactions of their pen pals to these locales gave the American students new perspectives on their region.

The ESL students commented each quarter that the thing they appreciated most about the letter writing project was that they got to meet Americans. One of the common complaints heard from ESL students prior to the letter exchange regarded their lack of American friends. International students constantly asked how they could develop friendships with Americans. The letter writing project turned out to be one answer to this problem. Although not all of the pen pals became close friends, a number of them continued to communicate after the project ended. Other ESL students expressed great enthusiasm about the opportunity to ask Americans questions through the letters about America, American families, and American social customs. One question asked regularly by the ESL students was why Americans want to move away from home so soon after graduating from high school. The information received through the letter exchange served to assist international students in forming more realistic perceptions of Americans and the American way of life, thus combating many of the grossly distorted perceptions they had formed based on their viewing of television and movies.

In an attempt to encourage interaction between students, the instructors arranged a lunch meeting one quarter at a restaurant on the last Friday of the term. In theory, students were to meet the pen pals they had been writing to all quarter; in reality, many of the students had already met their pen pals. Only about one-third of the students attended. Many were studying for final exams or had other commitments, but the ones who attended were delighted to meet their pen pals. Looking back on the experience, the instructors realized that a meeting earlier in the quarter, perhaps soon after midterm exams, might have been more successful.

The international students frequently asked for advice about the campus, about registration and drop/add procedures, and about extracurricular activities. Two questions frequently asked were "Could you explain the sorority/fraternity system?" and "What is Homecoming?" The American students were also quizzed in detail about football and basketball. Holidays were also favorite topics. During winter quarter, some students seemed always to be writing about holidays—Chinese New Year, Presidents' Day, Valentine's Day, Easter. Students would sometimes invite their pen pals to participate in holiday-related activities.

Many ESL students learned much about the English language through their correspondence with the American students. They discovered, for example, that their American peers were a rich source of slang and colloquial expressions. Such expressions as "take a chill pill," "get a life," and "get a grip" were fascinating to the ESL students. Learning what these expressions meant gave them more confidence when they encountered American students. Slang words that were also "regular" words, such as "bad" (meaning "really good") and "fresh" (meaning "extremely special"), were particularly confusing to ESL students. Their American pen pals helped to demystify these words by explaining them. This "real-life vocabulary," as one ESL student described it, quickly found its way into the active vocabulary of the international students as well as people in the community and on campus. Being able to use colloquial English with Americans off-campus helped the international students feel that they belonged.

Conclusions

While the letter exchange between ESL students and freshman composition students helped the international students develop an understanding and awareness of American expression, it also proved useful in helping them see grammar and punctuation rules put into practice by living, breathing people. Because most of the students in the ESL classes would be mainstreamed into English composition classes, it was quite beneficial for them to see the writing of first-language English speakers. Some ESL students found it surprising, but at the same time comforting, to discover that American students also made grammatical errors. On the other hand, the American students gained a greater sensitivity to the struggle that many second-language writers face. Through the letters from their international pen pals, the Americans became more aware of the role of sentence and paragraph structure and of grammar and spelling in effective written communication.

The dialogue that has taken place between our classes by no means offers the ultimate solution to the cross-cultural difficulties existing on our campuses and in our classrooms. However, we are confident that this activity represents one important step that language arts teachers can take in providing opportunities for students of varied social and cultural backgrounds to explore, collaborate, and listen—using language as a mechanism for cooperative learning, self-actualization, and, possibly, social change. As we recognize the importance of a positive self-image and of self-confidence in language development and effective language use, we have sought through this collaborative language exercise to strengthen bonds and provide an opportunity for students to hear many different voices and to recognize varied perspectives.

Through their experiences of communicating with these different voices, the students feel more confident in their own ability to use written language to communicate. As they write about their experiences and beliefs, the letter exchange helps students to discover their own voices. They also become, in most cases, more tolerant or less afraid of people from other cultures, allowing lines of communication to open which were previously closed. The letter exchange project provides students with a nonthreatening but extremely rich language experience, one whose effects can be profound and far-reaching.

8 "Delicious of the New": ESL as Poetry, EFL as Literary Analysis

James W. Penha
Jakarta International School, Jakarta, Indonesia

Just as I cherish those unique phrases in *Heart Of Darkness* which Conrad derived from his Polish idiom, I have been charmed by the fresh formulations brought to English by my high school and university students whose first-language syntax and vocabulary predispose them to ignore banal constructions—on which native English speakers tend to rely—in favor of what makes sense to them and what makes music to me. When, for instance, a defector from Shanghai told me he had "seized refuge" in the West, I heard his struggle far more than I should have had he identified himself simply as a refugee.

Thus have I encouraged student writers and their peer editors to revere, save, and exploit such serendipitous language in drafts. Even as a teacher of mainstream English classes and one without any special TESL training, I knew that this pedagogical strategy had the happy effect of instilling in ESL students pride in their special abilities and, thereby, encouraging fluency in English.

The inspiration to shape this concept into a focused teaching unit came, finally, from my correspondence with a batik artist whom I had met in Yogyakarta, Indonesia. As is the case with many Asians I have encountered since teaching at international schools, first, in Hong Kong and, at present, in Jakarta, this young man eagerly sought to practice his English with a real-live American, so we wrote to each other regularly. I used excerpts from his letters in my classes as examples of the inventiveness of a writer new to a language.

Indeed, the examples affected my own craft. Teaching and writing do mutually inspire! As I, in search of paradigms, reread the sheaf of letters from Yogyakarta, I thought I might try to develop a pastiche that would work as a poem. Sections of the result, "The Apprentice," follow:

Thanks for your letter again,
comes with special
of wonderful words. I want
to hearing the often it . . .

I used the border of the language. Do you know?
Why I looking about you
astonished
of my works?
Thanks of your flattery,
I am living on the sky . . .

I want to show the best.
You will
delicious of the new.
May you heavenly
more happiness to me.

Enormous! . . .

To separate yourself from your country
also the family yourself.
Within I think it's impossible
and so I can't say of flattery,
exception
to put up my thumb! . . .

But for me
I am wrestling with the hot wax
and to frighten!
The event of language to use myself,
maybe I'll wordless
if I am speaking directly
because I haven't more the words.
The language of dictionary in I used it,

know is means it! . . .

Sincerely,
Roto

PS I am sorry if my words
do not take pleasure in your heart.

If *I* could do it, so could my high school students at Hong Kong International School. I developed the following unit in an elective creative writing course with a group of juniors and seniors who were microcosmic of the school's population. Slightly more than half of the class of twenty-five were Americans and other native English speakers, but a large minority came to Hong Kong and to an American-style, English-speaking school from many different Asian and European nations. English proficiency and academic ability ranged as widely as passports at HKIS, but that was hardly a handicap in a unit that celebrates and relies on linguistic diversity.

Unit: ESL as Poetry

1. Distribute and read "The Apprentice." The class should examine the poem as it would an American poem from the canon. (Typically, I divide the class into threesomes who are instructed to search for the poem's oddities—clues, I profess, to the nature of a work—and its striking lines and language.)

2. After each trio reports its findings, reveal the author of the poem and describe its genesis. (I always bring in the original letters in case it becomes necessary to convince the doubters.)

3. Using words and phrases selected by students, investigate with the class why Roto wrote them. What does "wrestling with the hot wax" or "to put up my thumb" or "delicious of the new" evoke in readers and listeners?

4. Use the dictionary to follow Roto's search for what he determined to be the *mot juste.*

Roto's ingenuous ignorance of the denotative and connotative aspects of English vocabulary allow him, after all, to blur the distinction and, thus, to create figurative language. I find this a dramatic demonstration of how figures of speech develop from the stretching of language and of meaning.

The next step in the unit derives from my belief, as a writer and teacher, that prose provides a path, a useful early draft, to poetry. Indeed, as an introduction to poetry writing, the students in my creative writing classes clip out provocative newspaper paragraphs, copy these excerpts by hand in formats that look and sound *poetic* to them, and ultimately reshape and revise current events into original verses. This exercise in "refined found poetry" (see Penha, "Refined") provides apt preparation for the following prose-to-poetry metamorphosis:

5. Invite students to ask why the poem has found the form in which it exists: Why do certain lines enjamb? Why are the different threads of Roto's messages separated in the poem, whereas each of the sources (the letters) focuses on one specific idea? How do these disparate stanzas connect?

What actually occurs is that students ask me why I did what I did. Because this personal interchange vivifies, rather than merely points to, poetic technique, I suggest strongly that teachers generate their own models rather than use mine. The ensuing colloquy responds at last to that traditional, anticlimactic query by students of literature: "But how do you know that's what the poet was thinking?" The question of intention is not fallacious here; it is formative! Students love to grill teachers. Let them. Let them meet a writer. You. And let them see that you have attempted the very assignment you are about to offer them:

6. Assign students to find a stretch of unrefined, unedited writing by a person relatively new to English or by someone whose nonstandard English is nonetheless communicative and/or entertaining. Suggest that perhaps they can find, like the source of "The Apprentice," a series of letters, a diary written by a friend, a relative, or by themselves, or perhaps the rough draft of something written in this or another class. If some students don't think they can get hold of a manuscript, encourage them to tape or take notes on an interview with someone whose English, like Roto's, is naturally imagistic in its striving to convey. (If the class contains several such living resources, I allow time for this in-house research.) Students who choose the oral approach might break the ice by asking their subjects to relate a favorite story. (Everyone has a pet anecdote she or he tells at the slightest prompting!)

7. When students return with their transcripts and manuscripts, ask them to read aloud to a partner, and instruct them to circle any phrases, sentences, or words that strike the reader or listener as beautiful or fun. If the student pairs find any of these passages difficult to comprehend in standard English, they should try to translate them as best they can and jot down the paraphrases in the margins for future reference.

8. Still in pairs, each student should again read the draft aloud, this time looking and listening for phrases, sentences, and words that seem irrelevant to the main thrust of the piece. (Referring to "The Apprentice," I remind students that some tangents provide important ironies or represent well the mind of the speaker; these should be circled and retained at this time.) But students should put a light line through useless irrelevancies.

9. Guided to try to retain the circled parts and eliminate the lined irrelevancies, students should write new drafts of their pieces—still in prose, but expanded, contracted, rearranged, and altered as they see fit.

10. Partnered with a classmate again, students should ask their colleagues to read their second drafts and indicate in writ-

ing *what's there*—what story, idea, conflict, or character struggles to reveal itself in the piece.

11. With the goal of clarifying and dramatizing *what's* already *there* in the piece, students should pursue the revising/editing process. ("Relax," I tell my students, "because all your decisions remain tentative until the final draft. And remember, too, what we learned when we 'refined found poetry': this piece now belongs to you. You found it; you have the responsibility to change it in any way that will enhance its style and allow it to communicate something to a reader.")

In that original high school creative writing class, I encouraged students to shape the pieces into poems by the final draft. When I later used this unit in a freshman composition course at a large New York City university, I hoped students would discover the nature of narrative and voice as well as the delights of diversity in diction. For these purposes, prose drafts sufficed.

I tell all my students that the success rate for this exercise—the percentage of students who will really like what they finally create—is about 55 percent. Since my students choose, from among all projects, which final drafts they wish to be graded, they are content with the prognosis. And as we read our works around and aloud, we are, as writers and individuals, amused, assured, and fortified by delicious eccentricities such as "the air smelled ambiguous" or "I released the stifle of my scream."

EFL as Literary Analysis

Students' native knowledge of languages other than English provides a special opportunity in the study of literature as well as in writing.

In the midst of preparing lessons on variant English renditions of the ancient Chinese "Cold Mountain" poems, I was struck anew with the scintillating art of translation and how translation requires, inherently, the adapter to interpret the original critically as much as linguistically. Translation is, in this way, our most venerable deconstruction!

Thus do I offer literature students the chance, as one of several project choices, to translate a canonical work into a non-English language in which they are fluent. Although conceived as a fair option for my American and European students, who are required to take United States literature as part of Hong Kong International School's curriculum, this assignment remains in my repertoire, stateside or overseas. I offer it to all of my literature students, secondary and university, beginning and advanced. Since it promises an engaging detour from the typical, the exercise attracts some native English speakers who are willing to practice their own second languages.

Inasmuch as my own fluencies beyond English are limited to rusty French and pidgin Indonesian, I claim no right to judge the accuracy of the students' translations. Happily, colleagues from modern language departments are usually eager to collaborate with me on this task. If no staff member possesses expertise to help me evaluate the achievement in a particular language, I require, prior to my approval of the project proposal, that the student find for me an incorruptible referee.

I assess the line-by-line diary, which is also assigned and submitted with the translation, in which the student documents how and why all translanguage decisions were made, employing the criteria and techniques studied in the course. In her work on Sylvia Plath's "Edge," Susan, an HKIS eleventh grader, discovered that "the sentences and lines of the poem had to be structured just as in Plath's original so that the reader could get the same feeling in Spanish . . . very brain-racking!"

Susan's classmate Alex, who translated Dorothy Parker's story "Soldiers of the Republic" into Spanish, reported that he had to use idioms unrelated to the English in order "to keep the natural mood and feeling of the original":

From "Soldiers of the Republic" by Dorothy Parker:

That Sunday afternoon we sat with the Swedish girl in the big café in Valencia. We had vermouth in thick goblets, each with a cube of honeycombed gray ice in it. The waiter was so proud of that ice he could hardly bear to leave the glasses on the table, and thus part from it forever. He went to his duty—all over the room they were clapping their hands and hissing to draw his attention—but he looked back over his shoulder. (165)

Alex's translation into Spanish:

Aquél domingo, en la tarde, nos sentamos con la muchacha sueca en el restaurante en Valencia. Tuvimos «Cinzano» en copas densas, cada cual con un pedazo de hielo gris de colmena. El camarrero tenía tanto orgullo del hielo que casi no pudo dejar las copas en la mesa, despidiéndose de ellas para siempre. Él se fué a su deber—por todo el cuarto la gente le daba una palmeada y silbaba para genar su atención—pero él miró por detrás de su hombro.

A colleague born in Seoul found flaws in Joon-Young's Korean transliteration of "The Act," but I think, nonetheless, the visual-minded William Carlos Williams would have appreciated the new look given to his poem. Certainly, it was thrilling for Joon-Young's classmates—and his teacher—to hear the colloquial language of Williams set to an Asian melody:

"The Act" by William Carlos Williams*:

There were the roses, in the rain.
Don't cut them, I pleaded.
    They won't last, she said
But they're so beautiful
    where they are.
Agh, we were all beautiful once, she
    said,
and cut them and gave them to me
    in my hand.

Joon-Young's translation into Korean

행위

장미 꽃 들이 있어요, 비속에.
베지 마세요, 하고 탄원 했읍니다.
    오래 못 가요, 그녀가 말 하녔다.
그렁나 너무나 아름다와요
    그들이 있는 곳에.
아. 우리도 어여뻤지요 한번, 그녀가
    말하였다,
그러면서, 그들을 베어 저에게 주었읍니다
    저의 손에.

Publication of these projects, in anthologies distributed throughout the school or as broadsides made public in classrooms and hallways, makes manifest students' esteem for, and an institution's pride in, interchanges among languages and cultures. Even though neither I nor most of my students can recite the calligraphic and pictographic

---

*From: William Carlos Williams: *The Collected Poems of William Carlos Williams, 1909–1939, vol. I.* Copyright 1938 by New Directions Publishing Corp. Reprinted by permission of New Directions Publishing Corp.

languages of Asia, we learn, as audiences to one another's projects, to relish the aesthetics of these once-foreign tongues.

In James Weldon Johnson's "The Creation," Michael, a Singaporean teenager, found "very powerful language that really shouts out at the reader. Imitating this style was the hardest part, as I had often to erase a Chinese phrase again and again to replace it with a stronger expression":

From "The Creation" by James Weldon Johnson:

Then the green grass sprouted,
And the little red flowers blossomed,
The pine tree pointed his finger to the sky,
And the oak spread out his arms,
The lakes cuddled down in the hollows of the ground,
And the rivers ran down to the sea;
And God smiled again,
And the rainbow appeared,
And curled itself around his shoulder.
Then God raised his arm and he waved his hand
Over the sea and over the land,
And he said: Bring forth! Bring forth!
And quicker than God could drop his hand,
Fishes and fowls
And beasts and birds
Swam the rivers and the seas,
Roamed the forests and the woods,
And split the air with their wings.
And God said: That's good!

Michael's translation into Chinese:

之后，草開始發芽，
小紅花亦開放了，
尖削的松樹直指雲霄，
而橡樹伸出它的手臂，
湖水擁抱着地面的凹地，
河水流入海中；
神再一次微笑，
天上出現了彩虹，
在他肩膀周圍卷起來，
神提起雙手並揮動着，
在天地和海洋之上，
他說：你們出現了吧！

在神把他的手放下之前，
魚類和雀鳥
和野獸們
皆撲進河和海洋里去，
於森林之間旅游，
翅膀拍動着空氣，
而神說：非常好！

Wrote Michael in his diary, "I was very excited after finishing the translation and reading it out loud, for the style was much like Johnson's. By imitating the tone of Johnson's voice, I had actually interpreted the poem as precisely as possible."

Precisely.

Works Cited

Johnson, James Weldon. "The Creation." *Soulscript: Afro-American Poetry.* Ed. June Jordan. New York: Zenith, 1970. 60–63.

Parker, Dorothy. "Soldiers of the Republic." *The Portable Dorothy Parker.* Rev. ed. New York: Viking, 1973. 165–69.

Penha, James W. "The Apprentice." *On the Back of the Dragon.* Cupertino, CA: Omega Cat, 1992. 19–21.

———. "Refined Found Poetry." *Teachers and Writers* 21.4 (1990): 5–9.

Plath, Sylvia. "Edge." *Sylvia Plath: The Collected Poems.* Ed. Ted Hughes. New York: Harper, 1983. 272–73.

Williams, William Carlos. "The Act." *The Collected Poems of William Carlos Williams, 1939–1962.* Vol II. New York: New Directions, 1968. 147.

9 "Break On Through": An Interdisciplinary Approach to Composition

Michael G. Battin
U.S. Grant High School, Van Nuys, California

Teaching English, especially writing, must be one of the most exciting professions possible. The depth and immensity of ideas that are generated through class discussions about related literature, film, and current events can be constant sources of amazement. An English teacher who teaches a novel, for example, often finds that he or she is also teaching the history of the era and, in certain instances, part of another discipline, say, science, as well. Any English teacher who teaches writing as a process finds students thoughtfully examining their own lives and their own knowledge to learn how to cope with life's changes. And good English teaching requires breaking through the walls of isolated classrooms and reaching out to other disciplines and to personal experience.

The short unit detailed here calls for students to examine what they have learned from social studies and science. It can also involve fine art or graphic arts such as drafting. Thus, it is an interdisciplinary approach to learning. The unit was first presented as a single lesson at a writing workshop for teachers by Sandra Rodgers, of the Long Beach Unified School District, and Sherryl Broyles, of the Los Angeles Unified School District. They presented this lesson as a prototype for the California Learning Assessment System (CLAS) test. The ideas presented at the workshop inspired me to expand the lesson into a unit, adapting it to my ESL and English classrooms.

I have taught this unit to students of varying abilities from the seventh-grade through twelfth-grade levels. To demonstrate the unit's versatility, I have included here writing samples from two diverse groups of students at U.S. Grant High School in the Los Angeles Unified School District. One set of samples is from a sophomore honors English class with an ethnic makeup of 50 percent Hispanic, 25 percent Anglo, 13 percent Asian, and 12 percent Armenian. The reading level and writing abilities of some of the students reflect the difficulty of their English language development. But these students are motivated and eager to do well. The other set of samples is from an English-as-a-second-language (ESL) writing class that is predominantly Hispanic, but which includes 10 percent Asian students. These students have been studying English for less than two years.

The ideas generated within this unit provide a common ground for all the students. The poem used in this lesson, "A Winter's Tale," by Ruth Lechlitner, is easily read and understood by a wide range of students. This poem addresses a common fear, the destruction of our planet, yet it furnishes hope by allowing the reader to see a solution. No poet writes a poem that is intended to be used at a certain grade or reading level, but this poem seems to suit students in the secondary grades.

Depending on the needs of the class and the goals of the teacher, this unit can take from three to more than five class periods. I have found that the ideas generated by the students are much too involved, too complex, to rush through. Preferring to explore the ideas my students present, I guide them through a series of prewriting activities which lead to a culminating writing assignment that incorporates the concepts brought forth during their reading and discussion.

I begin the unit by asking students to brainstorm all the possible reasons that could cause humankind to seek the shelter of a city underground. Students need at least a superficial understanding of the dangers that humankind faces to do well on this assignment, and a group brainstorming session allows them to tap into a range of ideas and experiences without fear of being "wrong." Answers usually include atomic warfare, the greenhouse effect, pollution, acid rain, as well as many other disasters caused by humans. As the students share their answers, I lead a brief discussion, giving the class a clearer idea of the differences in these dangers, sometimes categorizing them by type of disaster. Another option that I have used is to assign groups of students to research a topic, such as the ultimate effects of global warming, and then ask them to present their findings to the class.

The poem "A Winter's Tale" is then introduced to the class by telling the students that the people in the poem were forced to live under the surface of the earth. Several questions—such as "What do these people remember?" and "What have they forgotten?"—are presented as cues for listening. I then read the poem to the class while the students follow with their own copies:

A Winter's Tale*

Born in these metal tubes beneath
Abandoned cities where no seasons turn
You ask about snow: the great White
Our ancestors knew as winter in December
When men lived with the cold air high about them.
(We breathe the bottled day, take the false light
Sterile upon our eyelids)—how shall I tell you?
Snow is the naked past, snow is the dream
We had before the sky became hell's house
And these sealed rooms deep in the dying earth
Our last escape.

What is snow like?

I can't say, but your great-grandfather knows.
(That's why he weeps: we have lost the need for tears.)
Ask him: he's very old, but he remembers.

Some phrases provoke insightful reactions from the students. I ask what is meant by the "bottled day" or the "false light / Sterile upon our eyelids." I ask how does one "[lose] the need for tears" and how does the sky's becoming "hell's house" relate to the disasters discussed in class. I ask them to respond to the implications of the title. We also talk about the difficulty of describing snow to someone who has never been out of the underground city.

After the discussion, students participate in a quick-write to describe snow. They have about ten minutes to jot down their ideas, using the following guidelines:

Describe snow to someone who has never been outside the underground city.

What words will you use to make your explanation clear?

What comparisons can you make in your description?

How can you make your feelings about snow known to the reader?

Describing snow in a limited amount of time challenges the creativity of the students. How does one describe something we all take

---

*"A Winter's Tale" by Ruth Lechlitner. Copyright © 1981. Used by permission of Anne M. Corey.

for granted? Despite time constraints, the students are able to make apt comparisons as well as express the sincerity of their feelings. A student once described snow as being "like miles and miles of vanilla ice cream. Imagine a blanket of cold vanilla ice cream covering the land. Cold, wet, slushy. That's what snow is." Another student, an Asian American from an intermediate ESL class, also turned to food to provide a comparison for snow: "Snow is like a breadcrumb. That color is white. It's like salt or sugar." A young Armenian student was able to write: "Snow is a great thing, which you cannot live without. You're the unluckiest person if you've never seen or touched the snow." A student from the honors class described snow as being "Heaven's cold and frozen teardrops." Each student found his or her own way to meet the challenge of time constraints and description.

After the students describe snow, I then like to play Stephen Sondheim's song "I Remember." (From the musical *Evening Primrose*, the song can be found in a few of the Sondheim collections available in most record stores). "I Remember" is a monologue sung by a man remembering things like snow, rain, and sky, and being able to describe them only by comparing them with objects invented by people. The students sense and respond to the song's poignant, wistful quality, to its looking at those things we all take for granted, and they find the ending quite moving. They often model their own writings after Sondheim's description of snow.

I Remember**

I remember sky,
it was blue as ink.
Or at least I think I remember sky.

I remember snow,
soft as feathers, sharp as thumbtacks,
coming down like lint,
and it made you squint
when the wind would blow.
And ice, like vinyl, on the streets,
cold as silver,
white as sheets.
Rain like strings
and changing things like leaves.

**"I remember," words and music by Stephen Sondheim. Copyright © 1966 by Burthen Music Co., Inc. Copyright renewed by Chappell and Co. Used by permission of the Hal Leonard Corporation.

I remember leaves,
green as spearmint,
crisp as paper.

I remember trees,
bare as coatracks,
spread like broken umbrellas.
And parks and bridges,
ponds and zoos,
ruddy faces, muddy shoes.
Light and noise
and bees and boys
and days.

I remember days,
or at least I try.
But as years go by
they're a sort of haze.
And the bluest ink
isn't really sky.
And at times I think
I would gladly die
for a day of sky.

In their final writing assignment, composing a letter from an underground city, which I shall explain more fully later in this chapter, students voice their awareness of what they have found rewarding in their immediate environment. One honors student treasured her world in these words:

> You know, I never even realized how precious the trees and the birds and the sky were. I can only hold dear my memories of swimming in the ocean and swinging high on the swings in the park. Down here we have no parks. No beaches. No birds. No nothing. It's strictly survival down here.

> —Michelle

ESL students also express their longing for the beauty of nature. Sofia wrote: "I miss the food from McDonalds, the air, the snow at Christmas. I miss also the flowers, the clothes, and the rain in Fall." Carlos also was able to take the ideas presented in class and incorporate them into his composition: "I wish too we could get back to Earth but we can't survive there. I remember the blue sky and shine sun, and the cold air. You remember when it was raining hard, we would go outside to receive the cold weather." Granted, while McDonald's is not usually described as one of the beauties of nature, the point is for students to take ideas presented in class and make them their own.

It is extremely helpful to have students consider the differences and similarities that an underground city would have compared with those of today's cities before they attempt to describe the underground city in their final writing. The concept of limited space and its implications for the city in the poem are not apparent at first. The students' early designs and explanations of the underground city, which were made without first comparing and contrasting the cities of the future with those of the present, tended to resemble their hometown of Los Angeles stuck under a dome. The designs and explanations made after a more formal planning stage had a greater degree of creativity to them.

I have developed several methods to elicit ideas from students. For some classes, a comparison/contrast paper is appropriate. For others, I assign questions to be answered by the students. I have put students in small groups and assigned each group one question from those listed below; sometimes, I shuffle students so that they may teach other students what they learned in their first group. Right now, I am inclined to ask groups to create a Venn diagram that illustrates the similarities and differences between the cities of the present and the underground cities of the future. The similarities are listed in the overlap of the two circles, while the differences are listed in the outer portion of the circles.

As the students work through this section of the unit, they consider the following questions:

How will the underground cities of the future be different from the cities of today?

How will they be similar?

What is the purpose of a city?

What kind of government will be in power?

How will the cities be organized?

What new technologies will be needed to live underground?

What will the underground cities have to do without?

An example of a student's Venn diagram illustrating the difference between the cities of today and those of the future may look something like figure 1. A teacher who makes clear the distinction between a city whose purpose is to engage in commerce and make money and a city whose sole purpose is to survive will enlist the imagination of the students. Using their individual ideas of the city's needs as the basis of their Venn diagrams, the students are next put in groups

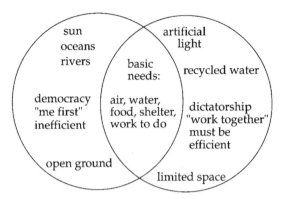

Figure 1. Example of a student Venn diagram.

of four and asked to combine their ideas for a plan of the underground city. I provide them with the following instructions:

> Discussion:
> Brainstorm the ways the underground city will look. How will the city be organized and arranged? How will the basic needs be supplied?

> Project:
> As a group, design the underground city. Draw the city as you think it will be arranged. Be prepared to present your plan to the class when you are finished.

I provide large pieces of paper and plenty of colored pencils, crayons, and markers. The idea is that everyone contributes to the design. To assure this, I wander about and listen to the group discussions, which can be very intense. I evaluate the students' designs on the basis of the effort that went into the work rather than on their appearance. I am interested in how the students account for the basic needs: air, water, and food. Once the designs have been completed, each group shares their creation with the class. From these presentations, interesting tangents will develop that can provide fascinating discussion: "Where will the best houses be found—close to the surface or deeper underground?" Because each group has selected the type of disaster that would force humankind underground, the answer to this question will reflect the nature of that disaster. A group once designed a city with a tanning salon, which sparked a class discussion on fashion and health that lasted almost the entire period: "Would the citizens of the underground city want to maintain a tan?"

The designs for the underground city in figures 2 and 3 illustrate the creativity of the students in addition to their comprehension of the underground city's needs. The designs appear vastly different, but both address the need to use space efficiently and eliminate luxuries of the present. One thing is clear: planning for efficient use of space is difficult for most students.

After all the preliminary assignments are completed, students are then asked to write a letter from another person's point of view. This assignment may be an in-class writing assignment or given as homework with several days to complete it. Each student is expected to write a well-organized letter that demonstrates an understanding of standard English. In addition to those standards expected in every writing assignment, each student is expected to incorporate the ideas generated in the class discussion, including:

> a clear understanding of the effects of the disaster;
>
> the possible methods that have been used to counteract the disaster;
>
> the society and government of the new community;
>
> a clear idea of the plan and layout of the underground city;
>
> a personal voice from one who remembers the past and has survived.

> Writing Situation:
> Imagine you are the oldest citizen in the underground city described in the poem, "A Winter's Tale." Of all the survivors, only you are old enough to remember life outside the underground city. You have received a letter from a friend on another planet who was one of the last able to leave Earth. Your friend has heard about the underground city and wonders how living there has changed your life.

> Directions for Writing:
> Write a letter to your friend. Create the sense of a personal voice as you describe some of the changes that have resulted from living underground. The changes you write about should include those in technology that have been developed, the society that has evolved, and an idea of how the city functions. Discuss the effects these changes have had on your everyday life. (The effects should seem possible or reasonable.)

The students in my classes have written of both mundane and unusual changes, addressing directly the problems of today as they project these problems into the future. Garen, an honors student, addressed the issue of privacy and personal space: "It is so populated, that we take shifts to sleep. My bed is used three times a day, each for eight hours. I have friends in high places and they promised me that I

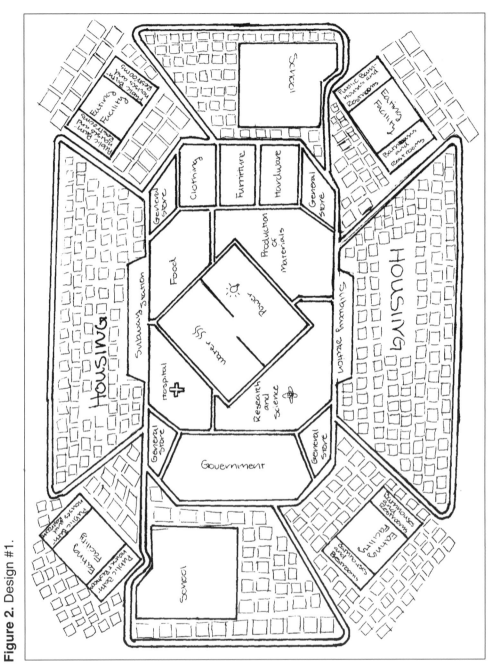

Figure 2. Design #1.

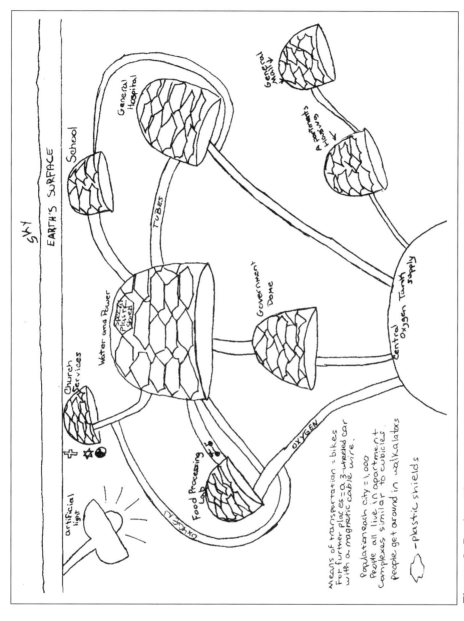

Figure 3. Design #2.

will soon get the night shift of sleeping." José, from the ESL class, saw the bright side of a new city: "The air we breathe is more natural and it's without smoke because we have clean transportation."

This unit also evokes humorous responses while still addressing the subject. Students who complained of eating tofu asked if there were cows on the moon. Taking an idea from the presentation of underground city designs, Justin wrote that he, as great-grandfather, had "won the Bio-Lottery. . . . The prize I won is ten steak dinners over the next ten years. Since there isn't that much meat around these days, a steak dinner is a rare thing."

Students are able to provide solutions to the problems that the underground city would face. Some of these problems are ones that we share. Shiva, an honors student from India, wrote that the underground city's energy source was "powered by a nuclear factory that draws energy from the nuclear debris that was left behind by the very atomic war which drove us beneath the Earth; it's almost ironic." Addressing directly the problem of overpopulation, Shaina described a world in which doctors "decide who is born and who should die. Only two children are allowed per couple. Those who can't produce, work, or help in society are killed by an injection. This includes the handicapped, old, and ill."

Optimistic voices may also be heard amidst all the doom and gloom. Providing a ray of hope for civilization, Maria predicted a future in which "our society doesn't have division of races or classes. Maybe its because we don't use money. . . . The children born here have grown up not caring for wealth, or racism."

The students' responses to this prompt continually amaze me. It does not matter what a student's grade or level of ability is; this unit strikes a common chord. The fear of Earth's destruction is one that has been shared since the first atomic bomb was detonated fifty years ago. Today's students have never lived in an age where that underlying fear has not influenced people's thinking. This unit allows students to face this unnamed fear.

Space only allows for one complete letter to be printed. Rather than show the finest papers my students were able to produce, I would like to share a paper by an ESL student from El Salvador. The paper has problems with standard English usage, but the paper responds to the prompt in a unique manner. This student captured the concepts discussed in class and found a way to put them into his letter while maintaining a personal voice:

Dear Dangela,

I'm going to answer all your questions that you asked me in the letter you sent me. Yes, I miss Earth because here in the underground city it is very crowded, not like on the surface.

I control the water machine. Here we do not use water like we did on Earth because here we don't have rivers, oceans, nor snow, so we have to recycle water. We have artificial air. We have a very high technology because we all know how to use computers. We have an artificial sun or light control by a machine. We do not suffer from a lack of food because we make our own. We have a special place where we grow them. We even have a place for cows, chickens, ducks, pigs, and goats.

But here is very crowded because we have five thousand people in only about three square miles. The animals and food have a mile to be. We have to share bathrooms. We have one hundred bathrooms for everybody but each bathroom has about twenty showers and twenty toilets. So some people have to go first, then other people go.

You know, I really miss Earth because on Earth are the dead bodies of my parents and brothers. If only the atomic war hadn't happened, I would still be on Earth. I'm very glad that you escaped to Mars because when you answer me this letter, you are going to tell me how is Mars and how you missed Earth.

Yes, we have fun here in the underground city. The children play all the games we used to play on the surface. But only here, the children have only one field for all of them. Children go to school only three days a week because parents need them to work at home. On weekends we go to church. Here in the underground city there is no hatred because we all work together. We have a hospital that if you get hurt, you don't have to pay anything.

Write when you can. I look forward to hearing from you.

Your friend,
Salvador

The students earn four grades in this unit: one for the quick-write description of snow, one for the group design of the city, one for the comparisons of the cities, and one for the culminating letter. Obviously, the weight given to each grade is increased as the student's time and effort spent increases.

This unit has been beneficial to students in a number of ways. The lesson was originally intended to prepare students for the California Learning Assessment System (CLAS) test, which is used to evaluate not only students' end products, but also the manner in which the students have been taught. By incorporating an assessment of prewriting and group work in addition to the final writing, teachers can better determine the strengths and weaknesses of teaching procedures and student effort. This unit also incorporates knowledge from several subjects, allowing students to break down the false barriers that separate the disciplines. The unit challenges students to draw upon their experiences and knowledge of other subjects, such as science, social studies, and art. It also reminds students of the need to remember their own past and the need to be able to describe it. Many of my students have come from different countries; they love their native lands but are unable to find the words to describe to others their countries as they remember them. This assignment serves to remind students of the need to remember and to find the words that describe something from the past. This unit provides a common ground for students from diverse backgrounds to work together, and they find that they enjoy working with one another in planning a new society.

Works Cited

Lechlitner, Ruth. "A Winter's Tale." 1981.

Sondheim, Stephen. "I Remember." *Evening Primrose.* New York: Burthen Music, 1966.

10 Environmental Writing and Minority Education

Luke Wallin
University of Massachusetts at Dartmouth

For eight years, my advanced composition workshop course, "Nature, Landscape, and Environmental Writing," has proven successful for African American, Native American, Hispanic, and Portuguese students. During and after the course, they have found ways to integrate personal environmental concerns within a wide range of career writing projects.

Environmental Writing Defined

Environmental writing ranges from personal essays which explore cultural and physical settings to such relatively objective forms as journalism and comprehensive community plans. There are always questions as to how much of oneself to reveal and about one's position along a line from impressionistic nature writing to impersonal-sounding environmental science. My course seeks to give students experience with different viewpoints, types of research, and levels of revealed social commitment.

The concept of environmental writing bridges gaps between personal memoir and objectivist, technical prose. For many minority students, there is a painful distance between the "environments" described in official bureaucratic/scientific documents and the ways these places have felt to them as home communities. Courses in nature writing or the literature of nature offer one kind of model, while those in journalism, science, and planning offer another. Students may feel an uncomfortable choice between indulgent poetics on the one hand and coldly authoritative rhetoric on the other. But upon graduation, they often have writing opportunities that partake of both extremes, yet require new syntheses; these include journalism, which explores community/environmental connections, and comprehensive and master plans, which will influence the futures of their home environments. When English and writing majors take this course, they tend to learn a good deal about the science and politics of local and regional planning. When science and planning students enroll, they tend to emerge with a stronger sense of how to include personal viewpoints in their professional work.

The Environmental Autobiography

This assignment is the cornerstone of my approach. It invites students to think and write about how the environment of their childhood, including the physical as well as the cultural landscape, has made them the unique individuals that they are. How might they be different had they come of age elsewhere? For young students, this can be a daunting question, so I have found it helpful to suggest the following structure:

A ——————————————— B

Point A represents a significant childhood event and point B, a poignant moment in adulthood which has been deeply influenced by point A. Older "returning" students often possess a rich integration of their life stages which they can work with in this assignment; undergraduates around twenty years of age also frequently appreciate the simplification of this structure as they focus on the role of environment in the formation of selfhood.

This beginning is important because it helps the students think through one of the great illusions of our culture, the idea that we are autonomous souls or minds, floating free of the environment. As anthropologist Richard A. Shweder put it in a recent study:

> By contrast [with the Oriyas of India], in the West . . . each person is conceived of as "a particular incarnation of abstract humanity" . . . a monadic replica of general humanity. A kind of sacred personalized self is developed and the individual *qua* individual is seen as inviolate, a supreme value in and of itself. The self becomes an object of interest per se. . . . The autonomous individual imagines the incredible, that he or she lives in an inviolate region (the extended boundaries of the self) where he or she is free to choose . . . where what he does is his own business. (151)

Such perspectives allow students to think about their own narrative viewpoints by introducing contrasting possibilities. For example, they may consider effects on the "selves" in their texts of experiences of sedentary emplacement versus those gained in significant travel. One of my goals is to lead students away from abstract identities, so I follow up with assignments which richly locate the narrative persona in a living world. (For an extended discussion of relations between identity and travel, see Leed, *The Mind of the Traveler*.)

A particularly fine model of writing which does not detach but rather situates the writer within a particular time and place is Isabel Allende's novel *Eva Luna*. Here is a passage from its opening:

> . . . I came into the world with a breath of the jungle in my memory. My father, an Indian with yellow eyes, came from the place where the hundred rivers meet. . . . Consuelo, my mother, spent her childhood in an enchanted region where for centuries adventurers have searched for the city of pure gold. . . . She was marked forever by that landscape, and in some way she managed to pass that sign on to me. (1)

Inspired by such spirited, confident examples, students begin to inscribe their own landscapes of childhood in language which gives them and their readers pleasure. For example, take this passage from Monica O'Malley:

> Our summer-filled days always began the same. After breakfast we rode our bikes around the driveway for a while, or maybe tossed the half-ripped baseball through the air, anxiously awaiting the thrill of seeing one more tuft of soggy grey stuffing escape and float like a feather to the ground. Mom sat on the back steps, keeping a cautious eye on all five of us, one hand nervously peeling the worn grey paint from her perch, the other soothingly caressing the neighbor's cat.
> We played all day with grass-stained skin and shoes so full of sand we could hardly walk. (1)

Environmental autobiographies are not always idyllic. In a recent class of fifteen students, two wrote about places in which they were molested as children. Whatever the effects of early landscape and environment on the adult character, beginning with such explorations can give students a base, a grounding, for the more objectivist kinds of environmental writing discussed below. Expressing where we came from, how we grew into our present identities, sharpens a sense of position and perspective on environmental issues—and helps liberate us from the illusion of the inviolate self, floating through life. This false view gives rise to the corresponding illusion of an independent, objective "nature," existing without humans and available to our knowledge without the labor of cultural interpretation.

In the environmental autobiography assignment, I stress the individual, separate identities of the students (not as abstract selves, but as unique ones). This is a place where anger, and sometimes rage, can be appropriately expressed, especially in revealing deep personal memories of the physical landscapes of poverty. Here, scenes of Indian reservations with a family surviving by eating prairie dogs, and of black Southern neighborhoods without sewerage or electric power find voice. But it is also true that we—separate minorities, majority-background students, and teacher—are joined together in a social enterprise, a hope and a search for common ground. I do not leave this as a fuzzy, sentimental "closure," floating over the class as a kind of official denial of the individuals' inscribed suffering. Rather, in the subsequent assignments, discussed below, we move together toward concrete solutions for specific environmental problems. I project an ideal of harmony and cooperation *in specific landscapes,* both cultural and physical. I do not presume to settle or decide the long-range movement of "our multicultural society," whatever that construct may turn out to be for each student in his or her personal future. But I know how to encourage the making of good stories from the painful, often silent lives my students have led. And I know how to bring people together in problem solving for very particular landscapes. Our discussions sometimes touch these questions of resistance versus harmony, but we do not attempt totalizing solutions. I make no secret of my own enthusiasm for our class itself, and I hope it may be a model for projects involving each writer—in strong personal voice—working with other people of diverse backgrounds, focused on particular intersections of community and terrain. The moment of transition from the environmental autobiography to the forms of writing discussed below is important in several ways, including the movement from recording isolated, personal, often painful memories to a shared focus on a common future. My goal is to "awaken" an environmentally informed self whose presence will henceforth be felt near the surface of the world described.

The Landscape History

The assignment is to take a particular site—a house, farm, waterfront, neighborhood, woods, etc.—and follow it through time. Or one may take a group of people through time and show how their treatment of the land changed. The inspirational model here is John Brinkerhoff Jackson, founder of the landscape studies field at Harvard. An excellent introduction is Clair Marino and Janet Mendlesohn's documentary video on Jackson's life and work, *Figure in a Landscape.* One of Jackson's revealing essays is called "The Westward Moving House," in which he traces several generations of a family through the houses in which they lived. Jackson begins in sixteenth-century pilgrim New England, moves through a generation on a Midwest farm in the nineteenth century, and finally describes their contemporary descendants doing feedlot cattle farming in Texas. For each generation, Jackson focuses on the house and the ways it reflects and shapes the culture and psychology of the family. For example, of the Texans:

> Now is the slack time of the year, and every afternoon the two men and Ray's boy Don, and once in a while a neighbor, go to work on Ray's new house. It is being built out of the best grade cement block, brought by truck some two hundred miles, and it is to be absolutely the last word in convenience and modern construction. It is to be flat roofed and one story high, with no artistic pretensions, but intelligently designed. It is located on a barren and treeless height of land on the outskirts of town. (31)

Jackson points out that, to them, the home is temporary; they think of house and farm as transformers of energy, nodes of secular convenience. They are as far from their God-fearing ancestors in the dark, bedeviled New England forest as they can be. The identities they experience are disconnected from both landscape and history; in their own minds, they are human processes, bound for travel and change.

Not all landscape history projects document increasing alienation, of course. But they concentrate the writer's attention on cultural—and temporal—ties between environments and their residents.

For her landscape history project, one of my students studied the history of the beaches in her community on the Massachusetts coast. She incorporated library research and family interviews:

> A legend concerning the sand bar gives Horseneck Beach its name. The tale is of a man who lost track of time and stayed on the island past low tide. In an effort to get back to the mainland, he led his team of two oxen, a cart, and a lead horse across the bar when the tide was too high. Half-way across, the cart began to float and the horse was lifted off its feet. The horse swam out into deep water, dragging the cart and the man along with it. The cart sank, and the horse and the man drowned. The oxen managed to break free from the cart and washed up into shallow water on Horseneck. They were half-drowned with the wooden yoke wrong side up on their necks. Men had to use ropes to pull them out from the undertow. (Fazzina, 2)

Another student researched the textile mills in Lowell, Massachusetts:

> Beginning at the 6:00 a.m. bell, the mill bustled with activity, each successive level in the factory serving a distinct phase of the manufacturing process. The "mill girls" labored on foot for eleven to fourteen hours per day, six days per week. (Signorello, 4)

Often, the students present their landscape history essays to the class along with old and new photographs (shown via an opaque projector) or slides. The relatively nonpersonal perspective of the historical study, following close upon the environmental autobiography, provides a balance and a sense of the diversity of possible approaches to any particular landscape.

Students discuss the possibilities of strengthening human/landscape ties, as opposed to passively watching these dissolve. Here, a minority student's knowledge of abused places and populations may begin to find an active, promising focus.

The Nature Essay

This form includes Thoreau's *Walden*, Annie Dillard's *Pilgrim at Tinker Creek*, and many of Barry Lopez's fine essays. The typical structure of the models is that of a journey, in which the writer leaves the built environment of civilization and travels into nature, has an encounter of some kind—with a wolf, a storm, an eclipse, etc.—and then returns bearing a new quality of understanding. The time encompassed may be a few hours or an entire year, but the experience is usually reported as a seamless, intense encounter. In his celebrated essay, "The Stone Horse," Barry Lopez recounts his solitary search, at dawn in the California desert, for a huge horse carved in stone by early native peoples.

> In the first moment of recognition I was without feeling. I recalled later being startled, and that I held my breath. It was laid out on the ground with its head to the east, three times life size. . . . The horse, outlined in a standing profile on the dark ground, was as vivid before me as a bed of tulips. (6–7)

Students are not bound by the essay structures of the models, but may begin from these and discover new forms for presenting their experiences. The nature essay, as I teach and attempt to practice it, combines intensely sensuous description with moral engagement between people and landscape. Far from escapist idyll, it should reveal cultural complexities in "the writing of nature."

The Landscape Perception Study

This assignment involves formulating a research question and investigating it through interviews. Many fine examples of such studies may be found in *Humanscape,* edited by Stephen and Rachel Kaplan. An extended account of research and evaluation methods is contained in their *The Experience of Nature.* Lawrence Hott and Diane Garey's video documentary, *The Wilderness Idea* (parts one and two), works well to introduce the diverse viewpoints that may compete for control of a single landscape.

This kind of project lends itself to teamwork. Four of my students combined their efforts to study the history of our university campus, focusing on the present-day feelings of the people whose land was taken by eminent domain when the institution was built almost thirty years ago. This passage is from their conclusion:

> Many years have passed since they lost their land and they have adjusted, but they still have feelings concerning the issue. It is very difficult and oftentimes painful to re-examine the past, but [these five people] have been extremely helpful and cooperative for the sake of this project.
>
> If there is one thing that we have discovered from our research, it is that this investigation is not truly complete until every previous owner has told his/her story. (Carlson et al., 10)

Environmental Writing in the Master's Thesis

Most minority students have experienced deep rifts between actual physical and cultural landscapes and those sung in the ideology of democratic America. The moment they are encouraged to explore this difference in their writing, they rise to the task. Each kind of environmental writing discussed above may be used effectively. I believe environmental writing assignments are of great value to students of all ages and levels, e.g., first-year to Master's. In all cases, the students awaken to possibilities of critical thinking and creative use of their writing skills for self-exploration and revelation; however, more advanced students may take an additional step, into proactive efforts to achieve a new vision for a community-in-environment. Examples from three projects follow.

James Edward Miller is a dynamic, young African American of great charisma. I worked with him in developing an environmental autobiography, and this process helped release a beautiful style which he later used in his Master's thesis, an exposé of corrupt black and white politics in the building of a nuclear power plant in his rural Mississippi county. James had terrible problems with grammar and spelling, but because his writing was integral to both his growing, powerful new sense of self and to the telling of his local environmental story, his confidence in the language bloomed. He wrote:

> An economy is a sometimes simple, sometimes complex set of institutions and social relationships that work to meet the material, social and cultural needs of its members. But it is also a system of power. Power is involved in decisions over who will get what, who will work for whom, and under what conditions. (12)

Not only did James Miller write a clear, scathing indictment of corruption in Mississippi, he did it without compromising his energetic and fluid prose.

James Bluestone is a Native American from the Hidatsa tribe. He is a person of intelligence, charm, and dignity, and all of these qualities show through in his writing. His Master's thesis is a clear, passionate account of his tribal history and prospects:

II. Introduction: The Problems

> This paper is concerned with the economic recovery of the Three Affiliated Tribes from the impact of the Federal government flooding the Fort Berthold Indian Reservation in 1954. Today—thirty-two years later—the reservation has never recovered from their removal, their loss of prime lands, and their break-up of unity, communication and organization. (7)

Like Miller, Bluestone moved from personal writing to objective subjects without the deadening loss of self that accompanies so much scientific and technical prose. He found a way, *within his writing,* to integrate his own stance in a unique place and time with his emerging professional life.

Linda D. Walton is an African American from a small town in Missouri. When the white superintendent of her district finally accepted integration, he built a bonfire of the black high school's history—the pictures, the yearbooks, everything of valued memory went up in flames. This experience left Linda with a fierce determination to fight for educational equality. In her Master's thesis, she sought to reveal the basic needs of students which are constitutionally guaranteed, then to plan for their implementation.

> The issue is not "better" compensatory education, or even "better" test scores; the issue is better education in the hour-to-

hour and day-to-day interactions between students and the teachers who serve them. (4)

My evolving course, "Nature, Landscape, and Environmental Writing," has provided some of the most satisfying experiences of my teaching career. Students continually open my eyes to the truth that nature and environment do not exist independently of people and cannot be described or planned for except from within cultural viewpoints. Minority students, having experienced their worlds with fewer cushions than many others, often contribute striking insights to the class dialectic. These lead to vigorous discussions of our common future and to a lean and active prose rather than a lyrical elegy for the passing scene. The disjunction between American dreams and realities drives the subject of environmental writing, and thoughtful students find endless ways of revealing themselves within the landscape, and the landscape within themselves.

Works Cited

Allende, Isabel. *Eva Luna.* New York: Knopf, 1988.

Bluestone, James. "Three Affiliated Tribes Program of Economic Recovery from the Impact of the Garrison Dam." M.A. thesis. Amherst: U of Massachusetts, 1986.

Carroll, Tracy. "Hard Realities on an Innocent Nature." Essay. N. Dartmouth: U of Massachusetts, 1991.

Carlson, Janet et al. "Another UMD History." Essay. N. Dartmouth: U of Massachusetts, 1991.

Fazzina, Nancy. "The Town Remains the Same." Essay. N. Dartmouth: U of Massachusetts, 1991.

Hott, Lawrence, and Diane Garey. *The Wilderness Idea.* Florentine Films, 1989. Video, 58 min. 2 parts.

Jackson, John Brinkerhoff. "The Westward Moving House." *Landscapes: Selected Writings of J. B. Jackson.* Ed. Ervin H. Zube. Amherst: U of Massachusetts P, 1970. 10–42.

Kaplan, Rachel, and Stephen Kaplan. *The Experience of Nature: A Psychological Perspective.* Cambridgeshire, England: Cambridge UP, 1989.

Kaplan, Stephen, and Rachel Kaplan, eds. *Humanscape: Environments for People.* Ann Arbor, MI: Ulrich's, 1982.

Leed, Eric J. *The Mind of the Traveler: From Gilgamesh to Global Tourism.* New York: Basic, 1991.

Lopez, Barry. "The Stone Horse." *Crossing Open Ground.* New York: Vintage, 1989. 1–18.

Marino, Clair, and Janet Mendlesohn, prods. and dirs. *Figure in a Landscape: A Conversation with J. B. Jackson.* Direct Cinema Limited, 1987. Video, 48 min.

Miller, James Edward. "The Transformation of the Political Process in Claiborne County, Mississippi." M.A. thesis. Amherst: U of Massachusetts, 1987.

O'Malley, Monica L. Untitled essay. N. Dartmouth: U of Massachusetts, 1991.

Shweder, Richard A. *Thinking through Cultures: Expeditions in Cultural Psychology.* Cambridge, MA: Harvard UP, 1991.

Signorello, Diana. "Lowell's Massachusetts Mill." Essay. N. Dartmouth: U of Massachusetts, 1991.

Walton, Linda D. "Creating Effective Schools for Minority Students." M.A. thesis. Amherst: U of Massachusetts, 1988.

11 Successful Teaching Practices for Sexual Minority Students in Writing Courses: Four Teachers at Work

Sarah-Hope Parmeter
University of California–Santa Cruz

Ellen Louise Hart
University of California–Santa Cruz

Paul M. Puccio
University of Massachusetts at Amherst

Ann Marie Wagstaff
University of California–Davis

As our profession pays increasing attention to the representation of marginalized groups in our multiethnic and multicultural society, more of our students find their lives reflected in the materials we ask them to read and write about. Despite our move toward diversity, too many teachers continue to ignore sexual minority students. Somehow, the profession has not seen the inclusion of lesbian and gay voices as necessary. This exclusion is particularly problematic given the pedagogy current in our profession that emphasizes process, narrative, and personal experience writing. When we employ such a pedagogy without making our courses explicitly lesbian- and gay-inclusive, we are placing sexual minority students at particular risk of failure: failure to identify the personally meaningful topic, to participate comfortably in a process-centered classroom, or sometimes to produce any writing at all. Raised in a culture that fears and hates them, sexual minority students have been taught to fear and hate themselves, to hide themselves, and to censor their writing. In addition, they usually lack the supportive, self-affirming home environments on which some students who are members of other marginalized communities can draw. At every grade level, lesbian and gay student writers are being forced to circumvent the drive for self-assertion and self-revelation, resulting in patterns that disable them as writers and affect their education in untold ways.

Like all students, sexual minority students need opportunities to integrate their personal identities with their academic work. They need to be able to write about the challenges they face as members of a community that is routinely denigrated, despised, and targeted for violence. But being a lesbian or gay man is much more than being a target of oppression. Being a sexual minority makes one a member of a culture that shares a common history and includes partnerships, households, business and professional associations, religious organizations, holidays, political movements, an alternative press, archives, music, art, theater, film, literature, and scholarship. Sexual minority students need to explore and celebrate this culture in writing.

The four of us are teachers on both sides of the country, three in California and one in Massachusetts, working to create learning environments where our lesbian and gay students find themselves represented in course materials and have opportunities to work comfortably and openly with their non-lesbian and non-gay peers. In the following pages, we offer views of our classrooms and the sounds of our students' voices as we describe the specific lessons we have learned.

Syllabus Re-Vision and the Sexual Minority Student
Paul M. Puccio

In our courses we design a reality for our students; the selection and arrangement of texts create a world which they will experience and reflect on. And so, we must deliberate on the kind of world we are creating, particularly for sexual minority students: Is it a world that excludes lesbians and gay men? Is it a world where they live only sad, blighted, self-destructive lives? Or is it a world where lesbians and gay men live satisfying, productive, potentially happy lives?

Along with strategically placing lesbian and gay texts in our courses, we also need to *choose* texts very carefully. If we hope to construct a reality that represents the true diversity of our culture, we have a responsibility to provide accurate, positive, and varied representations of lesbian and gay life. For most of our students, including sexual minority students, the texts we choose will be the first lesbian or gay texts they have read. For many, they will be the only ones they will ever read. Therefore, we should select literary representations conscientiously and responsibly: Will we show students the lesbian and gay experience of alienation, rejection, and oppression? Or will we offer them a glimpse of a world where sexual orientation does not impede personal happiness and fulfillment?

A text which foregrounds the oppression experienced by lesbians and gay men, as well as the pain and loneliness and hopelessness which can result from this oppression, presents a picture of *one* dimension of lesbian and gay lives. Just as African, Asian, and Hispanic American students need to learn about the historical experiences of African, Asian, and Hispanic Americans in a racist culture, sexual minority students need to learn about the experiences of lesbians and gay men in a homophobic culture. But such a picture of alienation and despair can be dangerous because it can reinforce the myth that lesbians and gay men cannot live as productive, contented members of our society. If we teach the literature of lesbian and gay despair, we must urge our students to reflect on how this despair results from social oppressions. Otherwise, we are abetting internalized homophobia.

I gained these insights about syllabus design when I was teaching "Man and Woman in Literature" at the University of Massachusetts–Amherst. When I was asked in 1988 to teach this course, I saw this as an opportunity not only to develop a course that would examine how literature can represent and challenge our cultural understanding of gender and sexuality, but also as one that would provide sexual minority students with a positive, self-affirming experience. At that time, I believed that in order to create such an affirmative classroom environment for sexual minority students, I needed to help heterosexual students become comfortable with lesbians and gay men. I thought I could do this best with an assimilationist approach: offering a syllabus that would first explore the heterosexual norm and then show how lesbians and gay men were, after all, "just like everyone else." To this end, I selected texts that included representations of long-term lesbian companionships, families with gay parents, even gay couples with "in-law" troubles. Referring to my experience teaching "Man and Woman in Literature," I hope to explain why I now believe that such an assimilationist strategy is not only intellectually narrow but also neglects the needs of sexual minority students.

I planned to include lesbian and gay narratives in "Man and Woman in Literature" because I believe that lesbian and gay students ought to read literary representations of their lives and to see these texts valued and treated seriously in the academy. Furthermore, I believe that an increasing visibility in the academy of lesbian and gay *texts* can be analogous to, and preparatory to, an increasing visibility of lesbian and gay *people.* Because my own vision of the world includes lesbian, gay, and heterosexual people living in harmony, I am committed to representing this vision to students. Accordingly, I ordered my books and designed my syllabus—determined to support sexual minority students by challenging the heterosexism I saw in the syllabi of most other literature classes. In addition to Bruce Chatwin's *On the Black Hill,* Paule Marshall's *Brown Girl, Brownstones,* Athol Fugard's *"Master Harold". . . and the Boys,* and Virginia Woolf's *A Room of One's Own,* I included Jane Rule's "The Day I Don't Remember," and David Leavitt's "Territory," as well as Stephen McCauley's *The Object of My Affection.* The Rule and Leavitt stories describe confrontations between parents and their lesbian or gay children. McCauley's novel depicts a gay man and a pregnant, unmarried, heterosexual woman struggling to understand how family, romance, and friendship might be redefined in contemporary American society.

My course description stated:

> Reading novels, plays, and short stories, we will examine how several writers of different racial, ethnic, and sexual affiliations understand the meanings of words like "masculine," "feminine," "romance," "marriage," "gay," "straight," and "family."

I was confident that this accurately described the course. And we did discuss masculinity, femininity, romance, marriage, and family for eleven weeks. Then, in the last three weeks, we talked about "gay." This creation of a "gay unit" was one of the biggest mistakes I made, ultimately resulting in a course that further marginalized, rather than included, sexual minority students.

Comments made by my heterosexual students revealed the flaws in my strategy. The placement of these texts in a separate unit (after the Thanksgiving holiday) isolated them from the rest of the syllabus. The students understood this isolation to be a sign of difference—a difference *I had created.* In her reading journal, one student commented: "I have . . . enjoyed much of what we have read in this class but I can see right now . . . I'm going to have a hard time reading this stuff." Another student, writing about the main character in "Territory," remarked: "It's funny how I naturally assumed that Neil was heterosexual. I wasn't shocked that he was not. I was just not expecting it."

Comments like these showed me that, by saving this material for the end of the course, I had communicated a number of inadvertent messages. I had implied that these texts were more "difficult" than the others and that their subjects were "alien" and "deviant." These messages not only subverted my own vision of a world where lesbians, gay men, and heterosexual people live in harmony, they also spoke exclusively to the heterosexual students in the class. Instead of creating a welcoming environment for sexual minority students, I had ignored them—and, ironically, I had ignored them through a facile inclusion of lesbian and gay texts.

After this experience, I found myself wondering if my students' experience in the course would have been more positive if I had integrated lesbian and gay texts throughout the semester. I reshaped the course the next semester, no longer isolating our discussions of sexual minority material. Although I kept *The Object of My Affection* as the last text of the course, I did not precede it with lesbian or gay stories. Instead, I placed John Cheever's "straight" story, "Goodbye, My Brother," before the McCauley novel in order to stress themes of familial alienation which are present in both texts.

Earlier in the course, I scheduled discussions of Willa Cather's "Paul's Case," Isaac Bashevis Singer's "Yentl, the Yeshiva Boy," and Merle Woo's "Letter to Ma." Although Cather does not spell out Paul's sexual orientation, many students confidently and sensitively maintained that the story describes the loneliness and despair of a young gay man in a working-class community. Singer's story of cross-dressing and marriage between women resulted in lively discussions of how gender and sexual attraction are socially constructed ideas. Woo's essay builds bridges between homophobia and other forms of social oppression. Furthermore, it shows a lesbian writer addressing issues not related to sexuality—racism, immigrant experience, and mother-daughter relationships. During this semester, students never expressed surprise or dismay at reading about lesbian or gay characters. These characters "fit" in the course, just as much as any heterosexual characters. For the sexual minority student, the course modeled a world in which lesbians and gay men are an integral and natural part.

As my experiences suggest, it is important not to stress an assimilationist position which merely tries to show how lesbians and gay men are actually "just like everyone else." Not only does this position preserve a heterosexual norm against which all sexuality and affection are compared, it also denies the existence of lesbian and gay culture within Western culture. Our sexual minority students deserve to see representations of their culture welcomed in our curricula. They need to know that they are a positive part of the academy's vision of the world.

Writing against Homophobia
Ellen Louise Hart

I teach a course at the University of California–Santa Cruz called "Writing in the Margins" that focuses on writing, identity, and difference. The title of the course exploits the pun on the work of teachers of writing, including students reading each other's papers, and is not meant to suggest that the writers we read are peripheral to U.S. culture or to university reading lists. In the course, we read articles and poetry by writers who represent marginalized groups, people who have experienced both literal and figurative "homelessness," the homeless on the streets and in the shelters as well as lesbians, gay men, and bisexuals who have been culturally homeless in this country. In the context of gender, race, religion, and class, we explore issues of sexual identity and lesbian and gay culture and experience.

The course attracts students who see themselves as different—in the society, at the university, in the curriculum. Those who enroll are students of color, Jewish students, working-class students, women and men challenging traditional gender roles, white students interested in exploring their ethnic and religious backgrounds, lesbians and gay men, and those with lesbian and gay family members. In each section of eighteen to twenty students, there are usually one or two students who identify themselves as lesbian, gay, or bisexual, and two or three who identify themselves as having lesbian, gay, or bisexual family members. Others describe themselves at the beginning of the course as curious about lesbian and gay issues and concerned about homophobia.

We begin the course with two readings. The first is Lawrence Langer's "The Human Use of Language," on the response of a composition teacher to the first attempt by a Holocaust survivor to write about the death of her parents in the concentration camps. This is paired with Audre Lorde's "The Transformation of Silence into Language and Action," on the courage it took for her—as a black, lesbian poet living with cancer—to continue to speak and to write. These essays, along with others, such as Maxine Hong Kingston's "Girlhood among Ghosts" and Gloria Anzaldúa's "How to Tame a Wild Tongue," are invitations for students to write about their own silences that may be linked to the kinds of discrimination they have faced. From here we move to readings that focus specifically on gender, essays by Virginia Woolf and Gloria Steinem, and poems by Charles Atkinson on being a father and raising his sons. Students write about their parents as role models, about sexism or overcoming sexism in their families, about friendships between women and between men.

Although I open the course with an essay by Audre Lorde, a lesbian writer, it is the third writing assignment and set of readings that focus specifically on lesbian and gay culture and experience. There are two important reasons for this sequence. I want to start the course with a lesbian writer, who is clearly identified as lesbian, writing about a topic that is not exclusive to lesbians. Furthermore, it is essential that material concerning lesbian and gay issues be presented strategically and not just dropped into a writing course. Students need to be comfortable with each other before they can discuss and write honestly on a subject about which there is so much ignorance and fear, and lesbian and gay writers, in particular, need time to discover that they can trust their readers.

We begin this unit with interviews of lesbian and gay teenagers and adults, an approach that brings many non-gay students, for the first time, face-to-face with a gay person telling a story about being treated unfairly—by parents, employers, or teachers—because of his or her sexual identity. Out of a sense of fairness, students come to identify with these stories. We follow the interviews with a chapter from Paul Monette's *Borrowed Time: An AIDS Memoir*, poetry by Judy Grahn, Lesléa Newman's short story "A Letter to Harvey Milk," and student papers from previous "Writing in the Margins" sections on recognizing and overcoming personal homophobia, making connections between racism and homophobia, finding out a friend is gay or lesbian, reading lesbian and gay literature, coming out at home or at school. The next assignment is to write persuasively about some aspect of the problem of homelessness, using articles from the collection *Homeless Not Helpless*. The final paper is an essay in which research on an issue raised in the course is used. Many return to the topic of homophobia and lesbian and gay experience, and write about representations of lesbian and gay men in film, historical periods such as the Holocaust, gay politics, lesbian and gay teenagers on the street, AIDS education, and lesbian and gay teachers. I have found that the assignment to write about homophobia gives all students the opportunity to explore issues which may be contributing to their own silences as writers. Evaluations of the course consistently show that students find the exploration of lesbian and gay culture and experience personally rewarding, particularly because non-gay students feel challenged by writing about what they term a "sensitive" or "difficult" issue. Meanwhile, the non-gay students are learning to be better readers of gay student writing.

The story of Emma, a lesbian student, highlights the isolation a lesbian or gay writer can feel "in a class full of straight people," no matter how safe the environment, and shows the indecision and blankness that can result even when a student is a confident and talented writer. On the first day, Emma wrote that she was taking the course because she was a lesbian and "would be writing in the margins" all of her life. "I have always found writing relatively easy, and I enjoy it immensely," she added. She came out to the class during one of our first discussions on lesbian and gay issues and described the group as neither hostile nor homophobic. And yet this is what happened when she tried to talk about her topic and then sat down to write:

> . . . I didn't know where to start. The class went around talking about the ideas people were thinking about. As I heard the ideas I began to feel more isolated. I knew I was probably the only lesbian in the class, but suddenly I really felt it. Frustration was silently pulsing through my veins as my turn to speak was coming close. As the words came out of my mouth, my shoulders were knotting up and my once clear idea started to get fuzzy as I heard my voice.
>
> My first reaction was: make a good impression. Soon after I realized the absurdity of this. I decided to talk about a topic that really interested me to write about, and I tried not to care about making any impression. As I spoke about internalized homophobia I felt like I couldn't articulate what I was wanting to say.
>
> When the discussion was over I felt like I was even more confused about what I was going to write about. I wasn't thinking about writing something for myself, instead I was thinking about how I would represent a gay perspective in a class full of straight people.
>
> When I finally sat down to write, my brain felt like a blank slate.

The open-minded behavior of a class engaged in the process of informing themselves about lesbian and gay experience can make a difference for a writer like Emma. When she arrived at the stage of revising her draft, she was able to ask the group for responses. "It was important for me to share my work with other students," she commented in her self-evaluation. "This was very helpful in developing confidence in my writing." With an audience of educated readers, lesbian and gay students can move through difficult moments and emerge as more confident and authentic writers.

Students with lesbian and gay family members often suffer from a kind of isolation in school similar to that experienced by lesbians and gay men. Sam, whom I met nearly ten years ago in a summer institute for teachers of writing, first impressed upon me the needs of this group of students. Here is his response to my question, "How can educators better serve lesbian and gay students?"

> . . . My father is gay. He has lived with the same man for almost fourteen years, one year less than my parents' marriage lasted. Ellen tells me that 25% of the population has an immediate family member who is gay, 10% are gay themselves. I never knew this as a teenager. No one ever talked about it. We never dealt with it in school.
>
> For me in adolescence—a time of great pain and change for even the happiest of us—my father's homosexuality was something I had to bear alone. It was something I discussed with no one. It increased my sense of isolation. Running was my place of belonging and to a great extent my coach played the role of my father. I believe if I could have written about this, it would have helped me to accept my father on his own terms much sooner.
>
> Homophobia is a prejudice that must be dealt with in the classroom. To ignore it is criminal.

As teachers of writing we may not be aware that there are students like Sam who would welcome the opportunity to write this kind of "coming-out" story, or that there are those like Gwen, who, in describing the fear she experienced telling the class her story, sounds very much like Emma:

> I am eighteen now, and am ready to tell you my story. I have held it back for so many years because I was scared, ashamed, and embarrassed. Of what, you wonder? Of what people would think when I told them my mother is a lesbian. Wow! I can't believe I'm actually writing about this, about my feelings, about my experience. What was even more unbelievable is that I told my whole class that she is a lesbian. That took guts. Let me tell you, it was something that I would never do. I was sitting in my chair thinking, should I tell them? What will they think? Each minute it was getting closer and closer to my turn. My hands started sweating, and I could not only feel my heart racing, but I could also hear it pounding. It seemed so loud to me I thought my neighbor could hear it. My turn finally came and I just

blurted it out. Nothing happened, nobody freaked, and my heart stopped pounding. I sank back down in my chair with a feeling of relief and no regrets. So now I must begin my very long awaited story.

Our students have "long-awaited" stories of many kinds, and it is our responsibility as teachers of writing to create classrooms where these stories, at last, can be written.

Introducing Sexual Minority Issues
Ann Marie Wagstaff

I use the model described below to introduce a unit on labels and stereotyping. The model encourages students to play with and analyze labels through a series of exercises designed to help them discover for themselves the limitations of labels and the difference between labels and people. In my use of the model, I am particularly interested in showing how the label "lesbian"—a label that can accurately be applied to me—distorts and obscures the deeper complexity of the individual to whom it is applied.

Prior to class, I select four persons to serve as "guinea pigs." These persons represent both genders, have different cultural roots, and belong to groups that are stereotyped frequently. The four I typically use are myself, Senator Bill Bradley, and two friends of mine— one an illegal alien and the other a Jew from the South. I then make a list of five labels that could be applied to each of the four persons I have selected. For example, Bill Bradley's list might include "Rhodes scholar," "politician," "male," "basketball player," "white." My own list typically includes "lesbian," "Bible study leader," "daughter," "writer," and "student."

When students arrive for class, they find the twenty labels listed on the chalkboard in random order. Their first task is to select one of the labels and to free-write their associations with that particular label. After students have written for about five minutes, a few volunteers read what they have written. Students tend to select the more potent labels (illegal alien, Mexican, Jew, lesbian, southerner) and write associations that are primarily stereotypical. This sets the stage for the evolution from label to individual that is to follow.

The students' second task is to select an additional four labels from the board, assume that the five labels describe attributes of one person, and write a story (beginning "Once upon a time . . . ") showing how this imaginary person integrates these attributes into his or her life. When the stories are complete, and after students have shared theirs with each other in small groups, we discuss the difference between a list of labels and a story. Students discover that as they create their stories, characters emerge who are more than the sum of their parts.

I then rearrange the labels on the chalkboard into the four original lists and tell students that each describes a particular person I know or know about. Immediately, the classroom atmosphere changes: we are talking about people who have feelings and who are connected to other people (perhaps even to the teacher). Next, we analyze each list in terms of the "potency" of its labels. For example: Which would be most or least visible to a stranger? Which would be most important to the individual who lived with the labels? Which labels on the list seem to be in conflict with each other? Finally, I ask the students this question: What one label applied to a person would include all the others? The answer is (and I have never had a student guess it): the person's name. We go on to discuss what difference it makes to know someone's name, what difference it would make to know the names of the four persons whose labels are listed on the board, and, finally, what difference it would make to know the four persons themselves. In other words, what happens as the person behind the labels begins to emerge as an individual?

After a thorough discussion, I turn my back to the class and write the names of the four individuals above their lists, including, of course, my own name above my list. By the time I turn again to face the class, something has happened. In that moment, the students and I experience the difference between labels and people.

I talk briefly about the relationships among the different dimensions of my life listed on the board and about the three other persons who now also have names. When I give my students an opportunity to ask me questions about myself and the three others, they are most interested in my list—particularly in how a lesbian could be a Bible study leader. So now they hear a piece of my story, which I conclude by telling them about the interfaith Bible study group that I lead. And I tell them that it is in that group that I met Victor (the illegal alien) and Risa (the southern Jew).

I follow up this in-class exercise with a journal assignment—one that gives the students an opportunity to respond to the class session, create a list of labels that could be applied to themselves, and write an analysis of the potency of their own labels, including a discussion of how they integrate the parts of themselves which the label represents.

In their responses, students write most about religion and how their particular religious background has taught them to view homosexuality. A number of students have written about gay relatives or about friends or relatives they suspect might be gay. Two students have identified themselves to me as gay. Later, students have the opportunity to expand this journal assignment into an essay, and many do choose to write about the particular ethnic, cultural, and religious tensions in their own identities. I particularly like this model because, in addition to allowing students to confront stereotyped notions about lesbians, it helps create a safe space for students to explore their own lives.

Obviously, a teacher need not be gay in order to use the model. A teacher with a gay friend or acquaintance or one who is familiar with the work of a prominent gay writer, artist, politician, or religious leader could easily adopt the model.

One can evaluate the exercise in a number of ways. Personally, I rate it a success because I am still in contact with the two lesbian students (neither of whom know any other lesbian faculty members), because it permits me to come out to my students without allowing the label "lesbian" to rob me of my deeper complexity, and because all my students now benefit from the opportunity to explore their own beliefs about homosexuality in a safe environment. I am satisfied.

Building Community When the Minority Become Majority
Sarah-Hope Parmeter

As is true for many teachers, my classroom practices are strongly influenced by my own experiences as a student and writer. Some of the strongest memories of my life as a student writer are of the clear distinction I drew between "writing" (small "w"), which I did for my classes, and "Writing" (with a capital W), which I did extensively, sometimes obsessively, on my own, and which very few of my classroom teachers ever saw. I didn't always perceive my work in this divided way, but in high school and college, as I became aware that I was a lesbian and as this aspect of my identity found its way into my written work, the split became clear. I knew that most of my teachers, even those who normally encouraged creative work, would not want to see the love poems I wrote for other women or the essays I drafted for myself exploring the meanings of love and desire. Yet, aware as I was of the "dangerous" nature of the identity I was uncovering, I felt compelled to write, to create on the page a space where I could name myself, where I could *celebrate* who I was.

When I first began teaching, I knew that a substantial proportion of my students—at least 10 percent—were wrestling with the same issues I'd faced some ten years earlier. I didn't have any models of pedagogies that would help support these students, that would keep them from feeling split between being writers and being Writers, but I was determined to try to develop them. My search for successful classroom practices for working with sexual minority students has affected virtually every aspect of my teaching, but it is most apparent in a course I taught at the University of California–Santa Cruz, created specifically for lesbian and gay students: "Writing Ourselves: Toward Lesbian and Gay Identity."

Although I didn't publicize the course widely, the simple presence of the course texts on the shelves of the university bookstore was enough to fill the class with students—most of them sexual minorities—eager to begin reading and writing in a lesbian- and gay-focused context. The readings for the course were six book-length works by lesbians and gay men: *Take Off the Masks,* the autobiography of the gay Episcopalian priest, Malcolm Boyd; *Zami, A New Spelling of My Name,* an autobiography by the black lesbian, activist, poet, and essayist, Audre Lorde; *The Normal Heart,* a play by Larry Kramer depicting the beginning of the AIDS crisis and the accompanying governmental disinterest in the face of the rising death rate; *Sinking, Stealing,* Jan Clausen's novel about a nonbiological mother's attempt to maintain child custody rights after the death of her lover, the child's biological mother; *Behold a Pale Horse,* Lannon D. Reed's novel depicting the internment and killing of gay men in Nazi Germany; and *Leave a Light on for Me,* Jean Swallow's novel of a lesbian couple, one of whom is a recovering alcoholic coming to terms with the sexual abuse she experienced as a child.

The course structure emphasized discussion. I knew that most of the lesbian and gay students would not have had previous opportunities to articulate sexual minority experiences in an academic setting, and I wanted to allow ample opportunity for this to become "normal" and comfortable. Rather than giving students specific writing assignments, I encouraged them to propose their own topics on the basis of issues raised in our discussions of the course readings.

In class, we would begin by "checking in," telling each other how the issues being raised in the course were reflected in recent events in our own lives. This allowed both sexual minority and heterosexual students repeated opportunities to articulate how the course was leading them to reconsider the nature of the academy and their role in it. From these personal reflections, we would move on to a discussion of the day's readings. These discussions were student-led and often highly personal, drawing on the required reading journals. The second hour of class was most often devoted to writing groups, which provided students with forums for their written work.

Even though I'd been teaching lesbian- and gay-inclusive courses for years, offering sexual minority texts along with readings from other marginalized communities, I was surprised by the intensely positive effects this specifically lesbian and gay focus had for sexual minority students. A few of them had taken courses before that included lesbian and gay material, but as they explained in class discussions, in those courses they'd been intensely conscious of their status as "other." Their instructors may have presented sexual minority material in a supportive manner, but these students complained that, while they might be "free" to identify themselves as lesbian or gay in the classroom, and while they could speak to lesbian and gay experience, they were expected to do so in a way that would explain that experience to the heterosexual majority. For all the lesbian and gay students in "Writing Ourselves," the course offered their first academic opportunity to speak and write about their lives without feeling a burden to explain themselves to a larger group of presumably straight teachers and peers.

"Writing Ourselves" offered a frequently repeated lesson on the value of community. Sexual minority students took great pleasure in being able to write about their experiences for an audience of genuine peers. They could critique their community, question its values, even poke fun at it. Ricardo could write an essay about his rethinking of the gay men's cruising scene for other gay men who had been a part of that scene, as he had. In this piece, Ricardo could move quickly into his analysis, both acknowledging the pleasures this lifestyle had brought him and exploring his growing lack of trust of other men as the AIDS epidemic spread. He knew his ambivalence wouldn't be misinterpreted as an attack on the gay community, which he was quite content to be a member of; it was, rather, simply an examination of the life he wanted to lead within that community. Tonia delighted the class with "A Field Guide to Monterey Bay Dykes," a satire on the foibles of the local lesbian scene. Because other students knew and were a part of the community she described, they could easily laugh at it with her. Her jokes needed no explaining.

The writing the students produced during the course highlighted the ways in which the sexual minority community is a rhetorical community, and the importance that entering into the rhetoric of that community had for the growth of sexual minority students as writers. Many of the lesbian students wrote poetry just as full of the clichés of lesbian erotica as my own early work had been—sea caves, an ocean home, warrior women, clenched fists, proud breasts. While any sophisticated reader of lesbian literature would recognize the clearly unoriginal nature of much of this material, writing it was a necessary first step for the lesbian students. They were claiming the language and images of their culture. Similarly, most students began early in the quarter by writing their own coming-out stories. The coming-out narrative—a naming of one's self as a lesbian or gay man, accompanied by the story of the individual process of discovery—is a rite of passage into the lesbian and gay literary world and is a fundamental sexual minority text. So it is not surprising that students in "Writing Ourselves" began by naming themselves in pieces of this sort before moving on to more analytical or argumentative work.

For the sexual minority students enrolled in "Writing Ourselves," the course became a kind of home, a place in which to relax, enjoy, and celebrate a shared culture. But the class was not always peaceful, and the common ground students shared did not always guarantee harmony. The fact that it is genuinely dangerous to live as a lesbian or gay man in this society meant that there were tensions among the sexual minority students—was it really safe to come out? Would someone's privacy be violated? Students from different circles or who identified with different cultural groups outside the lesbian and gay community were hesitant to trust each other. Because of this, class meetings could be explosive and debates about a seemingly theoretical subject often masked personal divisions between students. But this too offered an opportunity for strengthening community ties. By the end of the quarter, the sexual minority students, while still having some divisions, were able to articulate how such divisions served to further the oppression they faced in the world outside the classroom.

"Writing Ourselves" stands out in my memory not only as a class in which students produced excellent work, but also as a class in which students who were members of a highly disenfranchised community had an opportunity to change their own relationships with both the written word and with the academic community in radical and empowering ways.

Concluding Remarks

We want to emphasize that in order for sexual minority students to prosper, it is essential that they be able to build bridges between their cultures and communities and the academy. As teachers of writing, it is our obligation to prevent students from becoming articulately *distanced* writers and to teach them to be engaged with what they have to say. We encourage all teachers—those unfamiliar with or new to this work and those who have already developed strategies for working with sexual minority students—to reflect on our practices. We hope they will provide effective models for your own teaching. As we change our syllabi and our teaching practices to include sexual minority students, classrooms will continue to become more challenging and productive learning environments, to the benefit of students from all cultures.

Works Cited

Anzaldúa, Gloria. "How to Tame a Wild Tongue." *Borderlands = La Frontera: The New Mestiza*. San Francisco: Spinsters/Aunt Lute, 1987. 53–64.

Boyd, Malcolm. *Take Off the Masks*. Philadelphia: New Society, 1984.

Cather, Willa. "Paul's Case." *The Troll Garden*. New York: McClure, Philips, 1905. 211–53.

Chatwin, Bruce. *On the Black Hill*. New York: Viking, 1982.

Cheever, John. "Goodbye, My Brother." *The Oxford Book of Short Stories*. New York: Oxford UP, 1981. 466–86.

Clausen, Jan. *Sinking, Stealing*. Traumsburg, NY: Crossing, 1985.

Fugard, Athol. *"Master Harold" . . . and the Boys*. New York: Knopf, 1982.

Kingston, Maxine Hong. "Girlhood among Ghosts." *The Borzoi College Reader*. 5th ed. Ed. Charles Muscatine and Marlene Griffith. New York: Knopf, 1984. 547–52.

Kramer, Larry. *The Normal Heart*. New York: New American Library, 1985.

Langer, Lawrence. "The Human Use of Language." *The Borzoi College Reader*. 5th ed. Ed. Charles Muscatine and Marlene Griffith. New York: Knopf, 1984. 5–9.

Leavitt, David. "Territory." *Family Dancing*. New York: Knopf, 1984. 3–27.

Lorde, Audre. "The Transformation of Silence into Language and Action." *Sister Outsider*. Traumsburg, NY: Crossing, 1984. 40–44.

———. *Zami, A New Spelling of My Name*. Traumsburg, NY: Crossing, 1982.

Marshall, Paule. *Brown Girl, Brownstones*. New York: Feminist, 1981.

McCauley, Stephen. *The Object of My Affection.* New York: Washington Square, 1988.

Monette, Paul. *Borrowed Time: An AIDS Memoir.* San Diego: Harcourt, 1989.

Newman, Lesléa. "A Letter to Harvey Milk." *Women on Women: An Anthology of American Lesbian Short Fiction.* Ed. Joan Nestle and Naomi Holoch. New York: Plume, 1990. 177–94.

Paschke, Barbara, and David Volpendesta. *Homeless Not Helpless: An Anthology.* Berkeley, CA: Canterbury, 1991.

Reed, Lannon D. *Behold a Pale Horse.* San Francisco: Gay Sunshine, 1985.

Rule, Jane. "The Day I Don't Remember." *Outlander.* Tallahassee, FL: Naiad, 1981. 15–19.

Singer, Isaac Bashevis. "Yentl, the Yeshiva Boy." *Short Friday and Other Stories.* New York: Farrar, 1964. 131–59.

Swallow, Jean. *Leave a Light on for Me.* San Francisco: Spinsters/Aunt Lute, 1986.

Woo, Merle. "Letter to Ma." *This Bridge Called My Back: Writings by Radical Women of Color.* Ed. Cherríe Moraga and Gloria Anzaldúa. Watertown, MA: Persephone, 1981. 140–47.

Woolf, Virginia. *A Room of One's Own.* New York: Harcourt, 1991.

III Affirming Voices: Literature of Society and Self

This section focuses on the use of literature to expand, explore, and inform in a multicultural context. Each of the chapters examines ways in which traditional literature can be used to broaden and deepen the student's understanding of self and society.

The first five chapters depict programs for secondary school students or, in one case, a summer orientation session for at-risk prefreshman at the university level. "The Western Illinois University Minority Summer Tutoring Program: A University/Junior High School Collaborative Effort" details a summer program where successful university minority students tutor junior high school minority students by using story as a vehicle to develop academic skills—reading and writing—within a setting that supports questioning, shared interpretation and analysis, and self-monitoring of reading and writing strategies. "Real Voices: Action and Involvement in Secondary English Classrooms" describes successful lessons using traditional core works of literature that teacher-trainees and their mentors have employed with various groups of secondary English students from many different ethnic, cultural, and language backgrounds. "When Wordsworth Is Too Tame: Merging Minority Literature with the Classics in the Secondary Language Arts Curriculum" describes a program within an advanced placement course in high school. Here students study parallel works of literature from the traditional canon and from ethnically diverse authors. The central pairing is *Raisin in the Sun* and *Three Sisters.* The author also suggests other pairings that can prove useful in teaching these students. The next chapter, "Teaching *The Thief of Bagdad* as an Interdisciplinary, Middle School Unit," explains the use of film to teach literary concepts. The film and the concepts taught serve as a support to a reading program in an inner-city junior high school that uses a humanities-based curriculum. Next, "An Approach to Teaching Four Poems about Education: A Thematic Unit for Pre-Freshman Minority Students" shows how using four poems about ethnically diverse students and their experiences in school helps students in a summer orientation session for university "pre-freshmen" explore their own experiences. Using Sedlacek's theory of noncognitive variables in the success of minority students in higher education, these students reanalyze the poems and look at long-range goals for the speakers in the poems and for themselves.

The last three chapters explore the use of nontraditional literature at the community college or lower-division college level. "Caribbean Literature as Catalyst in the Composition Classroom" describes how incorporating the literature of African Caribbeans enriches the college English experience for students of African Caribbean descent and, indeed, for all students. "A Fiesta of Voices: Regional Literature in the Multicultural Classroom" describes how using the literature of northern and central New Mexico interests and involves students from a range of backgrounds in a community college setting. Finally, "Expanding the Literary Canon through Perceptions of Diversity and the American Dream" describes a course that provides a wide range of literature and experience for mainstream students from a somewhat homogeneous environment and helps them to explore the concept of "difference" and how it affects achieving the "American Dream."

12 The Western Illinois University Minority Summer Tutoring Program: A University/ Junior High School Collaborative Effort

Kathy H. Barclay
Western Illinois University

William Mosley
Morehead State University

A high percentage of minority students from Illinois public schools complete high school and enter universities lacking the reading and writing skills necessary to be successful university students. As a response to this problem, the Western Illinois University Summer Tutoring Program seeks to provide a greater number of minority students with the reading and writing skills necessary for success at the university level. Additionally, the program seeks to enhance students' motivation and desire to successfully complete a degree program. Our program utilizes as tutors successful minority students who are currently enrolled at Western Illinois University. These Western tutors work with junior high minority students in an intensive four-week summer program, held at junior high schools in cooperating districts. During each subsequent summer prior to their high school graduation, these same junior high students are invited to attend a week-long tutorial (staffed by university faculty members) and held on the main campus. In this essay, we discuss our tutor-training effort as well as the instructional program offered to the junior high students.

William Mosley's chapter is published posthumously by permission of Faith Mosley.

The Western Illinois University Tutors

The Western Illinois University Minority Summer Tutoring Program exists to accomplish two major goals: (1) to develop and refine the reading and writing skills of minority students prior to college entry; and (2) to enhance their chances for completing a degree program once they enter a university. An important aspect of the program involves the placement of seventh- and eighth-grade students into small, cooperative-learning groups led by successful minority students who are currently enrolled in their junior or senior year at Western Illinois University. The tutors are both male and female, pursuing various majors, including sociology, engineering, business, education, law enforcement, and foreign language. We feel that interaction with these bright and successful university students aids the junior high students in the program by providing positive role models and good academic examples.

The tutors are selected through an interview process held during the spring semester. There are no special qualifications required, other than a personable nature and an overall GPA of 2.5; however, we do inquire as to the prospective tutor's extracurricular activities, former experiences with younger students, and availability to participate in the training program. We also ask for two faculty references.

The WIU students selected for participation in the program receive a stipend of $1,000.00. In addition, room and board are provided for those students who wish to reside on campus during the five-week period. Some of the students do elect to take university courses during the program; however, they do so with the understanding that they are not to enroll in classes meeting before 2 p.m.

The Tutor-Training Component

The one-week training program is conducted by university faculty from the Department of Elementary Education and Reading. The interns, or tutors, receive a training module that delineates the program's goals and objectives and contains specific information as to the implementation of cooperative-learning and reading and writing strategies. The module also contains a suggested daily and weekly schedule.

One of the objectives of the program is to enhance cooperative learning within small groups of students, primarily through the implementation of reciprocal teaching (see Palincsar and Brown). In reciprocal teaching, students are taught how to monitor and regulate their own comprehension by "acting as a teacher." In the group setting, students are first taught directly four activities that an effective reader might do—summarizing, questioning, predicting, and clarifying ambiguous or unknown concepts. Initially, these four processes are taught and modeled through teacher-led instruction. Gradually, the students in the group take larger responsibility for conducting the lessons. Serving as "teacher" in this way is intended to aid students in self-regulation of their own comprehension. The material used for this component includes works of adolescent literature, such as *Roll of Thunder, Hear My Cry* by Mildred Taylor, *The War Between the Classes* by Gloria Miklowitz, *The Crossing* by Gary Paulsen, and *The Pearl* by John Steinbeck.

An important, related objective is to increase oral communication and discussion skills. The program also seeks to engage students in reading, discussion, and writing tasks that will foster students' constructing meaning from information derived from reading and from the discerning use of their own prior knowledge and experience.

During the training sessions, the tutors are asked to participate as students. That is, they assume the role of the junior high students while the university professor assumes the role of the tutor. It is through this role-play that tutors come to understand and feel comfortable with the instructional strategies utilized in the program.

"Setting the Stage for Cooperative Learning" is one of the first topics addressed during the initial tutor-training session. Since the tutors have not, as a rule, known each other prior to the program, the university professor fosters a spirit of teamwork and cooperation. The junior high instructional program and the tutor-training component both utilize cooperative-learning strategies in an attempt to lead the students toward the accomplishment of common goals and objectives by encouraging them to interact with each other. All students are expected to participate in and contribute to group discussions by raising questions, discussing answers, and articulating their understanding of the topic, story, or passage being discussed.

The group of tutors discuss and agree on some general rules pertaining to individual behavior in the group. These rules are generated by the group, with input from the university professor. The professor records the rules on a poster and displays them in the work area. Some of the more typical rules include: (1) each member must make a serious effort to contribute to the group discussion and to participate in all group activities; (2) a member may disagree with an answer that another member provides, but only if he or she can give specific reasons based on the text or prior experience; (3) no member may dominate or withdraw from the discussion; (4) each member must display a positive and encouraging attitude toward every other group member. The rules can be added to as the need arises, and the university professor models behaviors for encouraging their enforcement during the work sessions. During the first session with the junior high pupils, the university tutors follow these same procedures for establishing a cooperative-learning environment.

Since the tutoring program is aimed at helping junior high students improve their attitudes toward school or particular aspects of school as well as their reading and writing skills, tutors and their professor discuss the role of the tutor during the initial training session. The tutors discuss characteristics of a successful university student and effective means of conveying these characteristics to the junior high students. Tutors also discuss ways for gaining the trust and respect of the junior high students. Each tutor prepares his or her introduction to the young students, including information concerning personal and career interests, extracurricular activities, life as a university student, and study habits. The following is a sample introduction prepared by one of the tutors:

> Hello! My name is Joyce Coleman. I am a senior majoring in Business and Accounting. I chose this field because I have always liked working with numbers and I would like to be an accountant for a large firm. I am from a suburb of Chicago, where I live with my mother and two brothers. When I was your age, I thought a lot about going to college. I realized that I needed a good education if I wanted to have much of a future. Being a college student hasn't always been easy for me. I've had to work very hard, but I can honestly say that I believe it has been worth it.
>
> Since the five of us will be working closely during the next four weeks, it is important that we feel comfortable with each other. I have a bag of M & M's with me. I want each of you to take several M & M's and hold them in your hand. (Pass bag around.) Now, for each M & M you have, you are to tell us one thing about yourself. (Give time for everyone to have a turn.) I would like everyone to know that we can learn from each other. We may each have an area that we are particularly strong in. If we share this knowledge with each other and help each other out, we'll all be better off. It really helps to have someone you can turn to for advice . . . and we have the advantage of having four other people we can turn to. Now, let me tell you a little about what we'll be doing together each day.

During the training sessions, the tutors are actively involved in the reading, writing, and integrated reading/writing experiences that are provided throughout the tutoring program. For example, tutors participate in various writing activities, including journal writing and the development of a persuasive essay and a story. The professor models strategies for responding to written text, whether narrative or persuasive, evaluating peer writing, and providing feedback through individual and group conferences. The tutors first participate in group-dictated writing experiences, followed by independent writing. The professor models the introduction of each stage of the writing process—planning, drafting, revising, and editing—and guides writing at each stage. Finally, the tutors are engaged in peer conferencing for the purposes of revising and editing their writing.

The reading component includes teaching strategies for implementing the reciprocal learning goals—predicting, question generating, summarizing, and clarifying—and a discussion of the literature to be used during the program. Reciprocal teaching, a method that encourages students to become the "teacher" during a group discussion of a passage read silently, is modeled by the university professor. The procedure used in our program combines the four cyclical stages of predicting, questioning, summarizing, and clarifying (see Palincsar and Brown) with the four categories of question-answer relationships—right there, think and search, author and me, on my own (see Raphael). The tutors read John Steinbeck's *The Pearl* during the training week. Using this book for discussion purposes, the university professor balances the use of explanation, instruction, and modeling with guided practice as the tutors learn to move from one stage of the reciprocal-teaching strategy to the next, and applies the question-generating strategy. Similarly, the tutors learn to apply and then to teach the strategies. Figure 1 shows a sample plan used by the university professor to invoke discussion and writing based on *The Pearl.*

The integration of five aspects of language—listening, speaking, reading, writing, and thinking—is achieved through a unit involving the reading of African folktales, followed by the writing of original "folktales." During the training component, the university students read the folktales used in the unit and participate in the writing of a group-dictated folktale. In preparation for the writing of the folktale, the tutors discuss the parts of a narrative story and the characteristics of folktales. Using a story map, they delineate the story elements for each of the African folktales read and then create elements for their

---

Dramatic Expression/Writing
The Pearl

(Address the group, in role, as the chairperson of the Medical Professional Ethics Board.)

Ladies and gentlemen of the Board. Thank you for taking time from your busy hospital schedules to gather here today. We have a very full agenda this afternoon, so we must get started. I hereby call to order the June meeting of the Medical Professional Ethics Board. The first item on our agenda is the Kino case. You have all read the brief. As you will recall, a complaint has been filed against Dr. X for refusing to administer treatment to the Kino family. The complaint has been filed by a citizen action group in Kino's community on behalf of Kino, his wife and child. The complaint charges Dr. X with unprofessional conduct and neglect of duty because of his refusal to provide medical services in a life-threatening situation. Dr. X has gone on record stating that scorpion bites are a common malady, and a natural hazard associated with life in the particular neighborhood in which the Kino family resides. Furthermore, he maintains that he is in much demand as a physician and therefore cannot meet the needs of all of his paying patients, much less those who cannot afford to pay for even a fraction of the cost of the medical supplies used.

As you know, it is the task of this board, the Medical Professional Ethics Board, to determine a ruling in this case. If we rule against Dr. X, he may lose his license, thus rendering him unable to practice medicine . . . and also leaving the community without the services of a qualified physician. If we rule in favor of Dr. X, we risk further alienation and prejudice of the people living in this community—not to mention the continuation of life without adequate medical services. Your task is to study the case, determine a ruling, and make recommendations toward the improvement of this unfavorable and harmful condition regarding medical services in this community.

At this time we will recess, and I will leave you to your deliberations. We will reconvene in approximately thirty to forty-five minutes, at which time you will be asked to share your written report with the other members of the Board. Thank you.

Figure 1. Sample plan used to invoke discussion and writing on *The Pearl*.

original tale. A copy of this piece of writing is retained by each of the tutors to use as a personal example during the tutoring program.

The university professor models several of the suggested reading and writing activities for using the folktales. The tutors are encouraged to adapt and modify the plans to fit their own interests and personalities as well as those of the students in the program.

The Junior High Tutorial Program

Approximately fifty to seventy-five minority students enrolled in the seventh and eighth grades are recruited into the four-week summer program each year. Although the majority of the students enrolled are African American, we do have some Asian and Hispanic students participating in the program. All students are recommended by their classroom teachers because of their high ability or academic potential. These are the students whom we expect to see enrolling in a university following matriculation from high school. As was discussed earlier, our goal is to provide an early intervention program that will, hopefully, raise the probability that these youngsters will become successful university students.

The groups of students meet for three hours daily during a four-week summer session held at junior high schools in three cooperating public school districts. Although the program emphasizes reading and writing skills, students compose aloud and indicate their comprehension of material presented in oral as well as written form. Thus, the overall focus is on the development of thinking skills, whether students are reading, writing, speaking, or listening. The instructional procedures and materials utilized in this tutorial program are based on the following assumptions:

1. Both reading and writing are acts of composing—similar processes of meaning construction (Tierney and Pearson).

2. Mature readers and writers actively and purposefully select and utilize appropriate "before reading/writing" strategies, "during reading/writing" strategies, and "after reading/ writing" strategies (Baker and Brown; Armbruster, Anderson, and Ostertag; Brown and Palincsar; and Palincsar and Brown).

3. In order to improve comprehension/composing, tutors and teachers need to help students increase control of their own strategic behaviors in reading and writing (Tierney and Pearson; Stevens et al.).

4. Support and guidance from a successful minority university student promotes program effectiveness in terms of student achievement, motivation, and attitude toward school and higher education.

These assumptions are made explicit to the junior high students during the initial tutoring session. Throughout the program, continued emphasis insofar as the application of each assumption occurs as students participate in the various reading, writing, and discussion activities.

Reading Experiences

During the four-week, cooperative-learning experience, the students read, on the average, three to four novels using the reciprocal teaching method. Students read the first novel, *The Pearl*, during the initial introduction and modeling of the strategies. Next, students apply their understanding of the reciprocal learning and question-generating strategies as they read and discuss other literature selections, such as *Roll of Thunder, Hear My Cry; The War Between the Classes;* and *The Crossing.* A variety of multicultural novels are provided, from which the group may make their selections. Oftentimes, students elect to read one or more novels in addition to those selected by the group. Students also read a number of African folktales and selections from a variety of expository text materials, including the content-area textbooks adopted by the local school district, which are used by the students as they learn to apply various study-skill strategies such as notetaking.

Several considerations led to the choice of the literature selections: reading-level appropriateness; high interest; the ability to make social/ethnic identification; clear themes; and, more generally, a solid introduction to good writing that permits the exploration of universal themes. The African folktales and the novels certainly meet these criteria.

Writing Experiences

As indicated by the results of the National Assessment of Educational Progress (see Applebee, Langer, and Mullis), students have difficulty with narrative and persuasive writing tasks. Although we have no reason to believe that these students have greater difficulty than other students, the improvement of narrative and persuasive writing skills is seen as an appropriate objective for our program. Throughout the program, the emphasis in writing is placed on content before form. Students are guided through the stages of the writing process. Tutors model various prewriting strategies such as brainstorming, story mapping, and clustering. They lead the younger students in group-dictation experiences and then ask the students to continue writing independently or with a partner. The tutors, who model each stage of the process along with the junior high students, are the first to share their compositions in draft form. Tutors model as students are led to verbalize ideas for revising each piece of writing shared in the group. Suggestions for revision generally include many ideas for adding greater detail and substance to each piece. The tutors use what we refer to as a "bare-bones" piece of writing to elicit student comments and suggestions for improvement. The tutors generally find the need to model specific questions that might be asked by a listener or reader. Students learn to ask the author for clarification and elaboration—that is, to ask about parts that were not clear and to suggest areas where they would have liked more information. Once students are satisfied with their pieces of writing, the emphasis shifts away from content toward form or mechanics—spelling, grammar, punctuation, sentence/paragraph structure, and so on. The goal is to make the writing as "readable" to others as possible; therefore, students work with each other and with the tutor to proofread and correct their writing. Finally, students share their completed writing with each other and with the university personnel.

With respect to narrative writing, the students are taught to recognize and utilize story structure in the development of original stories. Students proceed through each stage of the writing process as they develop their narratives. To help students develop persuasive writing ability, tutors provide students with various writing prompts that ask the students to state their beliefs and opinions in a clear and concise way and then to support these beliefs and opinions in a way that could be used to convince, or "persuade," someone else to understand and/or adopt their point of view. Again, tutors model the writing of a persuasive essay and then lead the students in the development of a group-dictated essay before the students are expected to develop individual persuasive essays. Planning for the persuasive essay includes determining the position to be argued; generating several key points and reasons that support the position; providing support and elaboration for each point; and organizing the ideas to be presented in a logical and sequential manner. The tutors model each of the above planning steps and then proceed to compose the essay—thinking aloud while writing. Following is a typical prompt for modeling the development of a persuasive essay:

> The principal has recommended to the school board that school uniforms be required. As a member of the student council, you have the opportunity to make a speech at the next school board meeting. Do you agree or disagree with the principal? Write a paper for the school board in which you agree or disagree and explain your position.

Tutors then provide another prompt and ask the students to participate in the planning and writing of a second essay. After the development of this second essay, students usually have little difficulty with successive persuasive writing tasks. Prompts are often derived from the plot of one of the novels being read, as was the case with the prompt based on *The Pearl*, described in figure 1. Students elect to work alone or with a partner to respond to the various prompts, often taking opposite viewpoints—which leads to excellent discussion and debate!

Integrated Reading/Writing Experiences

Integrated reading and writing experiences are based on selections from Roger D. Abrahams's *African Folktales*. The strategies employed are adapted from the listening-to-reading transfer lessons developed by Cunningham and Cunningham. In these lessons, the students listen for a specific purpose to a short story or passage of text. Following the listening experience is a guided practice activity in which the teacher models a strategy for either (1) determining the main idea of the selection heard; (2) ordering the events in the sequence in which they occurred; or (3) making inferences about the story. Once the students have demonstrated an understanding of the task, they are asked to apply the strategy to a second short tale, which they are to read silently.

To integrate reading and writing, the Cunningham listening-to-reading transfer lessons are extended into writing experiences. After students have successfully applied the three strategies to a number of the folktales, they discuss characteristics of folktales and analyze several selections according to narrative story structure: characters, place, time, initiating event or problem, response or goal, action or events, conclusion and reaction. Once students are able to identify the parts of these African folktales, they are guided to use their knowledge of narrative story structure as a framework or blueprint for developing their own original folktales.

Use of the African folktales in conjunction with the three listening-to-reading transfer lessons provides highly motivating and successful instruction for the junior high students enrolled in our program. They are able not only to apply the reading comprehension strategies taught through the use of the folktales, but also to plan, draft, revise, edit, and share their own original folktales.

Monitoring the Summer Tutoring Program

Although the tutors are responsible for the daily tutoring sessions, an experienced junior high reading teacher is hired by the university to remain on-site during the entire program. This teacher, also a member of a minority group, receives the training prior to the tutors. Her role during the tutoring sessions is to assume legal responsibility for the presence of the junior high students as well as to provide general supervision to both the tutors and the junior high students. Problems regarding attendance and behavior, though minimal, fall within her realm of responsibility. At no time does this teacher participate actively in a group; rather, she observes each group and provides daily feedback to the tutors following each session. She also briefs the university faculty members who administer the program when they conduct their on-site visits. These visits from university faculty are conducted two to four times each week for the purposes of group observation and interaction with the tutors. On occasion, a university faculty member may join a group for a brief period of time, sharing in the current discussion; however, more often than not, the faculty members are engaged in observation, note-taking, and videotaping activities designed to determine and document program effectiveness. The university faculty members also provide continuing feedback to the tutors.

Measuring Program Effectiveness

Our Western Illinois University Minority Summer Tutoring Program represents the successful interaction of several key components. As of this writing, the program is beginning its sixth year and has proven itself to be very effective in motivating young minority students to develop and consciously apply effective reading and writing strategies. Observations and videotapes procured throughout the four-week program attest to the growing skill with which the junior high students apply the strategies they are taught. Book discussions are very animated and indicate a high level of thinking and an independent application of the reading strategies. By the fourth week of the program, tutors are very much in "backseat" positions as the junior high students conduct their own discussions, passing the role of "teacher" among themselves in a very easy and relaxed manner.

As early as the beginning of the second week, much progress can be noted as students begin their discussion of the second novel, *Roll of Thunder, Hear My Cry.* In the following excerpt transcribed from videotape, the students are discussing the first chapter of the book. The tutor, at this point in the program, still has a very active voice in the book discussions; however, the students are beginning to assume responsibility for applying the four strategies of questioning, clarifying, predicting, and summarizing.

> *Student One:* On page 22, it talked about "she was still considered by the others as a disruptive maverick." I didn't quite understand it. Could someone help me? It's in the first paragraph. I didn't quite know what it meant.

> *Student Two:* I would like to say it probably meant she was always interrupting people when they talked. Or something. Everybody knew her as interrupting people all the time. So maverick is another way to say that she interrupted people.

> *Student Three:* I was thinking when it said *"disruptive* maverick" that . . . like . . . all the other teachers were strict and she was like . . . kind. They called her radical. Her ideas were different and out of the way. And it disrupted their teaching and the way they disciplined children.

> *Tutor:* So we could say the system they were involved in was kind of conservative. They wanted to keep everything the same, and she wanted to bring some new ideas and to tell everyone that things weren't going as well as they thought. She was kind of like an outlaw—just like her kids! That brings me to a question: How would you have reacted to those books? Now, you have to think about how it was back then—the racial climate and everything like that. How would you have reacted? Could you see yourself getting upset like Little Man and Cassie?

> *Student Three:* I would have been upset. No doubt about it; I would have been upset. But knowing how it was back then . . . and knowing I couldn't do anything about it . . . I probably wouldn't say anything about it.

> *Tutor:* But Little Man was in a position where he thought he could. He didn't know how things were. So, could you see yourself ever being like Little Man?

> *Student Two:* Yes, he really didn't know how things were back then.

> *Student One:* And even when people explained it . . . it was like he really didn't quite understand it. He still asked questions and stuff.

> *Tutor:* Why is that? I mean, even though someone might say, "Little Man, this is the way it is. This is the way it is!" He's still like "No! Why is it like this?" Why is he feeling this way?

Student Three: Because, it's like they said later in the book, he never got a satisfied answer. Nobody ever sat down and told him. He's just going into first grade, so how's he supposed to know? His father's been gone, and his mother hasn't answered it to his satisfaction yet, so he really doesn't understand it yet. He doesn't know how it is.

Student One: And even though he is just six, he feels that everyone should be treated equally.

Tutor: Yes! Little Man is so upset and he has so much energy because what he's experiencing is wrong. Everything he's seeing is wrong—and it's wrong to everybody else, too, but nobody else wants to say anything about it. It seems like Little Man and Cassie have their mother's "rebellious spirit" quote unquote—whatever that means.

Careful perusal of journal entries, stories, and essays written both at the beginning of the program and near the end of the program indicates an increase in the length of written pieces and a higher, overall quality of the writing presented. The students definitely incorporate elements of style and content modeled by the tutors. For example, when modeling the revising and editing of a persuasive essay, the tutors emphasize transitions between paragraphs and model the use of several different transitional phrases. The subsequent writings of the students include more transitions between paragraphs. The students also become comfortable with using writing as a tool of self-discovery and knowledge. During the second week of the program, students are asked to record their predictions and summaries for the chapters read in the novel. They are also to jot down their questions as well as any portion of the text that needs to be clarified. In addition, students begin to write lengthier passages in their journals. For example, following a discussion concerning future goals, one junior high student pretended to be a university student. He wrote:

> I am a senior at Arizona State University and my major is Pre-Law and my minor is Economics. I picked these fields because I'm interested in law and worried about the economic status of the United States. I picked Arizona State because I like the football team. I like the football team because they are a tough team to beat in the NCAA. I like it too because of our basketball team. We have the hardest team to beat and we won a National Championship. I hope after I graduate that I will go to a good law school. I want to be a lawyer because I like the way the law works and it's a good paying job. I hope to be at the top of my profession. I want other lawyers to be in fear when they hear I'm handling the same case they are. I want to have lots of

money so I can give my family everything they ever wanted. I want to become an international lawyer and handle cases all over the world. I want to at least have two children. I want my Mom to never have to worry about not having enough money when she gets old and I want my Dad to never have to work again. I want my brothers to always have enough money for their families. I want to have family reunions every year in Hawaii. Well, I have a dream and it's gonna come true!

In addition to analyzing videotaped material and random samples of student writing, a faculty member from the Department of Elementary Education and Reading conducts weekly on-site observations throughout the program. These observations include the tutor-training component as well as the tutoring sessions. Interviews are also conducted with the junior high teachers, the tutors, and with a number of the junior high students. The use of a rotating journal to record the observations and reactions of the tutors, site coordinators, and other visitors to the program was begun in the fifth year of the program. This journal provides yet another vehicle for documenting insights and questions. For example, during the second week of the program a site supervisor wrote: "I saw a lot of teaching and learning going on today. The students have found their comfort level with the tutors, which makes it safe for them to take risks." The data obtained from these multiple sources have provided a thorough and very positive picture of the program and its results.

As we attempt to determine the effectiveness of our program, we must, of course, consider the impact on students' attitude and motivation. Through their relationships with the successful minority tutors, these junior high students have gained some valuable insights into the importance of a positive attitude, good study habits, and developing a spirit of cooperative learning. Although we have little direct evidence as to the extent that tutors function as worthy role models, we can infer their success from student response in two types of tutor-student interactions. The first type occurs at the annual banquet held at the end of the program each year. Here, the junior high students actively seek out their respective tutors. They wish to talk to them and spend their time with them in a social context. For tutors who are not able to attend the banquet, we are always besieged by numerous questions as to their whereabouts. The second type of interaction is seen in the amount of written correspondence that takes place between tutor and students once the program ends. Each year, we read letters from students to tutors that point to a strong, positive interaction developed between them. It may be that anyone who takes a fairly strong interest in the students (and in the perspective they bring to learning situations), is supportive and empathetic, and genuinely and systematically attempts to teach these students is likely to experience such success. Yet, because the learning context for these students, with few exceptions, is decidedly monocultural and "Anglocentric," the minority tutors are, perhaps, more effective because they too live in two cultures and, unlike these students, have achieved full membership in the dominant culture. Thus, they provide models of success and motivation that are not generally available with Anglo tutors.

Summary and Conclusions

The Western Illinois University Minority Summer Tutoring Program provides students with an introduction to reading and writing as keys to a larger world. It is also a program where junior high students come to understand the process of learning, of acquiring information, of generalizing, of evaluating, and of synthesizing. In short, the students work to acquire those higher-order skills that are necessary for success in high school and in colleges and universities.

While we are pleased with what we see as evidence of the effectiveness of our program, the success of the Western Illinois University Minority Summer Tutoring Program will not, obviously, be completely realized until these students graduate from their respective high schools and enter our state universities. Meanwhile, to echo the words of one of the students quoted earlier, we "have a dream . . . and it's gonna come true!"

Works Cited

Abrahams, Roger D. *African Folktales*. New York: Pantheon, 1983.

Applebee, Arthur N., Judith A. Langer, and Ina V.S. Mullis. *The Writing Report Card: Writing Achievement in American Schools*. Princeton, NJ: Educational Testing Service, 1986.

Armbruster, Bonnie B., Thomas H. Anderson, and Joyce Ostertag. "Does Text Structure/Summarization Instruction Facilitate Learning from Expository Text?" *Reading Research Quarterly* 22 (1987): 331–46.

Baker, Linda, and Ann L. Brown. "Metacognitive Skills and Reading." *Handbook of Reading Research*. Ed. P. David Pearson. New York: Longman, 1984. 353–94.

Brown, Ann L., and Annemarie Sullivan Palincsar. "Inducing Strategic Learning from Texts by Means of Informed, Self-Control Training." *Topics in Learning and Learning Disabilities* 2 (1982): 1–17.

Cunningham, Patricia, and James Cunningham. "Transferring Comprehension from Listening to Reading." *Reading Teacher* 29 (1976): 169–72.

Miklowitz, Gloria. *The War Between the Classes.* New York: Dell, 1985.

Palincsar, Annemarie Sullivan, and Ann L. Brown. "Interactive Teaching to Promote Independent Learning from Text." *The Reading Teacher* 39 (1986): 771–77.

Paulsen, Gary. *The Crossing.* New York: Dell, 1987.

Raphael, Taffy E. "Question-Answering Strategies for Children." *The Reading Teacher* 36 (1982): 166–90.

Steinbeck, John. *The Pearl.* New York: Viking, 1974.

Stevens, Robert J., Nancy A. Madden, Robert E. Slavin, and Anna Marie Farnish. "Cooperative Integrated Reading and Composition: Two Field Experiments." *Reading Research Quarterly* 22 (1987): 433–54.

Taylor, Mildred D. *Roll of Thunder, Hear My Cry.* New York: Dial, 1976.

Tierney, Robert J., and P. David Pearson. "Toward a Composing Model of Reading." *Language Arts* 60 (1983): 568–80.

13 Real Voices: Action and Involvement in Secondary English Classrooms

Lenora (Leni) Cook
California State University–Dominguez Hills

Training secondary English teachers for the urban schools of the Los Angeles basin poses many problems—not the least of which is the tendency on the part of the trainees to assume that their students will thrive and learn if they are taught about literature through the traditional questioning that emphasizes specific knowledge about genre structures and themes. It is a common premise, not even specific to English, but hazardous—even doomed—in today's classrooms. Such teaching denies that all students have something to say and to share, some prior knowledge that, if tapped, can spark an interest in literature and energize what happens in the classroom. Teaching *about* literature through genre structures and themes can also deny the students' need and capacity for understanding the relationship between literature and life.

Another myth that even highly experienced teachers sometimes bring to the classroom is that today's students, particularly those of ethnic or language diversity, are unable to understand and appreciate literature, especially the traditional canon. Teachers' remarks vary from "The material is just too hard" and "They just don't care" to "TV has made my students into surface readers; they don't see any relevance in something written even twenty years ago." Many of these teachers look toward simplified or "dumbed-down" texts, or they move away from reading entirely, using materials that stress the basic skills of filling out forms. Others use only multicultural young adult literature because they mistakenly believe that these assignments and/or these texts are "easier to understand," "more relevant," and "less challenging."

In order to challenge these and other myths about the learning potential and motivation of urban secondary English students, the English/language arts methods course at California State University–Dominguez Hills is designed to demonstrate that a *combination* or *core* of traditional, culturally diverse, and young adult literature offers the best opportunity for moving *all* students from being merely "text bound" to being involved. Trainees learn that working with today's students demands new strategies that connect the text to life experiences and that move from the concrete to the abstract. These trainees seek a balance between oral and written expression. They expect their students to respond to literature when these students see a connection to their own lives. Prior to the actual reading act, trainees guide students toward the themes and values of the literature by using students' personal experiences and by recalling ideas from young adult literature and traditional works already read. It is these themes and values that form the engagement points in the reading act, allowing students to relate their own experiences to those of the literature in reflective and expressive ways.

Secondary English trainees usually enroll in the specific methods course just prior to their field-experience semester. There they are expected to design and implement units of instruction which integrate the language arts, with literature as the core. Models are presented to them, models that focus on heterogeneous classrooms mirroring the diversity in culture, ethnicity, achievement, and motivation they are finding in their own teaching experience. The models are from the classrooms of their training teachers and the student teachers who have "gone before." Usually this methods course is the trainee's first opportunity to plan for an English course—to learn to design lessons that engage students, that provide a focus for responding to literature by using meaning-making strategies which support a highly interactive English classroom.

During a prerequisite general methods course, trainees master conventional instruction techniques and, through their own learning experiences, gain some expertise in the foundations of small-group work and the dynamics of small groups. Trainees use both structured cooperative and informal collaborative-learning activities in this course and in other prerequisite or concurrent courses such as "Content-Related Reading/Writing." Thus the trainees are ready to undertake the careful planning that is the basis for a successful lesson in English—or in any other content area.

This essay describes some of the trainees' successful lessons using traditional core works with various groups of secondary English students across the educational spectrum at all levels of achievement and from many ethnic, cultural, and language backgrounds. The schools where these lessons have been used mirror the demographics of the Los Angeles Unified School District—urban, multicultural, multilingual. In the school district and throughout the state of California, there is a recommended, staff-selected list of readings for each grade level. All genres are represented in this "core," which teachers use along with supplementary literature of their choice. The lists contain many of the same authors as they did forty years ago—Shakespeare, Dickens, Hemingway, Steinbeck, Frost, Whitman, Hawthorne, Hugo, Poe. There is a smattering of women writers—Harper Lee, Marianne Moore, Charlotte Brontë, Jane Austen; a few authors of color—Richard Wright, Maya Angelou, Langston Hughes, Rudolfo Anaya, Jade Snow Wong. Although many schools mirror their ethnic and language demographics with both core and supplementary works of literature, all schools seem to look to the traditional canon for the majority of their core works. Thus is posed a major problem for teachers—finding classroom practices that make traditional/classical literature accessible as well as relevant to today's urban, diverse student population.

The issue of accessibility of literature is perhaps the most difficult for the trainee to plan for. Even master teachers who are used to implementing core works find that they are often stymied when they encounter sophisticated and even arcane vocabulary and sentence structure in the literature they are to use. The most successful lessons and units, according to both master teachers and trainees, are those which have a thematic focus rather than a genre or chronology base. There is a prereading stage which emphasizes the relationship of the theme to both the student reader and to the work. Students are "led into the literature" through strategies that connect their present lives to the work itself. An environment for learning is established in this prereading stage as well. Vocabulary is always introduced in the context of the work to be studied. Rather than alphabetic lists of words to be defined and explained, vocabulary exercises connect to the theme for the lesson or unit. While students read, whether in class or at home, they keep dialectic journals where they question as well as respond to the literature. These journals feed the reciprocal teaching that takes place in small- and large-group settings as students work together to construct meaning from the texts.

Reading aloud is important, although underutilized, in the secondary English classroom. Teachers reading aloud to students is particularly effective in stimulating interest or communicating vividly the
feelings that a particular piece, especially poetry, evokes. Poetry and
short stories by such authors as Edgar Allan Poe, Ray Bradbury, and
Maya Angelou come alive as they are heard. Students can read aloud
in small groups, with each group focusing on a different part of a
selection. They can then share their reactions to what they've read
through large-group discussions about significant characters and/or
events.

Each of the teaching experiences described in this chapter began
as a "core" element in either a master teacher's or a trainee's course of
study. Each one was designed, taught, and evaluated by its author. All
of them can be effectively adapted to classrooms in all types of schools
at all secondary levels. Some of these lessons and others were presented in a videotape and discussion session at the NCTE Annual
Convention in Baltimore, Maryland, in 1989 (Cook and Gonzales).

The first teaching experience takes place in a comprehensive
three-year high school located near the harbor of Los Angeles, a school
which has a mainly Latino and African American student body. Other
ethnicities, especially Samoan and Filipino, make up the remainder of
the population. During their sophomore year, all students read *Julius
Caesar* in their English classes.

Initially, almost all the students were not only apprehensive but
even negative about having to read *Caesar*. Their written comments
were the usual—"Shakespeare, ugh." "He's dead." "He writes in
code." "Why do we have to read about dead men?" "What does he
have to say to me? He's a thousand year [sic] old!" They also wrote in
their journals about their inability to read the language. From their
comments, the teacher trainee[1] realized that he would have to provide
a scaffold of meaning for the students as they read. He did this
through various activities, including reading aloud, playing tapes of
key scenes, active summarizing using student input whenever possible, having small groups role-play key scenes, and, unintentionally yet
most meaningfully, creating found poems from key speeches. The
teacher-trainee selected segments from the play that he thought would
be meaningful to the students as well as crucial to their understanding
of the characters, plots, and themes. Students chose what they
believed to be key words and phrases from these segments and listed
them in a line-by-line fashion. The students enjoyed both scanning
these segments and pulling out words and phrases into an event- or

character-based found poem. In this classroom, the poems were mainly the result of small-group activity. During the unit, the poems were sometimes illustrated and posted on the bulletin board for reference.

In order to involve his students in this highly political drama, the trainee began his unit with a selection of articles about candidates and issues in the local election. The students read the newspaper articles and, through discussion, both in small groups and as a class, evolved a "feature analysis" instrument or chart which displayed the attributes of the candidates. They titled their instrument "The Good Guys and the Bad Guys." As the class read the play, act by act, the students listed the characters on their individual charts with + and - indicators, guided by the features that the group had identified using the modern politicians. They noted examples to substantiate their claims. They shared their findings with partners in their cooperative learning groups. Summaries of the attributes of single characters were written in "expert groups." Here students struggled with the complexity of Shakespeare's characters, finding that none of those chosen could be classified as "totally evil" or "totally good." It was necessary to weigh the attributes and decide the *relative* goodness and evil of each of the characters in the play. The students then defended their choices, sometimes loudly. Using the chart, they chose characters to compare and contrast such as Antony with Brutus, Caesar with Cassius. Their end question, which was an in-class writing, asked the students to speculate on the qualities that Shakespeare thought important for a "good person" to have and to describe either someone that the student knew or a character from the play and show, through example, that that person or character possessed those qualities. Students were allowed to use their charts, notes, and the play to help them, but this was an individual writing assignment.

The students' comments during the four-week unit were informative. Their dialectic journals were reviewed approximately three times a week so that the master teacher and the trainee were able to monitor the students' interest level both by their overt behavior and by their written responses. When the students were doing the chart that rated the local politicians, their opinions became questions, and there was a subtle change from negativism to thoughtful speculation: "Why aren't there any Black or Latino candidates?" "Why are all the candidates for city council either attorneys or real estate agents?" "What is corruption?" "No one from *my* street goes to candidates' meetings." After reading *Julius Caesar* and seeing a film of the entire play, the class literally took sides about the goodness or lack of goodness of the characters. These comments became arguments for and against Antony and Caesar, about the weakness of Brutus, and even about the intelligence level of the Romans. The students became totally involved in the play.

The trainee's comments ranged from anxiety to delight as he watched and led the students through their reading and study:

> I didn't want to teach Shakespeare; I felt that I didn't know enough about my students or about teaching. These kids lived with violence daily, but I didn't want to bring the murder of Caesar in as the play's focal point. I only understood the play after a college course where we analyzed the characters and compared them to the politicians in [Robert] Penn Warren's *All the King's Men*. I knew that I couldn't do that, but with my master teacher's help, I was able to design a unit around the local election. It went far better than I thought. I would change some things, especially if I didn't have an election to look at. I think that current events in general could be used as a basis or even the attributes of a president or a general.

The second teaching experience involved a teacher trainer[2] at a four-year comprehensive high school who organizes her humanities course by themes. In the "values" unit, among many essays, plays, and short stories, the students read a dialogue by Erasmus, "The Abbot and the Learned Woman." The student population at the school is approximately half African American, with the rest split mainly between Asian American and Anglo. The humanities course meets the English elective requirement for seniors, although it is open to all grade levels. The objective of the following lesson is for students to recognize that "every decision made, everything said, is a reflection of the values held by a person."

It is doubtful that any of the students in the class had ever heard of Erasmus, and their comments about who and what an abbot might be were hilarious. Because the literature was a dialogue, the teacher decided to assign an imitation as the final assessment. To engage the students and to provide a meaningful context prior to reading, the teacher had them, in small groups, discuss ways people solve problems at the personal, neighborhood/community, governmental, and societal levels. Students used their own knowledge to speculate on the ways that different people might look at the same problem. In their groups, they recorded and reported on how a person's position, age, and background could influence his or her values. They also talked about how a person's values might change over time. Those same groups read the dialogue aloud, sharing the reading responsibility. The vocabulary and structure of the dialogue posed no problems for them once they understood what an abbot was and the importance of religion in the lives of those living in Erasmus's time. After reading aloud, each group then assigned secretaries and recorders. The secretaries took the notes on the initial questions—Who in the dialogue spoke for Erasmus's point of view? What was Erasmus's message to his readers? Why does the author use a dialogue rather than a poem or a narrative? The recorder kept track of group participation on participation sheets, designed by the instructor. Each group summarized their discussion and reported their answers to the whole class; after this, the actual assignment was given: Imitate the dialogue with the same objective but for a modern audience. The audience choices were senior citizens, a church leadership conference, a feminist group meeting, a rural town (grange) meeting, peers (city high school students), or intermediate elementary schoolchildren. The students had two half-class periods to write and rehearse their dialogues. Every group then presented its dialogue to the class, and the teacher and the whole class, including the group presenting its dialogue, evaluated each presentation.

The student comments on this assignment were quite positive; the students seemed to enjoy the challenge and the opportunity to perform. One student wrote:

> Having been assign [*sic*] to rewrite the play was something different. I was assign [*sic*] to write for an audience who are senior citizens. It was kind of difficult to write for such audiences but with the help of my group, it turned out to be a sucess [*sic*]. I didn't think my group could operate without fighting but everyone's effort turned out quite an experience.

The teacher commented:

> I wondered if this large and noisy group would be able to use their time wisely. Some groups did have to meet outside of class, and I'm sure that the class felt rushed and unrehearsed when they presented their dialogues. But I was delighted with their scripts and with their understanding of the importance of audience in their planning. I could tell that they understood Erasmus's dialogue without having to read dull, safe paragraphs of explication. That might be the best part of all.

She has used the same type of assignment, with a high level of success, with juniors in an advanced placement language and composition course.

In a senior English elective course on modern literature at one of the training sites, a trainee[3] was given the short story "Eveline," from James Joyce's *Dubliners,* as one of the core works. She was fearful that the students would not be able to relate to the setting and that the language would be difficult in meaning and syntax. With the help of her training teacher and her university methods instructor, she designed and implemented a series of lessons using small- and large-group structures, questions to bring out the conflicts and attitudes of the characters in the story, and individual writing assignments.

The first activity, given prior to assigning the reading itself, was a journal entry about the meaning of a "promise" and was followed by voluntary sharing of entries. The reading assignment was introduced, and certain vocabulary, such as "cretonne," was defined and discussed. The students were given questions on character and conflict to guide their reading. As they read, they were to list images that Joyce used in establishing the tone of the story and to categorize them as light/lively or dark/heavy. After the reading, the students participated in small-group discussions about the guide questions, and new questions were given to them. These questions concerned the importance of setting and the author's attitude toward the characters' actions.

Another activity involved characterization, in which groups were given a character to analyze or "become." These groups became "experts" on their assigned characters and were questioned about their characters, using both teacher- and student-generated inquiry.

In the discussions, in small and large groups, it became clear that there were real differences of opinion about Eveline's decision to keep the promise that she made to her mother, to stay in Ireland. The backgrounds and cultural traditions of the students seemed to greatly influence their opinions. Although they had always looked to their teachers for "correct answers" about theme, the class members began to speak for themselves in this discussion. They were comfortable expressing their opinions and feelings—and the different points of view made the classroom an active forum for their ideas. As one student commented in his journal:

> I always thought that the teacher was right about what the story meant and I was usually wrong. I still don't like to read stories like this one where everyone is sad or dead at the end, but I understand why the authors do it this way. Will we ever read anything that has a happy ending? I'm glad I'm not one of the characters in the stories we read in this class.

The trainee was very interested in the oral discussions concerning this and other material studied in the class:

> I really understood the story from my point of view, but I got many more insights from them [the students]. Their cultural backgrounds really came out in the discussions; there were many differences of opinion, yet no one got hostile—I was afraid that might happen because of the different backgrounds of the kids.

The activities described are for all students and for all kinds of literature. The literature used by the trainees in this program, while not set in these students' cultures, provided opportunities for the students to connect with their own developing values. Teacher-trainers and trainees group literature by theme, building cross-cultural perspectives. By providing a scaffold of life and language experience, teachers can help students access literature in meaningful ways. For example, by looking at Twain, Knowles, Wright, Anaya, and Wong as authors whose topic of "growing up" in the United States has relevance for students' own maturation, teachers provide the connection which gives personal significance to their curriculum. When the students read "Eveline," they were able to look beyond the surface story to the fear of the unknown, the comfort of the known—even when that known is unhappy, bitter, and even violent. They could articulate through activities, journal writing, and discussion their personal interpretations of the events Joyce portrays. The story had individual meaning in the class; everyone could contribute, but more important, everyone had something valid, meaningful, and significant to contribute.

Validating students' experience and prior knowledge must not be underestimated. To understand literature, students need to portray their own feelings and to connect incidents and decisions in their own lives to those in the literature they read. In doing so, they become engaged in constructing meaning from text and then in articulating those meanings to others through the filter of their own cultural and ethnic heritage. Thus, the universality of literature is experienced rather than observed.

Notes

1. MD (trainee), spring 1988.
2. JK (trainer).
3. DA (trainee), spring 1989.

Works Cited

Cook, Leni, and Phillip C. Gonzales. "Teaching English/Language Arts in Multi- Ethnic Classrooms: Models of Excellence." Videotape and discussion session. NCTE Annual Convention. Baltimore, 19 November 1989.

Erasmus, Desiderius. "The Abbot and the Learned Woman." *The Humanities: Cultural Roots and Continuities. Vol. I: Three Cultural Roots.* Ed. Mary Ann Frese et al. Lexington, MA: Heath, 1985. 313–16.

Joyce, James. "Eveline." *Dubliners.* New York: Penguin, 1984.

Shakespeare, William. *Julius Caesar.* Ed. Arthur Humphreys. New York: Oxford UP, 1984.

14 When Wordsworth Is Too Tame: Merging Minority Literature with the Classics in the Secondary Language Arts Curriculum

P. L. Thomas
Woodruff High School, Woodruff, South Carolina

I n his Journal (August 18, 1841), Henry David Thoreau ponders, "It is only the white man's poetry. We want the Indian's report. Wordsworth is too tame for the Chippeway." In much the same manner, we as teachers today can claim that in our ethnically and culturally diverse classrooms and nation, the classics (though not necessarily tame) are simply not enough for our students, regardless of their grade/ability level or ethnicity.

Many students read Thoreau and Wordsworth, but far too few are even aware of "the Indian's report"—much less given an opportunity to read any minority works; we tend to assign the white man's report alone.

Though I was an avid reader and a successful student, I read virtually no minority literature until my senior English courses in college—where I discovered Ellison and Hughes, to my eternal delight.

All pairings of nontraditional and traditional works besides *Sisters* and *Raisin* were designed and submitted by a number of A. P. English teachers enrolled at the University of South Carolina–Spartanburg during the summer of 1989; hence, the credit for the ideas should be directed toward those teachers and not toward me, who merely compiled them for the benefit of others wishing to expand their curriculum to include outstanding ethnic works. The projects are described here with each teacher's permission.

Not until I had received a graduate degree and had been teaching for over six years did I learn of N. Scott Momaday and Zora Neale Hurston. I am richer for those experiences as a reader, a writer, and a teacher.

In "Teaching Multicultural Literature in the Reading Curriculum," Donna E. Norton offers justification for exposing students to ethnic literature:

> Through carefully selected and shared literature, students learn to understand and to appreciate a literary heritage that comes from many diverse backgrounds. Through this literature, students learn to identify with people who created the stories, whether from the past or the present. . . . Of equal value are the personal gains acquired by students when they read great works from their own cultural backgrounds and those of other cultures. They gain understandings about different beliefs and values systems. They develop social sensitivity to the needs of others and realize that people have similarities as well as differences. (28)

Norton adds that ethnic literature also teaches students to appreciate writers of many cultures and offers them alternative ways to learn history, geography, and sociology (29). Her article details a five-step procedure for studying ethnic literature with elementary and middle school students. With any age group, however, Norton's reasons for teaching ethnic literature are justifiable.

For secondary students, integrating ethnic and traditional literature maintains and enriches the integrity of the curriculum. Since all students need some exposure to the classics, minority works cannot simply replace traditional works in the secondary curriculum. The most effective approach is to incorporate minority works into the language arts reading curriculum as assignments paired with traditional works.

As my project for a graduate course designed to help advanced placement teachers adopt minority works into their courses, I studied the parallels in Anton Chekhov's *Three Sisters* and Lorraine Hansberry's *Raisin in the Sun*—seemingly incongruous works. Both works explore the theme of hope in the face of reality, and the plots of both works turn on the decisions of central, careless male characters. Whether in advanced placement English ("Literature and Composition") or any other English course, students learn, through analyzing and discussing the works, to understand better the ethnic and cultural diversities in the world, and, stimulated by the works, students realize and confront their own perceptions and prejudices. The result, as Norton argues, is awareness and understanding by students of ethnic and cultural similarity and diversity.

One obstacle for teachers attempting to pair nontraditional and traditional works is managing the actual instruction of the two works. A unit dealing with *Raisin* and *Sisters* can integrate traditional approaches to works with students' own exploration of their tolerance for diversity through carefully planned prereading, during-reading, and postreading instructional strategies.

Prereading instruction begins with students writing journal entries that narrate and explain experiences they have had with people of diverse ethnicities or cultures. The journal entries are then shared either in small groups or in classroom discussions. Next, to help students be better prepared for understanding the history surrounding plays such as *Sisters* and *Raisin,* students in pairs or small groups conduct research assignments on turn-of-the-century Russia and on 1950s and/or early 1960s America—with a focus on racial relations and tensions—to be shared with the entire class. Another project that may stimulate student interest is to have the class conduct a poll of racial attitudes throughout the school. The class could prepare and copy charts to share with all students through the student newspaper.

Next, during-reading instruction focuses on explication and analysis of each work. Students should read each play carefully, then view, or at least listen to, each play being performed. *Sisters* is most readily available on audio cassette, while a recent video version of *Raisin* is excellent (the cast includes Esther Rolle and Danny Glover). The reading and viewing of each play can be used in conjunction with the study guide (see figure 1). The students can use the study guide for journal entries or small-group assignments, or the teacher can use the study guide to lead classroom discussions and lectures. For example, early in each play, the dreams for the future of all the major characters are uncovered. Through lectures, group work, or discussion, these dreams can be explored before the outcomes are known. Students then begin to see the universality of dreams and goals in people of diverse cultures and beliefs. During-reading analyses vary by class level and purpose of the course. In advanced placement classes, the emphasis on analysis is heavy, but in all sections of our tenth-grade classes, *Raisin* is required and approached on varying levels. Class discussions, group work, and assignments are conducted with prompts such as those in figure 1.

Study Guide for *Three Sisters*
and *A Raisin in the Sun*

(1) (a) In the beginning of Act I of *Raisin,* Walter asks, "Check coming today?" What does the arrival of the insurance check mean for each character? Identify passages expressing those meanings.

(b) In Act I of *Sisters*—after Irena says, "Need we bring up all these memories?"—Olga reflects on Moscow. What does Moscow mean for each character? Which passages show the characters' feelings?

(c) In Act I of *Sisters,* Vershinin says, "So in two or three hundred years life on this old earth of ours will have become marvellously beautiful. Man longs for a life like that, and if it isn't here yet, he must imagine it, wait for it, dream about it, prepare for it, he must know and see more than his father and his grandfather did." How is this passage relevant to *Sisters?* To *Raisin?*

(2) (a) Early in *Raisin,* Act I, Walter says, "That's it. There you are. Man say to his woman: I got me a dream. His woman say: Eat your eggs." Later, Beneatha shouts at Walter, "What do you want from me, Brother—that I quit school or just drop dead, which!" What do these confrontations between Walter and his wife, then Walter and Beneatha, reveal about the relationships?

(b) In *Sister,* do conflicts exist between the sisters and Andrey? The sisters and Natasha? Andrey and Natasha? Mama and her children? Explain and support with passages from the play.

(3) List the parallels between Andrey and Walter (prepare textual support). How does each affect the realization of the dreams of the family/family members?

(4) In *Sisters,* Olga says, "Yes, but this is a cold place. It's cold here, and there are too many mosquitoes." How does her attitude about her present home compare with her earlier description of Moscow? What does the comparison reveal about the family? In *Raisin,* Mama describes both her present home and her newly purchased home in Clybourne Park (identify these passages). What do Moscow and Clybourne Park come to represent in the plays?

(5) Irena and Beneatha are both twenty years old in the two plays. Identify the characteristics of both characters. Are they more similar or more different? What qualities—age, sex, race, etc.—contribute to their similarities and difference?

(6) Irena says, "The truth is that life has been stifling us, like weeds in a garden." How is Irena's comparison relevant to *Sisters?* Can the comment be applied to *Raisin?* How? Explain.

(7) How are hope and despair presented in the ending of each play? Are the plays' endings parallel or opposite? Explain.

(8) Does the family's being black in *Raisin* and the family's being Russian in *Sisters* affect the plays? How?

Figure 1. Study guide for *Sisters* and *A Raisin in the Sun.*

Essay Topics

(1) Discuss the central symbol in *Three Sisters* and *A Raisin in the Sun* and how that symbol contributes to each play's theme.

(2) Parallel the words and actions of Andrey and Walter and explain how each affects the realization of the other characters' dreams.

Further Exercises, Writing Topics, or Comparisons

(1) Research the historical context of each play. How is it significant?
  (a) Turn-of-the-century Russia/*Sisters*
  (b) 1950s and 1960s America (race relations)/*Raisin*

(2) Discuss family conflict in the works listed below. Comparisons and contrasts with *Sisters*? *Raisin*?
  Death of a Salesman; "Everyday Use"; *The Glass Menagerie*;
  Look Homeward, Angel; *As I Lay Dying*; and *Romeo and Juliet*

(3) Discuss the American Dream as presented in the works listed below. Comparisons and contrasts with *Sisters*? *Raisin*?
  The Great Gatsby, Of Mice and Men, Native Son,
  Invisible Man, The Sun Also Rises

(4) Write a personal essay about a conflict between you and a family member. Circumstances? Helpful or harmful to relationship? Outcome? Different than conflict with a friend? Stranger?

(5) Discuss how the characters embody Thoreau's "The mass of men lead lives of quiet desperation."

Figure 1. *Continued.*

For postreading instruction, the focus shifts back to the students' perceptions of other cultures and ethnicities. Students review their original journal entries about personal experiences with people of other ethnicities and cultures and prepare an essay from the following prompt:

> America has long been called the Melting Pot for its blending of cultural and ethnic diversity. How has reading *Sisters* and *Raisin* affected your perception of other races and cultures? Include how the plays have changed your perceptions or confirmed your perceptions or both since reading the works.

What better lesson is there for students to learn than that turn-of-the-century, aristocratic Russians and mid-twentieth-century, economically struggling black Americans share common human conflicts with each other and, probably, with the students themselves, though all were shaped by diverse cultures?

When teachers pair minority and traditional works, students can explore each work better through comparison than if they were to study the works alone. Students can learn that, while cultural and ethnic differences do exist, humans are the same in their basic nature. The graduate course for advanced placement teachers enlightened me to the potential of pairing minority and traditional works, and the individual projects also provided many specific works for pairing—all of which are suitable for secondary language arts curricula at the appropriate levels.

Toni Morrison's *Song of Solomon* parallels several traditional works. One project explored the use of myth and the archetype in *Song* and in James Joyce's *Portrait of the Artist as a Young Man.* Both works incorporate the motif of flight, the myth of Icarus, and sustained allusion. Though race, gender, religion, and history separate Morrison and Joyce, the writers work through much the same technique and expose many of the same conflicts. *Song* also proves to be parallel to *Hamlet.* Both Milkman (from *Song*) and Hamlet experience a quest for identity, and both Morrison and Shakespeare reveal character through figurative language. Students can study not only the parallels between the two characters but also between the two authors, learning that the essential characteristics of the literary artist cross the lines of gender, race, and time.

Even when minority and traditional works are not parallel in theme or characterization, students can explore a pair of works using a variety of approaches to discover how one approach differs from another. For instance, one project grouped *Song* with Franz Kafka's *Metamorphosis* and had students divide into four groups, each group analyzing the works with a different approach—from formalistic, to psychological, to archetypal, to sociological. The culture and race of the authors can also serve as a basis for comparison and contrast of the works. Especially with Morrison and Kafka, the diversity between the two works and between the two cultures of the authors and their characters illuminates the works and the approaches for the students.

Martin Luther King, Jr.'s "Letter from Birmingham Jail" provides ample opportunity to discuss nonfiction and King's rhetorical style. An obvious traditional pairing with "Letter" is Thoreau's "Civil Disobedience." After students read Thoreau, they feel more comfortable with the comparatively concise language of King. They come to understand Thoreau better than if they had studied only Thoreau's work because King's writing reflects and his actions parallel Thoreau's ideas. These two works present students with a similar theme (the conflict between civil and moral obligation), a similar philosophy (nonviolent protest), a similar form of discourse (persuasion), and similar rhetorical devices (allusion, rhetorical questions, and parallelism). King's work echoes and justifies Thoreau's ideas; it also helps students apply those ideas to their own world—making literature relevant and real. With its persuasive techniques, King's "Letter" is useful as a companion piece to "The Declaration of Independence" as well.

Ethnic works by women also serve an additional purpose—to augment the traditional male point of view in literature. Even in classic works portraying strong female characters—*The Scarlet Letter* or *Macbeth*, for instance—the authors are predominantly male. The black female voice in literature offers both the black perspective and the woman's perspective, and secondary students often respond well to literary works exploring a character's search for knowledge or identity. Zora Neale Hurston's *Their Eyes Were Watching God* and Robert Penn Warren's *All the King's Men* are ideal for comparing and contrasting that search for identity. As both mature, Janie, in *Eyes*, and Jack, in *Men*, come to realize more about themselves after journeys through reality. In tandem, the works highlight every human's need for self-discovery, regardless of race or sex, and contrast the paths to that discovery since the roads *are* often shaded by gender and skin color. Janie could never have been in Jack's shoes and vice versa.

But what of Thoreau's "Indian's report"? A final example of pairing minority and traditional works is with the poetry of N. Scott Momaday, a Native American, and Emily Dickinson. Students can begin with Dickinson's "Further in Summer Than the Birds" and compare it with Momaday's "The Bear," "Angle of Geese," "North Dakota, North Light," and "The Burning." These poems lend themselves to an exploration of how diction and structure develop images and themes in a poem. The students thus learn about key elements of poetry and about the culture and mythology of American Indians—which are at least as important to be aware of as Dickinson's New England heritage.

With many of these pairings, the same instructional strategies detailed for *Sisters* and *Raisin* can be adapted and applied. Asking students about their perceptions of the world before and after experiencing great literature is fundamental to the purpose of literature, regardless of the ethnicity of the authors or the characters.

Teachers attempting to expand the reading curriculum may face stiff opposition from traditionalists: How do we know the pairing of traditional and nontraditional literature works? How do we know any ethnic selection is truly "literature"? As the 1990–91 school year was my first as the advanced placement English ("Literature and Composition") teacher, it serves as the only evidence I have of the program's success. The year's reading list included *Raisin*, Ellison's *Invisible Man*, and short stories and poetry by Bambara, Alice Walker, Hughes, Brooks, Lucille Clifton, Don L. Lee, and Nikki Giovanni; for the first time in the history of the program at my school, students in advanced placement English read nontraditional works along with traditional works— which included the classics *Metamorphosis*, *The Stranger*, *King Lear*, *Death of a Salesman*, and the like—as a major part of the workload.

On the free response section of the written portion of the advanced placement exam, eleven of the twenty-two students chose *Raisin* as their topic when answering the prompt dealing with contrasting places in a work of literature. Sixty-three percent of the students scored 3 or above, with two scoring 4 and four scoring 5 (with 5 being the highest possible score). Before this past year, the number passing the exam has remained at or just below 50 percent (the program began in 1981–82); only once before has any student scored a 5.

One of the students scoring a 5 in 1990–91 felt that *Invisible Man*, in conjunction with the traditional curriculum, had a profound effect on his ability to achieve the top score on the advanced placement exam. He explains:

> As a white, middle-class American [I saw] the tone and point of view of F. Scott Fitzgerald's Nick Carraway in *The Great Gatsby* . . . [as] universal. Upon first reading *Gatsby*, I failed to realize it even had a tone. The point of view was essentially mine. . . . Ralph Ellison's *Invisible Man*, however, has a visibly different tone from that in *Gatsby*. . . . Students tend to identify with narrators and situations from cultures similar to their own. A different viewpoint provides students the opportunity to examine their own system of beliefs and values and to integrate them into a larger scale. Black literature (in the form of *Invisible Man* and . . . *Raisin in the Sun*) clearly defined tone and point of view better for me than the standard classics. . . . As a tool of cultural understanding, ethnic works are essential to the society we live in.

As this student notes, before being exposed to ethnic works, he was completely unaware of the diverse voices of all humankind—the voices that are given life in literature. In advanced placement English, where students *must* be aware of shifts in tone and voice to score 4s and 5s, ethnic literature is a vital contrast to the classics.

The ethnic works we discussed also had a significant impact on the dynamics of our classroom discussions. The black advanced placement students (four out of twenty-two students) were most involved in classroom discussions during our studies of *Raisin* and *Invisible Man,* while the entire class was more animated and interested in those works as compared with *King Lear* and *Tess of the D'Urbervilles,* for example. Such evidence is subjective, but racial and ethnic diversity is a concern of today's young people, and they seem eager to explore race relations when offered an opportunity to do so.

The list of examples for pairing minority and traditional works is as limitless as teachers' imaginations and experiences with ethnic literature—because all true literature explores universal themes. Now, as language arts teachers, we must strive for Thoreau's "Indian's report" some one hundred and fifty years after he recognized the need. Without being assigned to do so, our students are watching *Do the Right Thing* and *Boyz in the Hood,* listening to rap music, and struggling with racial themes. The English classroom must meet these students' needs and offer them a stable environment in which to explore these issues of racial diversity and tolerance. Exposure to ethnic literature makes our language arts students richer human beings, and by pairing ethnic works with traditional literature, teachers provide students with broader experiences and a better chance to survive and prosper in an ethnically diverse classroom and world.

Works Cited

Chekhov, Anton. *Three Sisters. Modern Drama: Nine Plays.* Ed. Otto Reinert. Boston: Little, Brown, 1962. 151–211.

Hansberry, Lorraine. *A Raisin in the Sun.* New York: New American Library, 1988.

Norton, Donna E. "Teaching Multicultural Literature in the Reading Curriculum." *The Reading Teacher* 44.1 (1990): 28–40.

Thoreau, Henry David. *Journal.* Vols, I–VII. Ed. Bradford Torrey and Francis H. Allen. New York: Dover, 1962.

15 Teaching *The Thief of Bagdad* as an Interdisciplinary, Middle School Unit

Martin Mullarkey
Pacoima Middle School, Pacoima, California

The 1940 classic film *The Thief of Bagdad* is an Arabian fantasy with magic carpets, genies, flying horses, prophecies, and evil spells. The movie is a natural in a fantasy unit, and I have used it as a segue between the myths-and-legends and fantasy units outlined in the Los Angeles City seventh-grade course of study. I have successfully taught this film for two years with African American and Latino seventh graders and for one year with advanced ESL students at Foshay Middle School, an inner-city Chapter 1 middle school in Los Angeles.

Teaching literature in inner-city English classes is challenging because many students within these classes do not read proficiently and therefore do not read for pleasure. Whenever we study a story or novel, I read it aloud to the class. This strategy makes grade-level appropriate literature more accessible to a class with limited reading abilities. These seventh graders have read, following my oral reading, *Where the Red Fern Grows* and *A Wrinkle in Time.* They reread parts of each novel on their own in connection with outlining plot structure and creating a new setting for *Red Fern* and with studying character development in *Wrinkle.* My classroom library consists of a large number of paperbacks purchased from book clubs. These books were chosen for a wide range of reading abilities and interests. I assign independent reading for homework and have students keep response journals that focus on the personal meaning the texts have for them.

Since most students today spend a great deal of their time passively watching television, I also incorporate film into my English classes as a means to advance critical-thinking and literacy skills. One advantage of teaching a feature film to students is that it permits the analysis of literary elements as they develop throughout a full-length work without the enormous time commitment it takes to read a novel aloud. My hope is to create viewers who will transfer the meaning-making strategies I generate in class with film to the written word.

After spending several weeks studying Greek myths and other legends from cultures around the world, the class reads an excerpt from *Sinbad the Sailor* in their social studies textbook *Across the Centuries* (Armento et al.), an excerpt that serves as an introduction to a chapter in a unit on Islam. I ask students to compare and contrast this story to the myths and legends they have been reading. We then predict what a movie entitled *The Thief of Bagdad* might be about, considering that it contains some of the same elements found in *Sinbad the Sailor* and that, throughout the movie, the main character wants to go exploring with Sinbad on his ship. Since the movie sparks interest in the history of Islam and its contributions to world culture, students concurrently study aspects of the Muslim and Arab world in their seventh-grade social studies class as part of an interdisciplinary approach to learning.

The class begins viewing the film on laserdisc. I stop the movie after the good king, Ahmad, is jailed by his evil aide, Jaffar, so that I can check for understanding and answer any questions the students might have about the film. We continue our viewing uninterrupted until the Princess must decide if she will surrender herself to the loathsome Jaffar so that her beloved Ahmad might regain his eyesight. At this time I have students write an "open mind," a graphic representation of the thoughts of a character, pretending that they are the Princess (see figure 1). While the students always groan when I cut off the movie at this crucial point, almost all of them do their homework that night and decide how they would act in the Princess's place. I poll the class the next day on their responses, and there is always a spirited discussion among students who made different choices. Afterwards we continue to watch the film to its conclusion.

Laserdisc technology permits teachers to manipulate sequences or scenes from a film for class analysis as easily as those in a written text. Within seconds of inputting the time of a selected scene on the laserdisc player's remote control, teachers can access any part of a movie that they want to include in their lesson. I exploit this aspect of laserdisc technology when I expose my classes to clips from the movie that contain difficult vocabulary words used in an easily understood visual and verbal context.

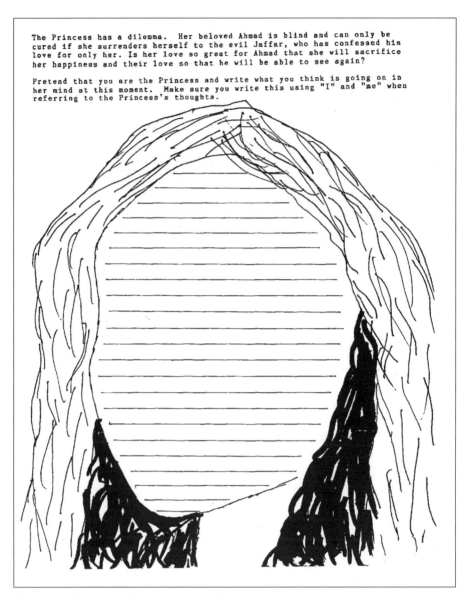

The Princess has a dilemma. Her beloved Ahmad is blind and can only be cured if she surrenders herself to the evil Jaffar, who has confessed his love for only her. Is her love so great for Ahmad that she will sacrifice her happiness and their love so that he will be able to see again?

Pretend that you are the Princess and write what you think is going on in her mind at this moment. Make sure you write this using "I" and "me" when referring to the Princess's thoughts.

Figure 1. Example of an "open mind" assignment.

In cooperative groups, students must figure out what the words mean and explain the reasoning behind the answers they chose. For example, I access the scene in the movie where the Princess's father enters his daughter's once beautiful garden and finds it abandoned and in ruins. The King says, "This is a place of *desolation*," as the camera shows an absence of joy in the previously lush garden. On a vocabulary sheet (see figure 2), I include the King's quote and offer four possible meanings: (a) beauty, (b) gloom, (c) wealth, or (d) peacefulness. I usually show the clip two times while the students discuss their possibilities and write their reasons for their answers. After the class decides the meaning of the ten words I have chosen from the film, we go over each answer and the reasons for their choices. We immediately review each clip after our discussion, and almost all of the students realize the correct answer without my having to identify it. Since we keep a tally of which group has the most correct answers, the students enjoy this activity enormously and inevitably ask me if we can always do vocabulary in this way.

Another advantage laserdisc technology has over video is that it allows instant accessibility to thematic elements in a film which are sequentially out of order. I created four separate indexes of scenes in the film: fantasy; foreshadowing; the eyesight/eye motif that runs throughout the film; and Abu's development as the movie's most sympathetic character. I begin this "literary elements" part of the unit by having the class discuss what makes a work of fiction a fantasy and by accessing two scenes from *The Thief of Bagdad* that showcase these properties, such as Jaffar casting a spell that makes Ahmad blind and Abu a dog.

Next, I ask the class if they enjoyed the end of the movie or if they felt cheated by Abu's ability to save the day. Since I have never met anyone who did not enjoy this classic film, I replay the prophecy at the beginning which states that a young boy will overthrow the evil tyrant. I ask the class why they believed Abu was capable of this extraordinary deed when no adult in the movie could accomplish it. This discussion leads us into the movie's foreshadowing of Abu as the hero, so I show the students two examples from my foreshadowing index to reinforce this concept. Scenes of Abu displaying his cunning—such as when he steals the key from the prison guard or tricks the vengeful genie back into the bottle—help the students grasp how the writer laid the groundwork for this ending to be both plausible and satisfying.

Vocabulary in Context

After watching the clips from the movie, decide what each vocabulary word means by the way it is used. Make sure you justify your answers by giving reasons from the film for your choices.

1. "They (the people) are fools and *knaves*. . . ." *Knave* means
   (a) merchant   (b) rascal   (c) hero   (d) an honest person
   because

2. "But a wise man among the sages of Bagdad comforted them with a *prophecy*. . . ." *Prophecy* means
   (a) prediction   (b) meal   (c) victory   (d) answer
   because

3. "And from the ranges of the sky he shall destroy this *tyrant* with the Arrow of Justice. . . ." *Tyrant* means
   (a) companion   (b) slave   (c) citizen   (d) cruel leader
   because

4. "Brother of Lions"—"Fountain of *hospitality*. . . ." *Hospitality* means
   (a) selfishness   (b) youth   (c) disease   (d) generosity toward guests
   because

5. "What do you want my daughter for?"—"I have to found a *dynasty*. . . ."
   Dynasty means
   (a) country   (b) ruling family   (c) secret   (d) army
   because

6. "This is a place of *desolation*. . . ." *Desolation* means
   (a) beauty   (b) gloom   (c) wealth   (d) peacefulness
   because

7. "My imprisoned spirit turned to *vengeance* on all that lived and was free, and I swore that I'd kill him that freed me to satisfy my hate."
   Vengeance means
   (a) loneliness   (b) forgiveness   (c) revenge   (d) wisdom
   because

8. "*Exquisite* . . ." *Exquisite* means
   (a) disgusting   (b) ordinary   (c)strange   (d) beautiful
   because

9. "We are the *remnants* of the Golden Age. Golden because gold was nothing. . . ." *Remnant* means
   (a) values   (b) remains   (c) strength   (d) future
   because

10. "And now, I do *homage*. For you are king. . . ." *Homage* means
    (a) honor   (b) disrespect   (c) depart   (d) remember
    because

Figure 2. Assignment in using vocabulary in context.

Finally, I explain to the class that a motif is an idea or subject repeated or developed throughout a work of art, as in music when the same melody is interpreted several different ways. I access for the class two examples from my motif index and ask them if they can figure out what the ongoing motif is in *The Thief of Bagdad*. A closeup of Jaffar's eyes mesmerizing Ahmad and the scene of Abu's capture of the All-Seeing Eye make this difficult literary element easier to comprehend. After this, I have the students work in groups to see if they can correctly categorize examples of fantasy, foreshadowing, or motif, each of which I access at random. The students greet the display of each scene with zeal and often see an overlapping of categories in scenes that contain more than one element.

Using correct plural and possessive forms is a particular problem for students who do not speak standard English as their first language or dialect. I include in this unit two paragraphs about how the thief becomes the most sympathetic character in the story. I then tell the students that there are a total of twenty-two errors in the paragraphs, and they must correct them. Words are written in their singular form when they should be plural, and words that should have an "'s" on their endings to show possession do not. Various irregular plural forms are scattered throughout the two paragraphs, and, after a brief review of the rules, I give students the assignment to finish for homework (see figure 3).

Another written usage exercise that I derive from the film involves sentence-combining using appositives. I explain how an appositive can be one word or a group of words that helps identify or gives additional information about one noun structure in a sentence; appositives follow that noun structure and are set off with commas only when the information they give is not necessary for identification purposes. I provide my students with several examples, and we combine a few pairs of sentences as a class to make sure everyone understands. (We have previously combined sentences with relative clauses, so this concept is not entirely new to them.) I then provide students with several pairs of sentences that contain information about the movie and its characters (see figure 4). Since all of the appositives I give them contain unnecessary, additional information, I remind them to make sure that they set off the appositives with commas. For example: "Abu was a thief. Abu stole the All-Seeing Eye" becomes "Abu, a thief, stole the All-Seeing Eye." After they complete this assignment for homework, I give extra credit to those students who can create

---

Editing for the Correct use of "'s" or "es"

The following paragraphs contain 22 errors. Words are written in their singular form when they should be plural, and words that should have an "'s" on their endings to show possession do not. Rewrite the following paragraphs so that all of the errors have been corrected.

Most story have main character who are law-abiding citizen, but *The Thief of Bagdad* is a movie titled after an outlaw. Although Abu steals for a living, most viewer like him above all the other character in the film. Abu friendship with Ahmad never wavers, even when Ahmad love for the Princess makes him break his agreement with Abu to sail on Sinbad ship. Abu never steals anything more than what he needs to eat or help Ahmad, even though Abu could probably use some more garment to wear. Abu cunning, carefree nature, and love for excitement are a pleasure to watch, especially when he is rescuing Ahmad the King, who is supposed to be wiser and more powerful than any of his subject.

Since the Princess role is not that important in the movie, the rest of the major character seem wicked, selfish, or loathsome when compared to Abu. Jaffar belief that all man are evil, Genie deserting of Abu after his three wish are finished, and the King trading of his daughter for a toy make none of these character very appealing. As a result, Abu charm steals the movie along with most people heart.

Figure 3. Assignment in editing for the correct use of "'s" or "es."

original sets of sentences from the movie's plot which can be transformed into appositives.

To prepare the class to write a persuasive essay, I ask students to brainstorm in groups about what qualities they look for in a good friend, and then we share our answers with the entire class. I tell them that they are going to choose one character from the movie that best fits our description of a good friend and convince the reader of their choice. Most of the boys decide initially that they would like the beautiful Princess as their friend, but I tell them to wait until they view all of the sequences from the character index. While seeing a series of scenes displaying Abu, Ahmad, and the Princess, the class discusses the characteristics exposed in the clips and unanimously agrees that only Abu demonstrates the necessary traits of loyalty, courage, compassion, generosity, and dependability. This assignment usually takes three days as I teach the students how to organize their thoughts to make a persuasive argument for their choice. I then give them a day to work on peer editing in groups, with a revision checklist as a guide. Essays including the correct usage of plural and possessive forms, appositives, and vocabulary words from the movie will receive a higher grade.

Use of Appositives

An appositive can be one word or a group of words that helps identify or gives additional information about one noun in a sentence. Commas are used with appositives when the appositive gives additional information about the noun it follows. <u>Example:</u> *Mr. Mullarkey, my English teacher, enjoys reading.* By using appositives in our sentences, we can combine two short sentences into one.

<u>Example:</u> *Abu was a thief. Abu stole the All-Seeing Eye.*

Abu, a thief, stole the All-Seeing Eye.

Combine the following pairs of sentences using appositives. Since all of the pairs listed below include appositives that give additional information, make sure you set them off with commas.

1. Jaffar was Ahmad's Grand Vizier. Jaffar had magical powers.

2. Jaffar betrayed Ahmad. Ahmad was the King of Bagdad.

3. *The Thief of Bagdad* is an Arabian fantasy. *The Thief of Bagdad* was made in 1940.

4. Abu and Ahmad sailed to Basra. Basra was the home of the Princess.

5. The Princess was a kind of Sleeping Beauty. The Princess needed Ahamd to break her trance.

6. Abu lived to regret his first wish. Abu's first wish was sausages like his mother used to make.

7. Genie flew Abu to the Temple of the Dawn. The Temple of the Dawn was the home of the All-Seeing Eye.

8. The Old King was a wise and generous man. The Old King gave Abu the Arrow of Justice.

9. The flying carpet was the Old King's prized possession. The flying carpet helped Abu rescue Ahmad from the executioner.

Figure 4. Assignment in sentence combining using appositives.

"The Third Wish," a short story by Joan Aiken, lends itself well to closing the unit on *The Thief of Bagdad* and beginning one on fantasy. In the story, a man rescues the King of the Forest and demands the three wishes that are his due. The King warns him that he has yet to meet a mortal who has made wise wishes and that most people spend their third wish undoing the first two. When the genie in *The Thief of Bagdad* grants Abu three wishes in return for his freedom from imprisonment in a bottle, even the shrewd Abu chooses unwisely and almost pays for his rashness with his life. I access for the class the three sequences in the movie where Abu makes his wishes, and then I ask them to predict whether they think the character in "The Third Wish" will fall victim to a similar blunder. Almost all of my students incorrectly believe that he will. After we read the whole story, I ask the class to write down what they would have wished for if they were in Abu's place and the reasons why they would not live to regret those choices in the future.

Since the movie exposes students to many aspects of Islamic customs that are foreign to life in contemporary America, it offers an excellent opportunity for an interdisciplinary approach to learning. Students have been studying an Islamic unit in social studies, and, as a culminating project, they decide upon an aspect of Arab or Muslim culture which they encountered during the film or in their social studies textbook that particularly interests them. They spend two periods in the library researching such topics as clothing, food, religion, justice, commerce, government, architecture, mythology, transportation, gender roles, geography, and the veil. Their history teacher and I work together on this assignment, and the students present their findings as oral reports in their social studies classes. Most of my students inevitably remark that they never realized they could learn so much from such an entertaining movie.

Having also taught *The Thief of Bagdad* in its video format, I am amazed at the way laserdisc technology opens up possibilities for teaching. Video restricted me from teaching the film in any other way but a linear fashion. Since I could not access different scenes from the movie without wasting class time searching for them by rewinding or fast-forwarding tape, I omitted all of the activities that required instant access. As a result, I relied more on the students' memory of the film than actual examples from the movie itself to teach literary concepts and skills. This approach led to mutual dissatisfaction because students cannot possibly be familiar enough with the different aspects of a film after only one viewing, when they are focusing most of their attention on following the storyline. In the past, every time my class watched a video, I would spend the entire period standing by the TV and pointing out dramatic or cinematic elements that I wanted them to notice. These constant interruptions during an initial viewing annoyed and distracted students, but I believed that they would not remember these points otherwise after the movie was over. Video limited the film's role in the classroom to that of an enhancer of literature rather than a rich source of literature in and of itself. Just as when I read a book with my classes, we explore vocabulary in context, consider literary elements, and engage in critical-thinking activities related to our reading. Thus, with laserdisc's instant-access capability, these opportunities for learning with visual media become equally viable. Considering that a vast majority of my students receive most of their information about the world through the visual media, I believe it is essential that we incorporate directed teaching of TV and film into the curriculum to motivate and develop critical thinking among our students.

If students can learn to become active viewers who constantly question and appraise what they are watching, then they will have learned a skill that can be transferred to the reading process, and they will be more likely to become better readers as a result. After I teach this unit and ask students to figure out a word's meaning through its context in print, I only have to remind them of how we did it in *The Thief of Bagdad*, and they understand the assignment immediately. The only difference, I explain to them, is the medium.

My endorsement of teaching films on laserdisc in the language arts classroom in no way means I plan to abandon the written word. Instead, visual media provide another avenue for engaging students in a learning process that involves listening, speaking, thinking, writing, and even reading. Difficult concepts, like foreshadowing and motif, become easier to grasp initially because students are more familiar and comfortable with visual images than with the written word. In addition, this approach appeals to the different learning styles that are present in all classrooms.

The success my students felt in identifying literary elements, utilizing context clues to uncover an unfamiliar word's meaning, and writing about an enjoyable story and memorable characters left them wanting more and asking me when we could do this again. The significant increase in class participation and the 50 percent jump in homework completions during this unit (particularly by those class members who rarely turned in their assignments) showed me that my students were sincere about wanting to "read" another film. The enthusiasm for learning regularly demonstrated throughout this two-week unit has inspired me to create more units utilizing laserdisc technology to complement the literature and themes middle school students traditionally study.

Recently, two of my seventh graders asked me if they could sit in on my sixth-period class when I was beginning to teach a different film unit.

"Why," I inquired, "when you have already seen the film third period? Won't you find it boring to see it again?"

"No," one answered. "We want to make sure we see everything in it like you do."

"Besides," the other added, "our sixth-period teacher is showing us one of those cheap movies."

"Cheap movies? What are those?" I ventured to ask.

"You know, like *Home Alone* or *Three Ninjas,* where you don't have to think."

For just a moment, before the bell rang and my sixth-period students nearly trampled me at the doorway, I thought I had died and gone to teacher heaven.

Works Cited

Aiken, Joan. "The Third Wish." *Prentice-Hall Literature: Bronze.* Ed. Roger Babusci et al. Englewood Cliffs, NJ: Prentice, 1989. 3–10.

Armento, Beverly J. et al. *Houghton-Mifflin Social Studies. Vol. VII: Across the Centuries.* Boston: Houghton, 1991.

The Thief of Bagdad. Dir. Michael Powell, Tim Whelan, and Ludwig Berger. 1940. Embassy Home Entertainment, Laserdisc.

16 An Approach to Teaching Four Poems about Education: A Thematic Unit for Pre-Freshman Minority Students

Mary Sauter Comfort
Lehigh University

Every summer, Lehigh University's Challenge for Success (CFS) program provides a six-week orientation session for pre-freshman Hispanic, African, Asian, and Native American students. In noncredit courses, they study computers, calculus, chemistry, and psychology or sociology. They also complete "Introduction to Literature: The Minority Experience," a three-credit course designed to increase appreciation of multicultural literature, prepare students for a first-year writing course, as well as suggest strategies for dealing with the "minority experience" in higher education.

Since 1987, the syllabus for this course has changed to meet student needs. Ellison's Invisible Man in "Battle Royal" has replaced Hawthorne's Robin Molineaux as an example of an alienated youth in an unfamiliar environment. Instead of *Othello,* Alice Childress's *Wedding Ring* is used to dramatize interracial relationships. Milton's "When I Consider How My Light Is Spent" has given way to Gwendolyn Brooks's "Kitchenette Building" as a meditation about unrealized human potential. This evolution reflects an increased awareness of the ways in which multicultural literature can prepare these students to meet the unique challenges awaiting them in a predominantly white, academically demanding university setting.

During the summer, CFS instructors from all disciplines meet regularly to discuss strategies to help the students meet these challenges. Instructors from the noncredit courses report that students confess to enjoying the readings and claim to be better-prepared for writing-intensive courses in other disciplines. In course evaluations, students point to their own self-confidence and readiness for "real" courses as a measure of the course's value. In the semesters that follow, instructors in freshman composition comment that CFS students refer to characters from summer readings as examples in their "personal experience" essays.

Students respond most enthusiastically to a unit on education. Readings are from the text, *New Worlds of Literature,* and other anthologies.[1] The unit includes prose and poetry and focuses on the minority student both in and out of school. Baldwin's "Sonny's Blues" and Jack Aquero's "Half Way to Dick and Jane" dramatize the plight of inner-city youth responding to peer pressures to drop out. In Inez Hernandez's "Para Teresa," a highly motivated minority student confronts a discouraged peer; in Antler's "I Raise My Hand" another minority student recalls his frustrated efforts to participate in class. Readings for this unit might include works like Claude McKay's "Truant," in which formal education seems to be only a peripheral concern, or August Wilson's *Fences,* in which differences in education, though discussed tangentially, motivate much of the action.

A short unit on education introduces diversity and, at the same time, the concept of a shared "minority experience." Students focus on four poems at first. In Richard Olivas's "[I'm Sitting in My History Class]," an Hispanic student is told that George Washington is the "father of his country." Since Spanish-speaking people arrived in America before George Washington, the speaker raises his "mano" and asks how Washington could be the father of a racially diverse country. Like other minorities, he experiences invisibility when the lecturer overlooks the contributions of diverse cultures. In "A Teacher Taught Me," by Anne Lee Walters, a student whose teacher calls her "pretty little Indian girl" expresses the feelings of minority students who realize they must suppress their anger or, at least, postpone its expression. In June Jordan's "A Poem About Intelligence for My Brothers and Sisters," the speaker, when told that I.Q. tests "prove" that African Americans are intellectually inferior, uses the values of her culture to "prove" that Albert Einstein was socially inferior. Intelligence tests have been used to diminish the achievements of African Americans in particular, but all minorities hope to discount such "evidence" used to justify discrimination. In Li-Young Lee's "Persimmons," a student's specific problems with language may be unique to Asian American students, but his efforts to regain his self-confidence when a teacher punishes him are shared by other minorities.

These four poems inspire students to participate energetically in discussions and to write with enthusiasm, comparing their experiences with those of the students in the poems. In each poem, for example, a teacher calls attention to a student's minority status; most CFS students can remember a teacher who ignored or insulted minorities.[2] Like the students in the poems, the CFS students struggle to discover innovative responses to isolation and anger and to respond creatively to the "minority experience" in education.

Although CFS students experience intense engagement with the poetry, they still exhibit two troublesome perceptions. First, when asked to inventory and evaluate the survival strategies described in the literature, CFS students insist that the characters' behavior was exceptional and, therefore, impossible to imitate. Second, they point out that even these extraordinary efforts are unsuccessful; whatever their innovative responses, the poets' speakers neither destroy nor avoid discrimination. Unable to initiate exceptional strategies and discouraged by the characters' failure either to "educate the oppressor" or to "beat the system," few of the CFS students find the poems encouraging. At this point in the course, the introduction of an educator's studies of actual students provides a frame of reference for the CFS students through which they can begin to see the literary characters' strategies as realistic. Within this context, the CFS students judge the literary characters as successful if they complete their education, whether or not they eradicate prejudice in the educational system; while the students in the poems do not change their teachers, they refuse to allow prejudice to compromise or block their academic success.

To help the CFS students focus on their own strengths, I share with them the research of social scientist William Sedlacek. Even though Sedlacek is not a literary critic, his studies nonetheless prompt CFS students to identify—and then to identify with—the strengths of minorities in literature. In its current form, this unit begins with small-group discussions in which students summarize and compare their responses to the teachers of the student speakers in the poetry. In journals, the CFS students summarize these discussions. Next, using Sedlacek's studies as models, they prepare a list of noncognitive variables that they would use to predict the academic success of minority students in higher education. Finally, in an essay for this unit, they analyze and evaluate the responses of the students in the poetry as examples of Sedlacek's variables and as predictors of academic success.

The Poems: Real and Imagined Minority Students

While doing their initial reading, CFS students describe in their journals the classroom incidents and the students' responses from the literary works. They also note specific connections to the minority experience as well as describe events from their own lives that have similarly challenged them. The structure of Richard Olivas's poem is particularly suitable for beginning this exercise. CFS students find a familiar complaint in each stanza and note Olivas's increasingly assertive responses.[3] First, a dull presentation style—the teacher's "rapping" pushes Olivas to the "verge of napping." Then, repetition of material inspires sarcasm: "I've heard it all before. / Tell me more! Tell me more!" The teacher's failure to engage Olivas in his own learning discourages participation: "Dare I ask him to reiterate? / Oh why bother." Finally, when he cannot find himself in the traditional history of America, Olivas raises his "*mano*" and challenges the familiar metaphor: "If George Washington's my father, / Why wasn't he Chicano?" Weary of the repetition and uninvolved in the material, the Hispanic student in Olivas's poem becomes a critic of pedagogy and a pioneer multiculturalist in his classroom.

Initially, of course, instead of on the gestures of self-confidence, students focus on the problems in this poem. They recall their own sense of racial invisibility in high school: minorities were absent from sociology texts, history lectures, literature anthologies, and even sample sentences in grammar texts. They recall their difficulty in identifying role models, their ambivalence about their own identity, and their embarrassment about their language and their heritage. Asked to make specific comparisons with the experience recorded by Olivas, one student, whose ancestors came from Africa, wondered whether the hardships on the Mayflower were similar to those on a slave ship.

Unlike Olivas's teacher, who seems oblivious to all students and especially to the cultural diversity of some of them, the instructor in Anne Lee Walters's "A Teacher Taught Me" notices diversity. But while this teacher avoids negative stereotypes of Native Americans, she calls attention to their appearance and race instead of to their educational development: the teacher patronizes the "pretty little Indian girl" and apologizes for "what we did / to the American Indian." Walters, "hating the kindness," tells her "cousins and friends" who, she trusts, will laugh with her, and she decides to remember the teacher's words. Whether or not they have ever gained strength from their family or ethnic community, student readers initially identify with the feeling of being singled out in class on the basis of race. They understand that such attention is not intended as an insult, but nonetheless they feel both diminished by the stereotype and embarrassed by their anger. A student from Peru, for example, recalled her embarrassment when, expected to be able to translate poems by Puerto Rican or Mexican American writers, she had to refuse because of the differences in dialects.

The possibility of a positive image functioning as a stereotype, such as the happy, self-sacrificing slave depicted in literature written in the plantation tradition, is unfamiliar to some students. The concept of a "model minority" or a victim of "racist love," therefore, can be introduced through Walters's poem. Students interested in the racism implicit in positive stereotypes might then view a videotape of *Charlie Chan at the Opera* or the opening scenes of *Birth of a Nation* for instances of such stereotypes as applied to Asian and African Americans. (For an explanation of the "racist love" implicit in the portrayal of Chan, see Elaine Kim's *Asian American Literature.*) Women students of color are familiar with this problem in the form of "hating the kindness" intended in evaluative comments about their "exotic" appearance.

In "A Poem About Intelligence for My Brothers and Sisters," June Jordan hears of the theory that African Americans are, according to I.Q. tests, intellectually inferior:

> A few year back and they told me Black*
> means a hole where other folks
> got brain
> it was like the cells in the heads
> of Black children was out to every hour on the hour naps

Her self-confidence shaken by this pronouncement, she goes to Mrs. Johnson, an "old lady live on my block," to ask about the wisdom of Einstein, who is, she has been told, "the most the unquestionable the outstanding / the maximal mind of the century." Even as she interviews her neighbor, the speaker senses that, although Mrs. Johnson is also judging her, she is using different criteria for excellence:

---

*From the book *Naming Our Destiny* by June Jordan. Copyright © 1989 by June Jordan. Used by permission of the publisher, Thunder's Mouth Press.

> . . . she know I ain'
> combed my hair yet and here it is
> Sunday morning but still I have the nerve
> to be bothering serious work with these crazy
> questions . . .

Instead of acceptance and reassurance, Mrs. Johnson represents further evaluation. Perhaps because her confidence is shaken, the speaker believes Mrs. Johnson disapproves of both her unkempt appearance and her research.

CFS students compare Jordan's speaker's desire to find an audience that will reassure her with Walters's speaker's repeated retreats to the sympathetic community of "cousins and friends." In journals, they recall their difficulties in sharing with less-educated family members their frustrations during the early weeks of the summer program. If, for example, they have read excerpts from Gertrude Bonnin's autobiographical work, students easily recognize in Jordan's speaker the double alienation of minority students—their native culture undervalued at school and their educational goals misunderstood at home.

Students are especially sympathetic to the speaker-as-victim-of-corporal-punishment in Li-Young Lee's "Persimmons." His punishment, they point out, is singularly unsuited to his mistake and encourages neither social immersion nor the personal confidence necessary for language acquisition. I discuss linguistic differences with the students, the lack of distinction in some Asian languages between certain minimal pairs of sounds, and, although CFS students recognize the difficulty of preparing to teach language in a culturally diverse classroom, they prefer to write about the plight of Lee's student speaker who remembers,

> In sixth grade Mrs. Walker
> slapped the back of my head
> and made me stand in the corner
> for not knowing the difference
> between *persimmon* and *precision.*

They trace to this experience the student's lost confidence in his language skills: "Other words / that got me into trouble were *fight* and *fright, wren* and *yarn.*" The students also see the punishment as the reason behind the student speaker isolating himself from his peers rather than sharing his knowledge that the persimmon, brought by the teacher, is not ripe. "I didn't eat / but watched the other faces," says Lee; "Bravo!" say the CFS students.

Ostensibly a penalty for failing to learn vocabulary and applicable to the entire class, this type of punishment isolates students for whom English is a second language. Although CFS students whose first language is Spanish have seldom been confined to a corner, some had problems like those described by Richard Rodriguez in the often-anthologized autobiographical excerpt usually entitled "Aria: A Memoir of Bilingual Education"—problems such as social ostracism, trouble learning English, the stigma often attached to being in "special" English classes. They are predisposed to be receptive to the youthful Lee, the speaker in "Persimmons," having seen him interviewed in Bill Moyers's *Power of the Word* series. They respond well to this complex poem, writing journal entries about times when they felt they were standing apart or alone because of language differences. One student who consistently answered correctly in discussions and then just as consistently failed written quizzes volunteered, after reading this poem, that his grasp of conversational English was much better than his reading comprehension. Given permission to bring a dictionary, he immediately improved his quiz grades.

Another student described his frustration when writing: "I can think bigger than I can write in English." Others agreed that linguistic alienation is, alas, an inexplicable problem. One explained that she knew the material and could express it well, but that she earned low grades in "classroom participation" because, by the time she planned her answer, a classmate had given the correct response. A student who grew up in Puerto Rico spent an entire paragraph distinguishing between English and Spanish terms for "mama." The distinction seemed unrelated to her family-celebrations essay, until she explained that, like Lee, she had once been misunderstood when she failed to make such a distinction.

In addition to inspiring personal narratives about negative experiences, these poems also serve as the basis for short research projects. Wherever practical, these reports are scheduled for the day the poem is introduced. For Olivas's poem, a group researches the contributions of Hispanic American explorers, including both missionaries and settlers. Reports on the histories of other minorities are appropriate as well. For the Walters poem, students outline "what we did / to the American Indian." Before their peers read Jordan's "Poem," one group reports on current debates about I.Q. tests or on the reception of Jensen's theory.[4] (When one innovative group of CFS students surprised their classmates with a difficult quiz on African American history, the class resisted even more vehemently the notion that intelligence test scores can measure intellect.) Additionally, a report on the status of laws on bilingual education should enhance a class's interest in "Persimmons," as should a mock TV documentary in which characters from the poem recall the historical-cultural background of Asian Americans. Since students attend classes all day during the six-week session and attend tutorial sessions in the evening, library research is impractical, so many students rely on my files of relevant materials and, less often, on audiovisual programs borrowed from the media centers of a consortium of five local colleges.

Sedlacek's Variables: Minority Students as Experts

Without ignoring racism or underestimating its damage, students welcome the shift in focus from errors and abuses to resources and strengths. After they list in their journals experiences and traits that promote academic success for minorities by drawing on their own backgrounds, their own observations of actual students and of students in poems, and on informal interviews with other minority students, they work in groups to combine similar items and, where appropriate, group-related strategies as well as to name more inclusive categories. When prompted by their peers to think of additional traits, CFS students always find more variables than the eight identified by Sedlacek which are described in this section.

Sedlacek has published many articles on minorities in higher education in professional journals (see, for example, Sedlacek and Brooks). In the title essay of *Teaching Minority Students,* he lists eight noncognitive variables that have been tested for validity and reliability to be "relevant to the retention of minority students but not necessarily useful in the retention of nonminority students" (40).[5] He lists each variable and describes it fully. Four of the variables are self-referential. First, students with a "positive self-concept" can be recognized by their self-assurance, racial pride, and expectations for academic success. Second, a "realistic self-appraisal" enables minorities to recognize the need for extra study to make up for weaknesses in their academic backgrounds. Minorities don't always receive rewards appropriate to their efforts. This practice should, of course, be remedied by instructors, but students who are aware and "prefer long-range goals to short-term or immediate needs" can resist measuring their self-worth by the recognition they receive. Finally, graduation is more likely if the student has "nontraditional knowledge . . . defined as unusual or culturally related ways of obtaining information and demonstrating knowledge" (47).

In addition to these four ways of seeing one's self, Sedlacek identifies four variables or patterns for relating to others. First, those who "understand and deal with racism" decide to correct prejudice rather than accept it, but they also resist enervating bitterness and hatred. Success is more likely for students who recognize and cultivate a relationship with a "strong support person," one who will initiate contacts and, if asked, offer guidance. Minorities who can plan and organize activities for friends and whose opinions are valued by their associates have the requisite "leadership experience." Those who share their personal gains with others of their race and study their racial heritage have "demonstrated community service."

Small groups can combine students' lists with Sedlacek's. Since discussion follows the introduction of each item, however, I usually work with the entire class. (They realize immediately that, having completed their lists moments or, at most, days earlier, their groupings contain Sedlacek's variables. They claim credit for identifying the same variables, not by empirical study, but by instinct, recent experience, or their reading of poetry.)

I treasure this class period and hope to design similar activities for other units. While combining lists, students become partners with the authority, expand on the expert's outline, add his ideas to their lists, and rename variables to emphasize their perspective or experience.[6] Many list good study habits, for instance, or a strong high school background. These they now see as enabling students to "prefer long-term goals." Some who list good looks and money explain that these qualities contribute to a "positive self-concept"; others say that recognizing the connection between academic achievement and wealth or beauty leads to "understanding racism." A sense of humor, they add, helps minorities accept their "realistic self-appraisal" and to "deal with racism." On their own, students recognize the interrelatedness of variables and appreciate their distinctness. This exercise in academic synergism liberates and empowers students whose ethnic and linguistic backgrounds often determine their position in established text-teacher-student hierarchies.

More important, however, when the students return to the poems and reread them in light of their list of Sedlacek/CFS student variables, they approach the poems as teachers, as "challengers," and see each speaker as a potential "success." In preparation for writing essays about their reevaluation of the poems, students complete journals and include the names of peers whose contributions they will acknowledge in their essays. These early drafts of essays are usefully organized by poem or by trait. Thus, some students list all traits demonstrated by Jordan or by Lee. Others list poems describing students with "positive self-image[s]" or "preference[s] for long-term goals." First in groups and then in class discussion, they read their lists and, upon requests from their peers, refer to specific lines to show a variable.

The Students' Essays: The Variables and the Poetry

Directly applying Sedlacek's theory to the poems enriches class discussion and increases students' understanding of the literature. Specifically, after they match the poets' student speakers to predictive variables, CFS students analyze those responses, think critically about theory itself, look for literary strategies, and discover thematic unity in the poetry. While Sedlacek's terminology serves as a common vocabulary for discussing the literature, it is flexible enough to allow for different opinions about character.

Students who write about a single character elaborate on the meaning of specific variables. For example, although they agree that Olivas has a positive self-concept and an understanding of racism, individual CFS students suggest different causal connections. Writing about Olivas, José (in his 1991 CFS final exam) said, "The first skill he has is that he is aware of racism. . . . By [raising his hand] the boy shows a positive self identity, he is proud of what he is and how he has been formed and raised by his culture, so he is courageous enough to raise his hand." Mariano argued that Olivas "succeeds (overall) because of his realistic and positive self-image. That fact that he knows that he is a Chicano, makes h[i]m . . . become aware of his idenitty [sic]." Sophie reversed the usual causality: "Raising his hand and asking . . . made him realize that by learning and participating in an American school you were not losing ties with your country. By posing that question . . . [he] realized that he should be proud of who he is, instead of being afraid or ashamed." (As usual, the CFS students were the teachers and, with these papers in mind, I asked the next year's class whether Olivas raises his hand because he feels confident or whether he feels confident because he raises his hand!)

Although they are willing to attribute student success to noncognitive variables, CFS students continue to evaluate the worth of the strategies. For example, in "A Teacher Taught Me," Walters clearly prefers long-term goals, understanding racism long before she deals with it. When the teacher calls attention to her race, she says nothing but resolves silently to remember these words and "to give them / back to her one day." She waits while "eight years' worth / third graders heard her," not expressing her anger until she slaps a boy "in jr. hi." Some students credit Walters with savvy, as well as patience, since direct retaliation against the teacher would have been unwise. Others doubt her assertion that one slap "across freckled face" reforms the boy, so that he "finally sees." Instead, CFS students think she overestimates the impact of her action, that it will have the same effect as Mrs. Walker's slapping Lee, sending the boy to his friends with whom he will enjoy a good laugh. Others argue that Walters should have responded immediately—but verbally—to the teacher's affront, that, in this case, a preference for long-term goals looks much like complacency and resignation. (Those who have read "Battle Royal" compare Walters's student's response to that of Ellison's narrator.)

Sedlacek's approach, when applied to literary characters, leads students to diction, imagery, rhythm, and structure for evidence of variables. For instance, they recognize that mixing informal and formal diction enables Olivas to characterize a student as being both reluctant to learn and determined to teach, that his mixing of English—the language in which he is "almost napping"—and Spanish—in which he challenges the teacher's metaphor—shows a positive self-concept. They see that the refrain, the chanted promise to "save" words in her hand, in "A Teacher Taught Me," represents both the girl's recurring pain and her efforts to postpone her response until it will be more effective.

CFS students delight in the use of juxtaposition and line breaks to illustrate the speaker's criticism of racism in Jordan's poem. In the opening of the poem, Jordan has no proof against Jensen and modestly announces her intention to run an experiment:

> Scientists called the phenomenon
> the Notorious
> Jensen Lapse, remember?
> Anyway I was thinking
> about how to devise
> a test for the wise.

Even as she announces his theory and her plan, however, Jordan subtly but soundly refutes Jensen's theory since, his view notwithstanding, Jordan, assumed to have a "hole" instead of a brain, "was thinking." In another richly ambiguous construction, she tentatively accepts the theory of racial inferiority and, at the same time, lodges her complaint against those who support that theory:

> And I'm struggling against this lapse leftover
> from my Black childhood to fathom why
> anybody should say so:
> E = mc squared?

At first, the lapse she struggles against seems to be her own, an inherent intellectual deficiency that makes it impossible for her to understand the theories of either Jensen or Einstein. "Black," in this context, attributes that deficiency to race. CFS students find another lapse here, a lapse in compassion, sensitivity, and wisdom by anyone who would "say so," either to minority students or to colleagues. In this context, "Black" describes the mood or the level of enlightenment during Jordan's childhood, rather than her parents' ethnicity. Jordan's assertion seems at first to reveal her "realistic self-concept," but most students decide that she demonstrates a "positive self-image" and a creative way to "deal with racism." (Walters, like the boy in Countee Cullen's "Incident," struggles for years against someone else's "lapse leftover.")

In essays identifying strong support figures, students focus on "A Teacher Taught Me," "A Poem about Intelligence," and "Persimmons." In "A Teacher," the similarity between the teacher's "pretty little Indian girl" and the boy's "squaw, squaw, squaw" point to their similar mindset and to the theme that racism is taught and learned. Walters's student's "positive self- image" and "strong support person" help her to withstand the insensitivity rooted in racism, her cousins and friends offering both empathy and support. In Jordan's poem, the speaker and Mrs. Johnson ultimately work together to measure Einstein against such cultural values as concern for personal appearance, community service, and hospitality. Mrs. Johnson's judgment, then, becomes evidence of the speaker's sensitivity to her mentor's every gesture. Lee's mentors range from his lover, Donna, to his mother, who made "wrens" from "yarn," to his blind father, who teaches him to see. Students repeatedly point out the skills required to benefit from the availability of these mentors and guides.

In some cases, the terminology helps a student identify a theme, which then generates further thought and writing. One CFS student, for example, identified community service and a support person in "Persimmons," but implied that it is the underlying morality of these people, not simply their presence, that promotes the success of the main character: "Li-Young Lee is a successful minority character because he has a strong support group," wrote Antonio. "His father is a strong representative of the straight and narrow. In his poem 'Persimmons' the author knows what is right as far as that the persimmon that the teacher brings in is not ripe." This CFS student did not develop the intriguing equation of ripeness and rightness. He did, however, discover the speaker's debt to a strong support person and identified the nontraditional knowledge offered. He identifies the father as a model for the speaker's self-confidence and as a guide for his refusal to internalize the teacher's misprizing of his intellect.

Longer prose readings would enrich a full-semester course. For example, chapters about school in Rudolfo Anaya's *Bless Me, Ultima* depict the Hispanic student's realistic self-appraisal, and Ultima epitomizes a strong support person. "Theme for English B" by Langston Hughes shows a positive self-concept comparable to that in "[I'm Sitting in My History Class]" and nontraditional knowledge similar to that in "Persimmons." In Ralph Ellison's "Battle Royal," in which the pursuit of education becomes a driving purpose, the narrator's preference for the long-range goal of giving his speech enables him to endure a series of racial slurs. Garrett Hongo's "And the Soul Shall Dance" juxtaposes sexual awakening in adolescence with personal awakening to racial identity, not unlike that experienced by Olivas. Antler's "I Raise My Hand" suggests a follow-up to Olivas's poem. In Toni Cade Bambara's "The Lesson," Miss Moore, a teacher, exemplifies Sedlacek's "support person" who subtly nurtures the variables in her reluctant students.

Paper topics on specific readings are implicit in the earlier discussion of student responses. Assignments with specified audiences, whose names students find in the university catalog, are particularly successful. For a review committee of the Student Forum, students defend Walters for fighting in school. For a professor in the social sciences, they paraphrase Jordan's poem and describe her experiment—the test she devises for the CIA. For a skeptical teacher, who judges these students to be troublemakers and wants to forbid them from attending classes, students enumerate forms of the speakers' nontraditional knowledge and suggest other ways to respond to them.

Most successful is the assignment to endorse one of these speakers for admission to the college. In this assignment, each has low SAT scores and lower high school grades, and each has submitted the poem as an entrance essay; however, only one student will be admitted on an experimental basis. The student essayists must recommend one, justifying the waiving of traditional requirements, identifying noncognitive variables, and predicting academic success.

Other assignments may be used to vary the length and form of responses. For a counselor's case study, students may analyze one variable as it is manifest in a student in each poem. On recommendation forms, students may predict the success of these students to those individuals who award scholarships. In an advice column, students may adopt the voice of one of the characters and advise the other three on how to deal with racism. In a pamphlet to be distributed to Mrs. Walker et al., a student may offer guidelines to teachers who want to help minority students. Following Jordan's plan to "devise / a test for the wise," students may suggest a test of noncognitive variables to be used by guidance counselors when recommending high school graduates. Next summer, I will ask students to respond to these lines from Lonny Kaneko's "Rooms": "Dignity can rise from dust / but not of its own accord." For one or more poems, students will describe the "dust" and the "dignity," the realistic self-appraisal and the positive self-image. They will describe who or what transforms dust into dignity. When they read these poems, students, at first, identify the racism and the poems' speakers' limitations.

When they reread them, they find strategies for dealing with racism, examples of positive self-image, and incidences of meetings with strong support persons. Some see poetry writing as a "nontraditional" skill, one they try themselves as a way to discover personal resources. All become better prepared for the academic Challenge for Success.

Notes

1. Unless otherwise noted, the assigned and optional readings are anthologized in Beaty and Hunter. June Jordan's "A Poem About Intelligence for My Brothers and Sisters" appears in Abcarian and Klotz (833–35). Anne Lee Walters's "A Teacher Taught Me" appears in Fisher (109–10).

2. The teachers in these poems are not typical and are not presented as representative educators. In addition to presenting students with opportunities to discuss "personal" experiences, these poems also attract student readers because, as professor of education Robert Mayer notes, "Kids love to hear about jerky teachers."

3. These poems are narrated by a speaker who is a student who may also be the poet. In class, unless they are certain the poem is autobiographical, CFS students refer to the "narrator" or to the "speaker." In this essay, how-

ever, when necessary to avoid confusion, I equate the "student speaker" with the poets.

4. For a summary of the reception of Jensen's work, see Ogbu (54–65).

5. All references to Sedlacek are from his "Teaching Minority Students."

6. This unit is useful in overcoming the assumption that "personal" essays are "private" essays and that academic writing is a collection of quotations. In "I Stand Here Writing," Nancy Sommers describes the goal: "Being personal means bringing their own judgments and interpretation to bear on what they read and write, learning that they never leave themselves behind even when they write academic essays" (425).

Works Cited

Beaty, Jerome, and J. Paul Hunter, eds. *New Worlds of Literature.* New York: Norton, 1989.

Jordan, June. "A Poem About Intelligence for My Brothers and Sisters." *Literature: The Human Experience.* 3rd ed. Ed. Richard Abcarian and Marvin Klotz. New York: St. Martin's, 1982. 833–35.

Kaneko, Lonny. "Rooms." *Coming Home from Camp.* Waldron Island, WA: Brooding Heron, 1986.

Kim, Elaine H. *Asian American Literature: An Introduction to the Writings and Their Social Context.* Philadelphia: Temple UP, 1982.

Lee, Li-Young. "Persimmons." In Beaty and Hunter, 511–13.

Mayer, Robert. Personal interview. Moravian College, Bethlehem, Pennsylvania. 4 October 1993.

Ogbu, John U. *Minority Education and Caste: The American System in Cross-Cultural Perspective.* New York: Academic, 1978.

Olivas, Richard. "[I'm Sitting in My History Class]." In Beaty and Hunter, 350.

Rodriguez, Richard. "Aria." *Hunger of Memory: The Education of Richard Rodriguez.* Boston: Godine, 1982. 19–40.

Sedlacek, William E. "Teaching Minority Students." *Teaching Minority Students.* Ed. James H. Cones, John F. Noonan, and Denise Janha. San Francisco: Jossey-Bass, 1983. 39–50.

———, and Glenwood C. Brooks, Jr. *Racism in American Education: A Model for Change.* Chicago: Nelson-Hall, 1976.

Sommers, Nancy. "I Stand Here Writing." *College English* 55.4 (April 1993): 420–28.

Walters, Anne Lee. "A Teacher Taught Me." *The Third Woman: Minority Women Writers of the United States.* Ed. Dexter Fisher. Boston: Houghton, 1980. 109–10.

17 Caribbean Literature as Catalyst in the Composition Classroom

Keith Gilyard
Medgar Evers College, CUNY

June D. Bobb
Queens College, CUNY

Joyce Harte
Borough of Manhattan Community College, CUNY

In the words of the Caribbean poet and Nobel laureate, Derek Walcott, "to have loved one horizon is insularity; / it blindfolds vision, it narrows experience" (79). More and more, today's freshman composition classrooms have become increasingly multicultural. Students from Haiti and Trinidad, Russia and Greece engage in dialogue with black and white American students. In the multicultural world of the classroom, it becomes the responsibility of the teacher of English to lure students away from "insularity" and encourage them to identify similarities of vision as they read and write about other experiences which are sometimes alien to their own cultures. This mutual sharing and entering into others' visionary worlds form a fundamental basis of cultural awareness and often inspire student writers to embark on their own journeys of discovery. In exploring the cultural heritage of others, student writers discover the strength of their own, and the "other" becomes familiar. As Geertz puts it: "Understanding a people's culture exposes their normalness without reducing their particularity. . . . It renders them accessible" (14).

To achieve this accessibility in our composition classrooms, students are introduced to readings in Caribbean literature—for literature exposes the student reader to this culture with an immediacy and a concreteness which cannot otherwise be duplicated. Our students' thirst for cultural identity is reflected in Paule Marshall's autobiographical essay, "From the Poets in the Kitchen." A native-born American of Barbadian parents, she writes:

> What I needed, what all the kids—West Indians and native black Americans alike—with whom I grew up needed, was an equivalent of the Jewish shul, someplace where we could go after school—the schools that were shortchanging us—and read works by those like ourselves and learn about our history. (11)

We often focus first upon the autobiographical voice because beginning students come to formal writing activities with a sense of themselves, the meaning of their own lives, and the desire to tell their stories. The first few weeks of the semester are spent exploring the autobiographical voice and learning narrative strategies. Readings are taken from such novels as Zee Edgell's *Beka Lamb* (Belize), Merle Hodge's *Crick Crack, Monkey* (Trinidad), and Jamaica Kincaid's *Annie John* (Antigua). (Students can build upon successes they achieve in the narrative mode by applying the same strategies to expository tasks.) By reading these selections, they come to realize what all good writers know: the more clearly you can conceive of a writing assignment as a personal statement, the better off you are.

In Kincaid's novel, there is an elusive grandmother who achieves mythic proportions. The following excerpt comes at the point when Annie John, the heroine, is seriously and strangely ill, and her grandmother, who lives on another island, comes to see about her—on a day when no steamer is due:

> When Ma Chess [the grandmother] leaned over me, she smelled of many different things, all of them even more abominable than the black sachet Ma Jolie [the local obeah woman] pinned to my nightie. . . . Ma Chess never took a bath in just plain water and soap. She took a bath once a month or so, in water in which things animal and vegetable had been boiled for a long time. Before she took this bath, she first swam in the sea. . . . Sometimes at night, when I would feel that I was all locked in the warm falling soot and could not find my way out, Ma Chess would come into my bed with me and stay until I was myself. . . . I would lie on my side, curled up like a little comma, and Ma Chess would lie next to me, curled up like a bigger comma, into which I fit. (123–26)

Strictly urban students approach this passage with much puzzlement and skepticism. But some students from the Caribbean, the southern United States, and Latin America, well-versed in the ways of santeria, voodoo, obeah, and conjure, are not at all taken aback; rather, they share their own experiences and stories with much enthusiasm.

Beyond generating vibrant discussions of content, these readings enable students to see narrative and descriptive techniques at work. For example, students become aware of the handling of chronology, the use of dialogue, and the appeal to the senses that are at the heart of description. Students also consider word selectivity, sentence sense, and overall organization. We focus on the richness of Kincaid's imaginary world by exploring the fictional elements she utilizes, such as her use of language and symbol. For example, we discuss her image of interlocking commas to illustrate the depth of connectedness between grandmother and granddaughter.

As a response to this literary selection and the classroom activities which surround it, students are asked to describe the oldest person who has influenced their lives and to re-create this person's world. The following are excerpts from students' first drafts:

1a

My grandmother's room was a hiding place or a secret room. Most of the time we were playing different games. She always told me what life is about and gave me examples from her own hard life. She made me understand and recognize the different faces of life. At night we sat together. At times there was a silence between us. I respected that silence.

2a

My grandmother touched people. She is no longer an exuberant woman. She is an aging woman looking back on her life.

3a

Memories of my grandmother enter my thoughts. I remember watching her sitting in her chair. She was very patient. She wore bright colored dresses, and at times the flowers on her dress seemed to come alive.

To demonstrate the importance of the process of revision, we return to the Kincaid selection, where the students are encouraged to see how the expansion of details and the use of imagery can enhance their own autobiographical worlds. Next, they experiment with the use of details and figurative language to clarify and enrich their own writing. The following passages illustrate this process of revision:

1b

My grandmother's room was a hiding place and a secret room. Here, out of sight, she kept the sacred things of her voodoo religion. Her life was very hard. Her parents died when she was ten years old, and she lived with an aunt who put her to work on a farm. Sometimes at night doing nothing we sit on the balcony of her room admiring the stars in the sky. Sometimes there is a silence between us, and we can hear the howling of the dogs. In the silence, I think she is thinking of her hard past life.

2b

My grandmother is no longer that exuberant woman who strode with the pace of a huntress, but an aging woman capable of looking back on thirty million things started and accomplished.

3b

Memories of my grandmother enter my thoughts with the singing of birds on a warm spring day. She loved birds. I remember watching her sitting in her rocking chair sewing a beautiful quilt. She collected pieces from everybody's old clothes. She would sit and sew with the patience of a saint. My grandmother always wore brightly colored flowered dresses, and at times the flowers on her dress seemed to come alive surrounding her with the faint scent of roses. Even on the most frigid winter days, she was like tall grass flowing in a warm breeze.

In the revised versions, the students not only expand their texts, but they capture the magic of the specific word and take chances with simile and metaphor. When the revised versions of students' papers are shared publicly, students naturally comment on the differences between the original and the revised versions, and compliment each other's work. Attention is then paid to grammar and mechanics.

Sometimes, as the journal entry below indicates, student autobiography gestures toward critique by means of evaluation and contrast:

4

As I read the book *Annie John* I became jealous of Annie at a certain point because of the mere fact that Annie was an only child who lived with her parents, and she had nothing to do except to feed birds and pigs. She even had her choice in the likes and dislikes of the food she ate. I remember my life as a child was filled with company. I had five sisters and three brothers, and I had a whole lot of household chores, such as bringing water in a container from a nearby standpipe that I would carry on my head cleaning the yard, doing the laundries and even cooking. Food was something we could not make choices on because, whenever it was eating time we were so hungry that we liked everything we ate.

To facilitate further movement from the autobiographical voice to the analytical voice, students read from such books as Simone Schwarz-Bart's *The Bridge of Beyond* (Guadeloupe), George Lamming's *In the Castle of My Skin* (Barbados), Earl Lovelace's *The Wine of Astonishment* (Trinidad), and Jacques Roumain's *Masters of the Dew* (Haiti). In writing about these works, students are encouraged to move away from storytelling and are expected to discuss specific characters, situations, or themes. To make this concrete, exercises are done involving writing summaries and reaction pieces and examining the differences between them.

Students eventually produce responses, such as the following:

5

There is a famous saying among the people of my country, Afghanistan, that man is softer than a flower and harder than a stone. In the meanders of life, he encounters hurricanes and breezes. Sometimes he has the power to resist the hurricane while at other times he will fall with a small breeze. Telumee, in *The Bridge of Beyond,* encounters happiness and sadness in her lifetime. Her first love leaves her; her second love dies; she is forced to work alone in the cane fields. She works for whites, the descendants of those who had once beaten and sold her ancestors. But with all of that she still resists life and continues to live. At the last hours of her life as she is waiting for death, she says: "As I struggled others will struggle, and for a long time yet people will know the same sun and the moon; they will look at the same stars. . . ."

6

In *The Bridge of Beyond* part of Telumee's life was the fact of slavery. Slavery was not a part of her present life but it still haunted her old age. She could not stop thinking about it. She saw herself in place of those who had been slaves. She felt that slavery had still been killing people silently: "I think of the injustice in the world, and all of us suffering and dying silently of slavery after it is finished and forgotten" (169). Telumee is a slave in many ways. She was a slave to the harsh land that didn't produce enough for her to survive; she was a slave to her first husband who had an affair with another woman which sent her mad. She was a slave in a world which didn't give women the independence they wanted. Telumee described her life in this way: "As I struggle others will struggle, and for a long time yet people will know the same sun and moon; they will look at the same stars. . . ." Women today are looking at the same stars.

Some instructors may prefer, as we ourselves have done on occasion, to utilize shorter, self-contained selections that can be read very quickly in class. Fortunately, there is an excellent body of work from which to choose. For example, Paule Marshall's "To Da-duh, In Memoriam" proves stimulating. Both a story of her trip to Barbados when she was nine years old and a tribute to her grandmother, this is the most autobiographical of Marshall's short works and is a rich exploration of cultural continuities and discontinuities. Karl Sealy's "The Sun Was a Slaver" treats similar themes. Ruth, her stance toward her grandpa and her ringing the bell upon his death, can be readily discussed in connection with Da-duh and her granddaughter.

Hazel Campbell's "See Me in Me Benz and T'ing," a wonderfully compact story set in 1970s Jamaica, illustrates the decadence of the privileged and the resentment of the masses toward the privileged class. It highlights the conflict generated by their respective value systems. Edgar Mittelholzer's "Sorrow Dam and Mister Millbank," set in Guyana, is another story about class conflict which students enjoy.

Because of its clarity and conciseness, Michael Anthony's prose is always an excellent choice. Sure to spark fruitful discussion is "Drunkard of the River," which raises questions concerning family relationships. "The Day of the Fearless," another work by Anthony, is a portrait of a young man trapped in a role from which there is virtually no escape. Both stories unfold in Trinidad. Students relate readily to such stories, seeing in the characters' struggles many of the same conflicts that surface in their own lives. Students write initially in response journals, and this material is eventually utilized in both their narrative and expository essays, thus facilitating their movement from personal narrative to expository writing.

Caribbean literature is a valuable resource for all students in multicultural composition classes. The use of such texts not only provides validation of the collective identity of the Caribbean student population, but it also exposes all students to a literature that lures them away from insularity toward a broader cultural awareness.

Works Cited

Anthony, Michael. "The Day of the Fearless." *Cricket in the Road.* London: Deutsch, 1973. 60–65.

———. "Drunkard of the River." *Cricket in the Road.* London: Deutsch, 1973. 54–59.

Campbell, Hazel. "See Me in Me Benz and T'ing." *West Indian Stories.* Ed. John Wickham. London: Ward Lock, 1981. 129–36.

Edgell, Zee. *Beka Lamb.* London: Heinemann, 1982.

Geertz, Clifford. *The Interpretation of Cultures.* New York: Basic, 1973.

Gray, Cecil. *Images.* Kingston: Nelson, 1973.

Hodge, Merle. *Crick Crack, Monkey.* London: Heinemann, 1970.

Kincaid, Jamaica. *Annie John.* New York: Farrar, 1983.

Lamming, George. *In the Castle of My Skin.* New York: Collier, 1953.

Lovelace, Earl. *The Wine of Astonishment.* New York: Vintage, 1984.

Marshall, Paule. "To Da-duh, In Memorium." *Reena and Other Stories.* Old Westbury, NY: Feminist, 1983. 93–106.

———. "From the Poets in the Kitchen." *Reena and Other Stories.* Old Westbury, NY: Feminist, 1983. 1–12.

Mittelholzer, Edgar. "Sorrow Dam and Mister Millbank." *Images.* Ed. Cecil Gray. Kingston: Nelson, 1973. 134–39.

Roumain, Jacques. *Masters of the Dew.* London: Heinemann, 1982.

Sealy, Karl. "The Sun Was a Slaver." *Images.* Ed. Cecil Gray. Kingston: Nelson, 1973. 171–74.

Schwarz-Bart, Simone. *The Bridge of Beyond.* London: Heinemann, 1982.

Walcott, Derek. *The Arkansas Testament.* New York: Farrar, 1987.

18 A Fiesta of Voices: Regional Literature in the Multicultural Classroom

Jeffrey Laing
Sante Fe Preparatory School, Santa Fe, New Mexico

Regional literature courses are most often the poor stepchildren of community college English departments. They are frequently perceived by administrators as unnecessary frills which undermine the FTE average and are offered only when budgets are more generous and when individual instructors persist in their demands. It is my experience, however, that regional literature courses provide an opportunity for multitalented, multicultural classes to tap already existing interests and then to develop academic skills that will benefit both the traditional and nontraditional community college learner. Furthermore, the heightened confidence and self-esteem of my regional literature students suggest that such courses should be an integral part of language arts programs. Using my experience with the development of English 270: "Contemporary Southwest Literature," I will share some thoughts on the functions and applications of regional literature in the multicultural classroom.

New Mexico community colleges have an especially varied student population. The state legislature has mandated an open admissions policy—any state resident eighteen years of age or older may attend classes—which is further complicated by the tricultural population mix—Native American, Hispanic, and Anglo (everyone else)—of northern New Mexico. My situation in the mid-1980s was a daunting, even schizophrenic one.

I was teaching English at the University of New Mexico–Los Alamos and at Santa Fe Community College. These institutions are within forty miles of one another, but they are radically different in student background, academic preparation, and career goals. The typical Los Alamos student is a middle- to upper-middle-class spouse of an employee at the Los Alamos National Laboratory; this student is usually of Anglo, East Asian, or Hispanic background and educated in an urban public or private school; the student has some postsecondary school education, with some students already possessing associate or bachelor's degrees; and the student is usually an ardently conservative Republican who is most likely working on a math or science degree or simply taking courses out of personal interest.

The representative Santa Fe student, on the other hand, is a lower-middle- to middle-class woman and single parent; this student is most often Hispanic and educated in a rural or small town public school; the student is usually beginning postsecondary school education or returning to complete a community college degree; and this student is quite often a progressive Democrat who is working within a wide range of academic and vocational programs.

I had a simple educational goal that seemed impossible to achieve: to develop a program that would speak to the needs and interests of my widely different student populations without sacrificing intellectual content or academic rigor. It is axiomatic that all Americans patronize the same films, televisions shows, and mass-market paperbacks. My goal, then, was to take this cultural given and develop a defensible academic course that would possess the same recognizable and accessible subject materials for my students as do popular literature forms and that would accommodate the varied experiences of my students.

English 270 was and continues to be an experiment. Trying to balance social, psychological, and academic concerns, I established minimal criteria for the selection of class materials. Works had to be set in the Southwest, preferably in New Mexico, and whenever possible, had to reflect the region's tricultural activities and concerns. More important, works had to be sensitive to the beliefs and politics of my students while simultaneously challenging these beliefs, and they had to be accessible in both form and content to any student who might elect to take this course. While English 270 follows sequentially the exit composition course and is a class that students are encouraged to take for honors credit, it is my philosophy as well as that of both colleges that any student who demonstrates an interest in English 270 may take this class. With this final qualification in mind, I structured my course on works of all genres that deal with characters in conflict, possess regional environmental detail(s), and raise pertinent social and/or moral questions.

The classroom activities in English 270 are varied. Since my primary interest is to create an atmosphere of trust and experimentation, I do little or no lecturing. Whenever pertinent background information is necessary, as in the case of some regional historical overview to place the literature to be studied in context, I provide photocopied handouts and arrange guest speakers from other academic disciplines. Adrian Bustamante, Santa Fe Community College's Dean of Arts and Sciences and a noted New Mexico historian, is a frequent early visitor to my English 270 sections. Most classes involve three activities: large-group questions and analysis in order to frame reader-response, written work in student journals, and small-group discussion of the literature. Early in the semester, students are reluctant to enter small groups; ironically, they are most comfortable with the teacher-presentation method they often found of little value in their previous academic careers. I generally make up the groups, trusting to early observation the formation of groups balanced among talkers, observers, peacemakers, fighters, and politicians. I do look to ensure that groups are composed of both men and women. By the end of the semester, the small groups usually achieve some degree of cohesiveness, and this is generally noted as the most satisfying part of the course in students' evaluations.

A typical class might be organized as follows: I distribute copies of Jan Morris's "Capital of the Holy Faith, Santa Fe, New Mexico" after reading Richard Bradford's *Red Sky at Morning.* I then ask students to write in their journals, discussing whether or not Morris's portrayal of Santa Fe is a fair and accurate one. I want the students to write expressively and to ignore any mere analysis of the piece. Then, armed with their observations, I ask them to meet in their groups to compare Bradford's Santa Fe with Morris's. The individual small groups then report back to the class at large or, depending on the question or class make-up, a free-wheeling, large-group discussion takes place. In these situations, I act only as a facilitator. I want the students to gain confidence in writing, speaking, and listening. Traditional literary analysis is begun only at midsemester (and sometimes even later) when students have experience in thinking and expressing themselves about literature. Intellectual rigor is not forsworn in this course. Students are continually being asked to challenge their definitions of meaningful southwestern literature and to build small-group and class consensus on the question of whether or not—and to what degree—southwestern literature is purely regional in influence or part of a larger canon of American literature.

Student evaluation is based on rather traditional criteria: student attendance and class participation (oral and written); essay tests in which short works by lesser-known authors or obscure pieces by more noted authors are read, summarized, analyzed, and, in the later part of the semester, related to the major themes of the course; and three major projects, two of which will be traditional papers of classic rhetorical types, for example, a critique and a comparison-contrast paper. The last major project must involve some student outreach to the immediate community and its rich cultural and literary heritage. Students generally work extremely hard on this project and have often demonstrated grit and initiative far beyond my expectations. Some of the most noteworthy of these projects (but by no means is this list exhaustive) are as follows:

1. Students have conducted telephone interviews with such northern New Mexico authors as Jim Sagel, Luci Tapahonso, Richard Bradford, Joy Harjo, and John Nichols. In one instance, Nichols gave a reading to the entire class at the request of a student.

2. Students have rewritten classic southwestern texts to reflect current social conditions and concerns after contacting the appropriate social agencies for information to justify their rewriting. One clever student updated Calamity Jane's *Letters to Her Daughter* from the perspective of a troubled, feminist single parent.

3. Students have compared actual and fictional descriptions of a place. One student took current photographs of the Santa Fe Plaza and then went to the New Mexico Photo Archives and had early photos of the same Plaza reproduced. The student then compared the photos from the 1940s and 1950s to the literary descriptions of the Plaza of the same time frame in Richard Bradford's work.

4. Students have visited area museums to critique the content and social importance of a particular exhibit. The contemporary southwestern art at the Museum of Fine Art and the traditional Native American exhibits at the Wheelwright Museum yielded some illuminating and thought-provoking work.

5. Students have explored the Anglo, Hispanic, and Native American music of a particular time period for similarities and differences. One talented individual used guitar and recorder to compare and contrast nineteenth-century pieces.

6. Students have visited literary and historical places of note and come up with their own theses. One student visited New

> Mexico ghost towns and, after documenting his trip, wrote a
> long poem that evoked the feel of the places. Another indus-
> trious student spent a few days in Taos, following in the foot-
> steps of D. H. Lawrence and speculating on how the village
> influenced the author's New Mexico work.

All of the student projects are not as successful or as thoughtful as
those listed above, but students do participate in the spirit of the program and find the assignment more challenging and enjoyable than
the usual literature course fare.

I have been pleased that, in English 270, theory and practice do
coalesce. The class does provide the reassurance and psychological coherence that mirror the popular mass-market genres. For instance, students possess a great deal of practical knowledge about geography
and, in many cases, actions and rituals of characters in this regional literature course. Thus, they feel competent to readily engage in discussions of course materials in ways that a course in Renaissance drama
could not duplicate. With increased self-esteem, students can better
master the technical and critical-thinking skills required of them in
their community college programs. One recent student, a perennial
composition course dropout, became so involved in English 270 that,
after passing that course, he retook the basic composition course he
had never completed and passed with a more than acceptable grade.

Students' fears of "great" literature and their preconceived notions of how difficult and/or "boring" it might be are eliminated in
English 270. Since the works studied are set in New Mexico locales no
farther than a four-hour drive for students, and since the characters
and action are seemingly the students' "own," they are more quickly
and more directly engaged during the semester. As with popular literature forms which generate patterns, stories, and symbols that are psy-
chologically reassuring to a wide and diverse audience, southwestern
literature provides my students with accessible and recognizable
forms that allow for a fuller and more complete understanding of the
course materials and more confidence in students to express their individual observations and questions. For example, my Native American
students immediately understand Tayo's plight in Leslie Marmon Silko's *Ceremony*. They, too, must determine to what degree they will embrace a traditional culture that no longer seems able to sustain them.
The buzzword of the late sixties was "socially relevant" course materials, and these kinds of materials are precisely the core of English 270.
Students will frequently vent their own psychological tensions and
frustrations when dealing with contemporary southwestern literature.

One angry male identified with the main character in Ortiz's "Killing of a State Cop"; after a heated monologue on society's injustices, this student, with the sensitive aid of his small group, realized he also identified with the main character in Silko's "Uncle Tony's Goat," who harnesses his anger with humor and success.

In my opening paragraphs I make much of the differences between my Los Alamos and Santa Fe student populations. There are, of course, differences in the focus and style of both groups. However, I am most struck by how both groups respond to English 270. For all my students, this regional literature course builds interest and confidence and seems to be a solid predictor for future academic success. English 270 excites the individual student's memory and imagination, urging him or her to discover what is valuable personally in the community. As they experience their different actual and "fictional" Southwests, my English 270 students, whether from Los Alamos or Santa Fe or Espanola or Wagon Mound, are forced to confront the other, as they do in their daily lives, and to reconsider their own philosophical and political positions. English 270 works.

The academic and social goals achieved in English 270 are applicable to other regional literature courses. (While living in New York City, I taught a course in immigrant literature with similar results.) Working from an inherent interest in the works studied, students sharpen their critical-thinking skills by reading, discussing, and writing about the thought and artistic achievement of regional authors. Equally important, along with increased academic self-esteem, students seem to be positively affected in their discernible attitude and behavior toward their fellow students. In a most significant way, then, regional literature courses become emblematic of the goal of a liberal education: Students become aware of and are encouraged to express differences in historical, cultural, ethnic, and even personal realities while simultaneously challenging the primacy of any and all categorical positions.

A Representative English 270 ("Contemporary Southwest Literature") Bibliography

The basic structure of English 270 is thematic, with a focus on works that reflect the region's tricultural nature and the resultant conflicts among Native American, Hispanic, and Anglo peoples. Four influential novels serve to introduce and investigate the major themes, with at least five other full-length works being used to reinforce and extend the focus introduced in the influential novels. Poetry, short fiction, and nonfiction are used weekly to provide both variety and entry into the major works.

Primary Texts

Anaya, Rudolfo. *Bless Me, Ultima.* New York: Warner, 1972.

> This is a first-person *Bildungsroman* narrated by seven-year-old Antonio Mares, who lives with his large Hispanic family in Guadalupe (Santa Rosa). Set in northern New Mexico in the 1950s, this work chronicles Tony's struggle for self-identity, personally and socially, in a changing, threatening environment. In this work of myth, naturalism, and imagination, Tony comes to an awareness of himself in relation to his family, his community, and his future through the moral guidance of a natural healer, Ultima.

Bradford, Richard. *Red Sky at Morning.* New York: Harper, 1968.

> This is another first-person *Bildungsroman* narrated by teenager Josh Arnold, a Southerner transplanted to Sagrado (Santa Fe) during World War II. Comically bittersweet in tone, Josh's narrative is a coming-of-age story in tricultural New Mexico.

Nichols, John. *The Milagro Beanfield War.* New York: Holt, 1974.

> This meandering, episodic tale of northern New Mexico in the village Milagro (Taos) tells of how an unforgettable group of Hispanic and Anglo eccentrics, who are usually at each other's throats, band together to defeat the seemingly unbeatable forces of entrenched political power and land-development capitalism. This comic work serves as a coda for the course in that reconciliation and mutual understanding among peoples are shown to be attainable.

Silko, Leslie Marmon. *Ceremony.* New York: Viking, 1977.

> This is a story of a Native American war veteran, Tayo, of New Laguna (Acoma Pueblo), New Mexico, who remains locked in continual combat with himself and his culture. Using the healing powers of his people's rituals and myths, Tayo breaks the cycle of self-hate and violence that was destroying him and the very harmony of his Native American world.

The following lists of full-length works, short fiction, poetry, and nonfiction are of necessity brief and highly selective. All selections are based on my own experience in the classroom and any biases or limitations revealed are my own and are unintended and nonpolitical in nature. The abbreviations NA (Native American), H (Hispanic), and A (Anglo) placed after a work reflect the major focus of the work and, frequently, the ethnicity of the author.

Full-Length Works

Abbey, Edward. *The Brave Cowboy.* New York: Dodd, 1956. [A]

Blacker, Irwin. *Taos.* Cleveland: World, 1959. [H & NA]

Cather, Willa. *Death Comes for the Archbishop.* New York: Knopf, 1945. [H & A]

Church, Peggy Pond. *The House at Otowi Bridge.* Albuquerque: U of New Mexico P, 1960. [A]

Cleaveland, Agnes Morley. *No Life for a Lady.* Santa Fe, NM: Gannon, 1976 [c. 1941]. [A]

Eastlake, William. *The Bronc People.* New York: Harcourt, 1958. [NA]

Fergusson, Harvey. *Grant of Kingdom.* Albuquerque: U of New Mexico P, 1975 [c. 1950]. [H]

Hillerman, Tony. *Dance Hall of the Dead.* New York: Harper, 1973. [NA]

Momaday, N. Scott. *House Made of Dawn.* New York: Harper, 1977. [NA]

Otis, Raymond. *Miguel of the Bright Mountain.* Albuquerque: U of New Mexico P, 1977. [H]

Waters, Frank. *The Man Who Killed the Deer.* Chicago: Sage, 1970. [NA]

[The Church and Cleaveland works are memoirs; all the rest are novels.]

Short Fiction

Apple, Max. "Research." *Harper's* 274 (January 1987): 66–71. [A]

Erdrich, Louise. "The Red Convertible." *Love Medicine.* New York: Holt, 1984. 143–54. [NA]

Ortiz, Simon. "The Killing of a State Cop." *The Man to Send Rain Clouds: Contemporary Stories by American Indians.* Ed. Kenneth Rosen. New York: Vintage, 1974. 101–8.

Sagel, Jim. "Tunomás Honey," "El Lupito," and "Whistling." *Tunomás Honey.* Ypsilanti, MI: Bilingual, 1988. 10–17, 48–55, 119–28. [H]

Silko, Leslie Marmon. "Yellow Woman," "Uncle Tony's Goat," and "The Man to Send Rain Clouds." *Storyteller.* New York: Little, Brown, 1981. 54–62, 171–76, 182–86. [NA]

Tapahonso, Luci. "The Snakeman." *Sáanii Dahataal: The Women Are Singing.* Tucson: U of Arizona P, 1993. 73–83. [NA]

Ulibarri, Sabine. "My Wonder Horse." *Voces: An Anthology of Nuevo Mexican Authors.* Ed. Rudolfo Anaya. Albuquerque: U of New Mexico P, 1979. 1–6. [H]

[All of these works reveal characters at war with themselves, their cultures, and/or society as a whole. Silko is the acknowledged master here. Sagel's work is unique in that he frequently writes in both an idiomatic New Mexican Spanish dialect and English in facing texts. See, for example, Sagel, Jim. *On the Make Again/Vez en La Movida.* Albuquerque, NM: West End, 1990.]

Poetry

Baca, Jimmy Santiago. "Meditations on the South Valley." *Martin and Meditations on the South Valley.* New York: New Directions, 1987. 51–100. [H]

Chavez, Fray Angelico. "Sangre de Cristo Range." *Selected Poems.* Santa Fe, NM: Press of the Territorian, 1969. n.p. [H]

Church, Peggy Pond. "Black Mesa: Dream and Variation." *Birds of Daybreak.* Santa Fe, NM: Gannon, 1985. 15–18. [A]

Cohoe, Gary. "Tocito Visions." *The Remembered Earth: An Anthology of Contemporary Native American Literature.* Ed. Geary Hobson. Albuquerque: U of New Mexico P, 1979. 312–14. [NA]

Littlebird, Harold. "Old Man for His People." *On Mountains' Breath.* Santa Fe, NM: Tooth of Time, 1982. n.p. [NA]

Mares, E. A. "Once a Man Knew His Name." *Voces: An Anthology of Nuevo Mexican Authors.* Ed. Rudolfo Anaya. Albuquerque: U of New Mexico P, 1979. 100–3. [H]

Ortiz, Simon. "Telling about Coyote." *A Good Journey.* Tucson: Sun Tracks and U of Arizona P, 1977. 15–18. [NA]

Sagan, Miriam. *Acequia Madre.* Easthampton, MA: Adastra, 1988. [A]

Sanchez, Carol Lee. "Conversations #'s 1 to 4." *The Remembered Earth: An Anthology of Contemporary Native American Literature.* Ed. Geary Hobson. Albuquerque: U of New Mexico P, 1979. 240–42. [NA]

Silko, Leslie Marmon. "Story from Bear Country." *Storyteller.* New York: Little, Brown, 1981. 204–9. [NA]

Tapahonso, Luci. "Feast Days and Sheep Thrills." *A Breeze Swept Through.* Albuquerque, NM: West End, 1987. 48–49. [NA]

———. "A Prayer." *Seasonal Woman.* Santa Fe, NM: Tooth of Time, 1982. 51. [NA]

[There is a strong lyrical strain in southwestern poetry, especially in the war songs, rain prayers, and corn dances of the Zunis, Hopis, and Navajos. Traditions, myths, and rituals—those which sustain and those now being called into question—are the focus of much Native American and Hispanic poetry. This is also true of the best drama and story collections, such as David Richard Jones, ed. *New Mexico Plays.* Albuquerque: U of New Mexico P, 1989, and Gerald Hausman, ed. *Turtle Dream: Collected Stories from the Hopi, Navajo, Pueblo, and Havasupai People.* Santa Fe, NM: Mariposa, 1989.]

Nonfiction

Hillerman, Tony. "The Great Taos Bank Robbery" and "The Conversion of Cletus Xywanda." *The Great Taos Bank Robbery and Other Indian Country Affairs.* Albuquerque: U of New Mexico P, 1973. 1–12, 44–50. [A & NA]

Lawrence, D. H. "The Dance of the Sprouting Corn." *Mornings in Mexico.* Layton, UT: Smith, 1982. 125–40. [NA]

Morris, Jan. "Capital of the Holy Faith, Santa Fe, New Mexico," *Journeys.* New York: Oxford UP, 1984. 144–51.

[There are two major strains of southwestern nonfiction: the cranks, curmudgeons, and crooks (lovable all) of Hillerman's work, and the serious, investigative, informative reporting of Lawrence. I frequently supplement this section with editorials and articles from Santa Fe's *The New Mexican* on issues of the moment—for example, water rights battles, ethnic conflicts, traditional politics, populist concerns, and religious debates—that are also issues of lasting importance.]

Readers interested in complete bibliographic information and further reading suggestions may write to any of the major New Mexico universities—the University of New Mexico—Albuquerque or the New Mexico State University in Las Cruces—or contact any of the state's public libraries for free, selected bibliographies. There are also many specialized lists (e.g., La Nelle Witt of Eastern New Mexico University at Roswell has compiled "southwestern children's" and "cowboy" bibliographies) and even some annotated lists (e.g., Barbara Dubois of New Mexico Tech in Socorro provided me with an invaluable list when I began English 270). A major source of such information (and perhaps the place to begin one's search) is the New Mexico State Library in Santa Fe.

19 Expanding the Literary Canon through Perceptions of Diversity and the American Dream

Eileen I. Oliver
Washington State University

For those of us who cut our teeth on the Eurocentric models of literary criticism and who continue to teach our students in the same manner, the issues of cross-cultural studies in teaching literature are problematic not only because most of us have not experienced more global exposure, but also because we share a common reticence to venture into what, for many of us, is unknown territory. Real cultural literacy in a multiethnic world means—at least to me—that an educated person must know something about the lives and literatures of the peoples that make up the macroculture. Thus, when we speak of "expanding the literary canon," we must be careful not to focus, as we usually do, *only* on students of color and those from diverse backgrounds to whom—because of the rapidly changing demographics of the United States—we are, all of a sudden, paying attention.

Few would dispute that nonmainstream students benefit in many ways from the infusion of multiethnic courses. But in our zeal to provide for "minority" populations, we tend to neglect what we might more fairly identify as the "culturally deprived" group—the mainstream students who are more typically educated in a homogeneous environment, devoid of knowledge and exposure to the diversity that makes up the fabric of our nation's rich culture.

While teaching at a midsized university in central Minnesota, far from the "big cities" of the nation, I found that my students' understanding of the immigrant experience in America was two or three generations old. "Difference" was defined by these students as non-Catholic or non-Protestant, non-Scandinavian, non-German, nonrural. In discussions of current issues of immigration and changing demographics, my students made a distinction between "us" and "them" when referring to any of the nonmainstream groups with whom they had experienced little interaction and less understanding.

Diversity and the American Dream

Troubled by these implications, I designed my honors English class as an attempt to provide a wider range of literature for these students, many of whom would soon fulfill their general education requirements and never take another literature course. Since the major goal of this freshman-level class is to collect data and prepare a research paper, focusing my course around the history and literatures of nonmainstream groups seemed appropriate. The course description read:

> The readings and research for this course examine the literature
> of diversity. Using both group and individual study, we will
> explore the concept of "difference" and how it impacts on
> achieving the American dream.

In the course, students were asked to select their own areas of literary analysis on the basis of the notion that the literature of a pluralistic society is diverse. Research would include relevant historical and cultural background, identification of appropriate characteristics of artistic excellence, and evaluation of the literature studied through application of recognized criteria.

Since the goals of the course were to examine the literature of diversity and to explore the concept of "difference" and how it impacts on achieving the American dream, we looked at issues of equality, immigration, assimilation, and alternative lifestyles from the perspective of those outside the mainstream. Our text was Colombo, Cullen, and Lisle's collection, *Rereading America,* a centerpiece from which students could branch out into their individual research areas. This text provided excellent insight into many nontraditional groups and gave rise to lively discussions intermingled with various input resulting from students' individual readings.

Initial class discussions reminded me of Kissen's description of the xenophobia from which many mainstream students suffer (211–18). Though my class was composed of honors students, bright and already successful in their academic pursuits, these individuals were also from very traditional, rural backgrounds and were often myopic in their perceptions of nontraditional groups. When I asked them if they'd ever been the victims of discrimination, they responded with examples from such situations as being "from the farm," "members of 'a different' religion," or "poor."

They tended to think of themselves as "the real Americans." When I asked them to talk about their own family histories, many of them shared stories of migration, pioneering, and problems of discrimination faced by their grandparents and great-grandparents due to their "improper" language abilities and traditional old-world religious and social customs. Clearly, they saw no relationship between their families' personal experiences and those of more recent immigrant populations. When I suggested that language might be a problem for many immigrants today, one student shared a "distasteful" experience at a check-out stand with "someone from some Southeast Asian country who had 'not bothered' to learn English."

American Indians were invisible to these students. Although one of this country's largest populations of Ojibwa people is located in Minnesota, and the Mille Lacs Indian Reservation is less than forty-five minutes from the campus, no one ever mentioned this Indian nation in any of our discussions of local diverse cultures until I finally identified it myself.

In presenting the course requirements, I said that I hoped that our text would stimulate some individual interest and ideas which would ultimately assist them in selecting a nonmainstream group. After several discussions, I asked them to choose their own areas of literary analysis on the basis of the notion that the literature of a pluralistic society is diverse and deserves a place in the macroculture's literary canon. Each student was first required to investigate the relevant historical and cultural background of a selected group and to give periodic progress reports based loosely around the notion that the rest of us needed such background information as the reasons for the group's migration, its history in America, and the individual characteristics of their literature. Each student's second task was to read and provide information on the literature of authors within his or her group. Finally, students would present their findings in groups on the basis of some common aspect of their work.

Selection of Topics

Students selected topics on the basis of a list of suggestions provided by me, the reference librarian with whom we worked, and several provocative essays from our reading collection. Some found specific authors; others picked groups. Only one student (the one who thought immigrants should immediately learn English or leave) resisted my efforts, selecting, unsatisfactorily, first George Orwell, then L. Frank Baum. Since neither of these choices was relevant to this assignment, he and I finally reached a compromise: Soviet dissidents and Jewish immigrants. Our selected list of authors and groups was impressive:

Asian American Writers	Black Writers of the Depression
Chinese American Writers	Malcolm X and Martin Luther King, Jr.
Japanese American Writers	W. E. B. DuBois and Richard Wright
The Homeless	Women Out of the Mainstream
Chicana/o Literature	Nineteenth-Century Immigrant Women
The Ojibwa	African American Women
American Indian Women	Native American Literatures
The Black Experience in the Changing South, 1940–1969	Soviet Dissidents and Immigrants

Toward the end of the quarter, we viewed the film *El Norte*, the story of a brother and sister from Central America who struggle to come to the United States, only to meet with misery and disaster. A tragic metaphor of the dreams and disillusionment from which so many of our country's immigrants suffer, this film had a profound effect on my students. The class also saw the movie *Glory*, the story of the first African American regiment to fight in the Civil War. Historically based and fascinating in its characterizations, the film provided another poignant example of what some call "fulfillment" of the American dream from the perspective of nonmainstream people.

Final Presentations

At the end of the quarter, the students presented their research and literary analyses. Grouping them loosely according to their topics, I asked them to pull together, under some consistent theme, the experiences and/or the literatures of the groups and authors they had read. I also requested that each group present a question to the class which would appear on the final exam.

This was the real test. Had the students grown as a result of their experience, or had my efforts been in vain? Could we actually accomplish cross-cultural approaches to understanding and recognizing literature? Or should we be satisfied with doing the best we can with what we've already got? These questions and several others plagued me as we approached our final days together.

What the students presented far surpassed my expectations. Those who worked on women's literature traced oppression through the eyes of women, using Anne Moody's *Coming of Age in Mississippi,* Toni Morrison's *The Bluest Eye,* Alice Walker's *The Color Purple,* Ignatia Broker's *Night Flying Woman,* and Sandra Cisneros's *House on Mango Street.* Treating the nineteenth-century immigrant experience, they presented Rose Cohen's *Out of the Shadow,* Gro Svendsen's *Frontier Mother,* and Marie Hall Ets's *Rosa.* Finally, identifying two women who, they felt, were socially and philosophically "out-of-the-mainstream," they presented Kate Chopin's *The Awakening* and Sylvia Plath's *The Bell Jar,* as well as the collected works of these two writers. We learned, through accompanying historical documentation and authors' accounts, of the differences and similarities suffered by nonmainstream women, of the relative absence of sexism in the "old way of living" in the Ojibwa community, and of the prejudices and stereotypes endured by Northern European women before coming to America.

The group who selected the lives and literatures of African Americans picked as their theme: "Methods of Survival of African Americans." This group pointed out the earlier efforts to fight discrimination, using the work of W. E. B. DuBois and Richard Wright. They also read Harlem Renaissance writers Langston Hughes and Zora Neale Hurston and reflected on the religious teachings of Martin Luther King, Jr., and the struggles of Malcolm X, contrasting their beliefs, intellectual development, and successes.

Those students who chose the topic of Asian Americans provided, in many ways, the most diverse group, both chronologically and geographically. Drawing from the histories and writings of several Japanese, Chinese, Filipino, and Southeast Asian authors, this group treated the class to discussions of such books as Chin et al.'s *Aiiieeeee! An Anthology of Asian-American Writers;* Louis Chu's *Eat a Bowl of Tea;* Maxine Hong Kingston's *The Woman Warrior;* Jeanne Wakatsuki Houston's *Farewell to Manzanar;* Yoshiko Uchida's *Desert Exile;* Mine Okubo's *Citizen 13660;* Joy Kogawa's (Canadian) *Obasan* and *A Choice of Dreams;* John Okada's *No-No Boy;* Carlos Bulosan's *America Is in the Heart;* and Maureen Wartski's *A Boat to Nowhere.* Rounding out this group was my "resistant dissident," who reported on Soviet writers, using Elena Bonner's *Alone Together;* Andrei Sakharov's *Progress, Coexistence, and Intellectual Freedom;* Alexandr Solzhenitsyn's *One Day in the*

Life of Ivan Denisovich; and Anatoly and Avital Shcharansky's *The Journey Home.*

By far the toughest assignment, or so I thought, was given to one student who chose to look at the military history of the Lakota land his grandfather had claimed. He read John Niehardt's *Black Elk Speaks;* Paul Radin's *The Autobiography of a Winnebago Indian;* Dee Brown's *Bury My Heart at Wounded Knee;* N. Scott Momaday's *House Made of Dawn* and *The Way to Rainy Mountain;* and Nancy Wood's *War Cry on a Prayer Feather.* This student, studying the American Indians of the northern Midwest, provided a three-page bibliography, including all of Louise Erdrich's work, Ignatia Broker's *Night Flying Woman,* Jim Northrup's prose collection, and numerous Ojibwa poems, short stories, and historical documents. Students acquainting themselves with Chicano/a literature read Rudolfo Anaya's *Bless Me Ultima,* the poetry of Gary Soto, and Sandra Cisneros's *House on Mango Street.* Another group worked on the plight of the homeless as identified through Jonathan Kozol's *Rachel and Her Children,* Fowler et al.'s *Out of the Rain* (a collection of drawings, writings, and photography by members of a San Francisco homeless shelter), and the Steinbeck classic, *The Grapes of Wrath.* After much thought, this group chose as their theme: "The suffering, pain, and indignation of certain groups can never be fully understood by people of privilege."

Assessing Student Outcomes

The institutional goal for this course was to expose students to research techniques through data collection so that they would learn the skills of term paper writing. My goals were to provide an opportunity for students to learn something about the lives and literatures of nonmainstream groups. How close did I come to achieving my goals? First, students read far more, used wider and more varied resources, and secured much more assistance from library staff than I had expected. In their evaluations, most of the students expressed their surprise and enthusiasm for conducting their own research. Many said they felt much more comfortable now after working on their own. One student began her presentation on African American women by telling us:

> When I first started this project, I'm embarrassed to say . . . that I
> thought it wasn't going to be worth my time . . . that the litera-
> ture of uneducated Black women would not have much to say
> to me. How wrong I was! The reading I've done has allowed me

into their lives and I'm much the better person for it. These women have endured and overcome far more than any of us will ever experience.

Another student shared that she was glad to have chosen American Indian women, commenting, "They write so well. They really have a lot to say." Another class member quickly corrected her by pointing out that her surprise displayed some residual stereotyping, to which the first speaker uneasily agreed. (We all still have much to learn!)

In their class evaluations, students commented:

- You tried hard to make us think about things we otherwise wouldn't have.

- This class has opened my mind to different people's cultures. Living in Central Minnesota makes it difficult to experience cultural diversity.

- Very beneficial . . . I learned much about my topic . . . and through others' presentations, an overview of the real American society. . . . Everyone should be exposed to this material.

- We incorporated the research with the literature in an interesting and informative manner. . . . I learned a lot about our society and reasons for discrimination and prejudice. It helped me look at literature I would otherwise not have known.

- I learned about minority groups through our readings and our individual research projects. I enjoyed the literature read and feel closer to my subject. I feel that some of my racial prejudice disappeared.

On the face of it, students accomplished much more than I had anticipated, and I look forward to teaching the course again. I recommend this approach as a step toward increasing students' awareness of our diverse population and developing their interest in an expanding literary canon. In all the years I have taught, I have seldom reaped the generous rewards I received from this course.

However, these classroom victories are not without problems. I thus conclude this narrative by providing some suggestions to those interested in teaching such a course. First, recognize that you do not have to be an expert on all the literatures of the world. I certainly am not, though I worried early in the quarter that I would shortchange my students because of this weakness. The readings and research of students (along with my efforts to fill in the gaps) proved more than adequate for their projects.

Next, realize that topics will be uneven and dependent upon library holdings, interlibrary loan conditions, local (and private) sources of materials, and the will of your students. Although our campus is well-equipped with information and works of earlier, recognized men and women of letters, our searches for more current nonmainstream writers produced meager results. Their works were difficult to find. Students must learn to accept these conditions as the nature of research and understand that perseverance yields rewards. They will also discover the advantage of collaboration when resources are scarce.

Finally, and this was my biggest fear, do not worry about venturing into new territories where students may, in many ways, end up educating themselves; do not worry that your doing so might reinforce some of the negative stereotypes and prejudices they already harbor. At first, I was concerned that, perhaps, my "hammer-over-the-head" approach to learning about others might backfire and create a class full of confirmed bigots—and I would be responsible! Many times I held my breath and hoped that my efforts would bring positive results. But when I looked over their final papers and read their class assessments, my faith in exposing learners to quality literature and letting them make up their own minds was restored.

If we give students the opportunity to see the world through the eyes of others, we are giving them a look at the American dream from everyone's point of view. In our efforts to expand the literary canon to provide a more realistic look at what American writers have to say, we discover for our students—and for ourselves—a vastly unappreciated, yet wonderfully broad-based literature that, heretofore, many never knew existed.

Works Cited

Colombo, Gary, Robert Cullen, and Bonnie Lisle, eds. *Rereading America. Cultural Contexts for Critical Thinking and Writing.* New York: St. Martin's, 1989.

Kissen, Rita M. "Multicultural Education: The Opening of the American Mind." *English Education* 21.4 (December 1989): 211–18.

Recommended Sources

Anaya, Rudolfo. *Bless Me, Ultima: A Novel.* Berkeley, CA: Tonatiuh-Quinto Sol International, 1972.

Bonner, Elena. *Alone Together.* Trans. Alexander Cook. New York: Knopf, 1986.

Broker, Ignatia. *Night Flying Woman: An Ojibway Narrative.* St. Paul: Minnesota Historical Society, 1983.

Brown, Dee Alexander. *Bury My Heart at Wounded Knee: An Indian History of the American West.* New York: Holt, 1971.

Bulosan, Carlos. *America Is in the Heart: A Personal History.* New York: Harcourt, 1946.

Chin, Frank et al., eds. *Aiiieeeee! An Anthology of Asian-American Writers.* Washington, D.C.: Harvard UP, 1974.

Chopin, Kate. *The Awakening, and Other Stories.* Ed. Lewis Leary. New York: Holt, 1970.

Chu, Louis. *Eat a Bowl of Tea.* New York: Stuart, 1961.

Cisneros, Sandra. *The House on Mango Street.* Houston, TX: Arte Publico, 1983.

Cohen, Rose [Gallup]. *Out of the Shadow.* New York: Doran, 1918.

Ets, Marie Hall. *Rosa, the Life of an Italian Immigrant.* Minneapolis: U of Minnesota P, 1970.

Fowler, Tom, Malcolm Garcia, and the Shelter Staff at the St. Vincent de Paul Ozanam Shelter, comps. *Out of the Rain: An Anthology of Drawings, Writings, and Photography.* San Francisco: St. Vincent de Paul Society, 1988.

Houston, Jeanne Wakatsuki, and James D. Houston. *Farewell to Manzanar: A True Story of Japanese American Experience during and after World War II Internment.* Boston: Houghton, 1973.

Kingston, Maxine Hong. *The Woman Warrior: Memoirs of a Girlhood among Ghosts.* New York: Knopf, 1976.

Kogawa, Joy. *A Choice of Dreams.* Toronto: McClelland and Stewart, 1974.

———. *Obasan.* Toronto: Lester & Orpen Dennys, 1981.

Kozol, Jonathan. *Rachel and Her Children: Homeless Families in America.* New York: Crown, 1988.

Momaday, N. Scott. *House Made of Dawn.* New York: Harper, 1968.

———. *The Way to Rainy Mountain.* Albuquerque: U of New Mexico P, 1969.

Moody, Anne. *Coming of Age in Mississippi.* New York: Dell, 1968.

Morrison, Toni. *The Bluest Eye: A Novel.* New York: Holt, 1970.

Neihardt, John. *Black Elk Speaks: Being the Life Story of a Holy Man of the Ogalala Sioux.* Alexandria, VA: Time-Life, 1991.

Okada, John. *No-No Boy.* Seattle, WA: Combined Asian American Resources Project, 1976.

Okubo, Mine. *Citizen 13660.* New York: Columbia UP, 1946.

Plath, Sylvia. *The Bell Jar.* New York: Harper, 1971.

Radin, Paul. *The Autobiography of a Winnebago Indian.* Berkeley: U of California P, 1920.

Sakharov, Andrei. *Progress, Coexistence, and Intellectual Freedom.* Trans. *New York Times.* New York: Norton, 1968.

Shcharansky, Anatoly, and Avital Shcharansky. *The Journey Home.* San Diego: Harcourt, 1986.

Solzhenitsyn, Alexandr Isaevich. *One Day in the Life of Ivan Denisovich.* Trans. Max Hayward and Ronald Hingley. New York: Praeger, 1963.

Steinbeck, John. *The Grapes of Wrath.* New York: Viking, 1939.

Svendsen, Gro. *Frontier Mother: The Letters of Gro Svendsen.* Trans. and Ed. Pauline Farseth and Theodore C. Blegen. Northfield, MN: Norwegian-American Historical Association, 1950.

Uchida, Yoshiko. *Desert Exile: The Uprooting of a Japanese American Family.* Seattle: U of Washington P, 1982.

Walker, Alice. *The Color Purple: A Novel.* New York: Harcourt, 1982.

Wartski, Marie Crane. *A Boat to Nowhere.* Philadelphia: Westminster, 1980.

Wood, Nancy C. *War Cry on a Prayer Feather: Prose and Poetry of the Ute Indians.* Garden City, NY: Doubleday, 1979.

Editors

Lenora (Leni) Cook is associate professor of secondary reading and language education in the School of Education at California State University–Dominguez Hills (CSUDH), where she teaches content-related reading and writing, language learning, and is the evaluation director for a California Beginning Teacher Support and Assessment Project. Prior to coming to CSUDH, she was a high school teacher of English, ESL, and drama for twenty years in the Los Angeles Unified School District, as well as English department chair. Active in NCTE and the International Reading Association (IRA), she is the co-author, with Phillip C. Gonzales, of a regular column in *Reading Today* on second-language issues in reading. In NCTE, she serves on the Standing Committee for Teacher Preparation and the NCATE Folio Review Advisory Committee. She was co-chair of the CEE Commission on Minority Education and Minority Educators and assistant general chair of the 1987 NCTE Annual Convention. She also served on the ESL Committee of IRA. The author of numerous chapters and articles focusing on teaching students from diverse cultures and language backgrounds, she has presented workshops and conference sessions on this topic internationally.

Helen C. Lodge taught English in secondary schools in Michigan and California. She is professor emerita of secondary education at California State University–Northridge, where she taught methods classes and supervised student teachers for many years. She received the 1984 Distinguished Service Award from the California Association of Teachers of English. She has been a curriculum consultant in many school districts, served as co-director of the Northridge Writing Project, and been a consultant for the California State Department of Education. Her most recent experience has been as a member of the Language Arts Development Team for assessment of English skills at the state level. She is also the co-author of a number of language arts textbooks at the secondary level.

Contributors

Susan B. Andrews is associate professor of general studies and journalism and broadcasting at Chukchi College, a branch campus of the University of Alaska–Fairbanks (UAF), located in Kotzebue, a predominantly Inupiat (Eskimo) community thirty miles above the Arctic Circle in northwest Alaska. She is a graduate in comparative literature from Smith College and holds a Master's degree in journalism from the University of Oregon. She has been news director at the CBS television affiliate in Fairbanks and produced TV documentaries on Alaska Native issues for the Northwest Arctic Borough School District. Since 1989, she has taught for UAF in rural Alaska while co-editing Chukchi News and Information Service, a writing project that publishes Alaska Native (Eskimo, Indian, Aleut) and other rural Alaskan students in statewide newspapers and magazines. This publication project was a winner of the 1991 Robert F. Kennedy Journalism Award for Outstanding Coverage of the Problems of the Disadvantaged.

Julia Stutts Austin is the director of the Scientific Communication Program at the University of Alabama at Birmingham.

Kathy H. Barclay is professor of education at Western Illinois University, where she teaches undergraduate and graduate courses in reading, language arts, and early childhood education. She has authored numerous articles in professional journals, including *Childhood Education, Young Children, Reading Improvement, Reading Horizons,* and the *Journal of Language Experience.* She is co-author of *Moving Toward Whole Language: A Handbook for School Leaders.* She is a frequent presenter at national, regional, and state conferences, including those of NCTE, IRA, NAEYC, ACEI, and the Whole Language Umbrella. She serves as an editorial advisor for *The Reading Teacher* and as a book reviewer for educational publishing companies.

Michael G. Battin received his B.A. in drama from San Diego State University and his teaching credential from California State University–Northridge. He currently teaches at U.S. Grant High School, Van Nuys, California.

June D. Bobb is assistant professor of English at Queens College, CUNY, where she teaches composition and Caribbean literature. She is currently working on a study of resistance strategies in contemporary Caribbean women's poetry.

Mary Sauter Comfort teaches at Lehigh University and Moravian College, both in Bethlehem, Pennsylvania. She has served as an editorial consultant to *An American Mosaic: Native American Literature; An American Mosaic: Asian American Literature;* and *An American Mosaic: Hispanic Lit-*

erature. Her publications include contributions to *The Mark Twain Encyclopedia* and *The Encyclopedia of British Women Authors.*

John Creed is associate professor of general studies and journalism and broadcasting at Chukchi College, a University of Alaska–Fairbanks branch campus located in Kotzebue, an Inupiat (Eskimo) settlement some thirty miles above the Arctic Circle in Northwest Alaska. A magna cum laude graduate of the University of Massachusetts at Amherst, he also studied at University College, Dublin, Ireland, the University of Montana, the University of Oslo, Norway, and the University of Oregon. He is the former editor, writer, and photographer for *Tusraayugaat,* an award-winning bilingual newspaper of the Northwest Arctic School District. He has also worked as a staff writer for the *Fairbanks Daily News–Miner* and since 1987 has taught by satellite-assisted distance delivery for the University of Alaska to mostly indigenous communities throughout the remote reaches of rural Alaska. He is founder and co-editor of Chukchi News and Information Service, a student writing project that publishes Alaska Natives (Indians, Eskimos, and Aleuts) and other rural Alaskans in newspapers and magazines statewide. In 1991, the project captured the Robert F. Kennedy Journalism Award for Outstanding Coverage of the Problems of the Disadvantaged, in addition to two other national awards and the Alaska Press Club's Public Service Award, the journalism industry's highest award in Alaska.

Bonnie O. Ericson formerly taught high school English in New York state. At present, she teaches English methods courses and content-area literacy and supervises student teachers at California State University–Northridge. She is the CEE liaison to the Secondary Section Steering Committee of NCTE and a member of the Executive Board of the California Association of Teachers of English.

Linda Flammer-Kassel has been an English teacher at John H. Francis Polytechnic High School in Sun Valley, California, since 1981. In her years of teaching, she has been involved with publishing and presenting for NCTE and other professional organizations, most recently with the Los Angeles Educational Partnership. In addition to her regular teaching duties, she also coordinates and teaches in an interdisciplinary program known as Humanitas. Over the years, she has provided workshops as a Fellow of the California Writing Project; she also maintains a close working relationship with California State University–Northridge, both as a training teacher for student teachers and as a curriculum/methodology consultant. She holds a certificate in clinical supervision, and she regularly plans and conducts in-services for faculty and staff members at her school in areas such as cooperative learning and sheltered instruction.

Keith Gilyard is associate professor of English at Medgar Evers College, CUNY. His articles on language, literature, and education have appeared in publications such as *Before Columbus Review, Black Ameri-*

can *Literature Forum, College English,* and *Community Review.* He is also author of the noted educational memoir, *Voices of the Self: A Study of Language Competence,* and a volume of poetry, *American Forty.* He is the CEE representative to CCCC and serves as chair of the NCTE Committee on Public Doublespeak.

Brenda M. Greene is associate professor of English at Medgar Evers College, CUNY, where she chairs the Department of Literature, Languages, and Philosophy and teaches composition and literature. Although the major focus of her research and writing has been in the areas of basic writing, multicultural literature, and writing across the curriculum, she has begun to teach and conduct research in African American, feminist, and modern literature. She was program chair for the 1994 NCTE Summer Institute for Teachers of Literature. She has conducted workshops and presented papers in composition and has published many articles and chapters in books, including those for NCTE, MLA, and the recent *When Writing Teachers Teach Literature.* She is also a key member of the National Black Writers' Conference Steering Committee and the Editorial Board of the National Council of Teachers of English.

Ellen Louise Hart has been a member of the writing program at the University of California–Santa Cruz since 1984 and currently teaches courses on "Writing and Place," "Multicultural Literacy and the American Detective," and "The Literature of Friendship." She has published essays on literacy and pedagogy, and on editing the letters of Emily Dickinson.

Joyce Harte is an instructor and deputy chairperson in the English department at Borough of Manhattan Community College, CUNY, for the academic year 1994–95. She will then be on sabbatical leave to complete a partly autobiographical dissertation for New York University on her colonial education.

Sarah Coprich Johnson is assistant professor of English at the University of Alabama at Birmingham. She has presented her work at a variety of conferences, including the Conference on College Composition and Communication.

Jeffrey Laing, who holds a Ph.D., is English department chairperson at Santa Fe Preparatory School and is on the creative writing faculties of Santa Fe Community College and the Union Institute. During the past twenty-four years, he has taught in New York, New Jersey, New Mexico, the Netherlands (Fulbright Teacher Exchange), and Scotland (University of Saint Andrews Schoolmaster Fellowship). He publishes fiction, poetry, and literary and theater criticism.

G. Douglas Meyers is chair of the English department at the University of Texas at El Paso, where he previously directed the freshman composition program. He has taught at the University of Maryland and Florida International University and has worked as a K–12 language arts consultant in Central America. A former high school English teacher, he has also directed a National Writing Project site, has published widely, and has made numerous conference presentations on topics related to the teaching of writing and English education.

William Mosley's chapter in this book is published posthumously. He was the original developer and director of the Western Illinois University Minority Summer Tutoring Program. He was professor and chair of the Department of Special Education at Western Illinois University. He was also a faculty member in the Department of Elementary, Reading, and Special Education at Morehead State University.

Martin Mullarkey has been teaching English and ESL in the Los Angeles Unified School District since 1989. He has a B.A. in cinema production from the University of Southern California and an M.A. in secondary education/English education from California State University–Northridge.

Eileen I. Oliver is an assistant professor of English at Washington State University. She has taught in high schools, continuation and correctional schools, community colleges, and university programs in California, Texas, New York, Minnesota, and Washington. Her interests in composition, English education, literature, and multicultural studies are reflected in her research. She is the author of *Crossing the Mainstream: Multicultural Perspectives in Teaching Literature* and has had articles appear in such publications as *English Journal, English Quarterly, Multicultural Education, Expanding the Canon: Bridges to Understanding, Meeting the Challenge of Cultural Diversity in Teacher Preparation,* and *Uncovering the Curriculum: Whole Language in Secondary and Postsecondary Classrooms.* She received a B.A. from the University of California–Berkeley and a Ph.D. at the University of Texas at Austin.

Barbara Osburg is a full-time English teacher at Parkway North High School, St. Louis, Missouri. She received her Ph.D. in American literature from St. Louis University and is currently an adjunct professor, teaching graduate courses in linguistics and methods for the M.A. in teaching program at Webster University. She is certified K–12 and has been teaching for over twenty years, with experience at all levels. Her most recent publications include contributions to *Missouri English Bulletin* and *Talking to Learn.* She has been honored as Teacher of the Year in two school districts, has organized numerous conferences for teachers, and has had many consulting and speaking engagements.

Sarah-Hope Parmeter teaches composition at the University of California–Santa Cruz. In addition to teaching lesbian/gay/bisexual-focused courses, she also teaches multicultural writing courses that include an early outreach component, pairing Spanish-speaking elementary students with University mentors. She is a member of and has served two years as the co-chair of the CCCC Lesbian and Gay Caucus. She is a former union organizer and vice-president of the UC-AFT.

James W. Penha, who earned his Ph.D. in English from New York University, has alternated between university and high school teaching for over twenty-five years. He currently lives on the Indonesian archipelago, a setting for his book of poems, *On the Back of the Dragon.* His other publications include the book *The Learning Community: The Story of a Successful Mini-School;* articles in *English Journal, Issues in Higher Education, Clearing House,* and other professional journals; and poetry and fiction in *We Speak for Peace, American Poetry Confronts the 1990s, Movieworks, Phoebe, Hawaii Pacific Review, Thema, Paragraph,* and many others. He currently teaches at Jakarta International School, Jakarta, Indonesia.

Paul M. Puccio is a doctoral candidate at the University of Massachusetts at Amherst; his dissertation examines the cultural ideals framing fictional representations of male friendship in Victorian and Edwardian England. He is the recipient of a University of Massachusetts Distinguished Teaching Award and a Pew Teaching Leadership Award. He has presented papers on teaching sexual minority issues, computers in basic writing, and teaching about AIDS, as well as papers on Victorian schoolboy fiction, the Gothic Novel, and E. M. Forster. He is a founding chair of the CCCC Lesbian and Gay Caucus.

Kyoko Sato taught for many years in middle schools and high schools in Los Angeles. At present, she teaches methods of teaching secondary English, supervises student teachers, and acts as a consultant and advisor to professional groups and school districts. Her publications include essays in *California English* and *The Yearling: A Teacher's Guide.* She has served on the NCTE Commission on Language.

P. L. Thomas is currently pursuing a doctoral degree in curriculum and instruction at the University of South Carolina. He teaches advanced placement literature and composition, American literature, and journalism at Woodruff High School, Woodruff, South Carolina, where he is also the department chair. He has published a wide range of material, from poetry and short fiction to articles on education and bicycling. His work has appeared in *Cumberland Poetry Review, Bicycling, Oregon English, Amelia, The Pinehurst Journal,* and *Western Ohio Journal,* among other literary and professional journals. He also served for several years on the Executive Board of the South Carolina Council of Teachers of English as the editor of the student publication *Carolina Writes.*

Ann Marie Wagstaff is a writer, teacher, and consultant living in Davis, California.

Luke Wallin is associate professor of English at the University of Massachusetts at Dartmouth, where he has directed the graduate writing program. He holds graduate degrees in writing, philosophy, and environmental planning. His eight novels include *Ceremony of the Panther* and *In the Shadow of the Wind.* Wallin's work has been honored by the American Library Association, the Rhode Island State Council on the

Arts, and other organizations. In 1994 he was nominated for a Pushcart Prize Award.

Smokey Wilson teaches at Laney College, Oakland, California. She is one of the founders of Project Bridge, an interdisciplinary basic-skills program for underprepared students, and also of Deaf CAN, a bilingual/bicultural program for deaf students. Her doctoral work in language and literacy at the University of California–Berkeley focused on theories of conversation and classroom interaction. Concerned with the link between theory and practice, she has worked closely with the Bay Area Writing Project's teacher research group. Her publications include *Struggles with Bears: Experience in Writing,* a composition text, and numerous articles. She is at work on an NCTE-sponsored study of resistance among basic writing students.

Titles in the Classroom Practices in Teaching English Series

NCTE began publishing the Classroom Practices series in 1963 with *Promising Practices in the Teaching of English*. Volumes 1–16 and Volumes 18–21 of the series are out of print. The following titles are available through the NCTE Catalog.

Vol. Title

17. *How to Handle the Paper Load* (1979)

22. *Activities to Promote Critical Thinking* (1986)

23. *Focus on Collaborative Learning* (1988)

24. *Talking to Learn* (1989)

25. *Literature and Life: Making Connections in the Classroom* (1990)

26. *Process and Portfolios in Writing Instruction* (1993)

27. *Ideas for the Working Classroom* (1993)

28. *Voices in English Classrooms: Honoring Diversity and Change* (1996)